THE PHILOSOPHY OF ENVY

Envy is almost universally condemned and feared. But is its bad reputation always warranted? In this book, Sara Protasi argues that envy is more multifaceted than it seems, and that some varieties of it can be productive and even virtuous. Protasi brings together empirical evidence and philosophical research to generate a novel view according to which there are four kinds of envy: emulative, inert, aggressive, and spiteful. For each kind, she individuates different situational antecedents, phenomenological expressions, motivational tendencies, and behavioral outputs. She then develops the normative implications of this taxonomy from a moral and prudential perspective, in the domain of personal loving relationships, and in the political sphere. A historical appendix completes the book. Through a careful and comprehensive investigation of envy's complexity, and its multifarious implications for human relations and human value, *The Philosophy of Envy* surprisingly reveals that envy plays a crucial role in safeguarding our happiness.

SARA PROTASI is Associate Professor of Philosophy at the University of Puget Sound. She has published essays on love, envy, beauty, pornography, and pedagogy.

T0382267

THE PHILOSOPHY OF ENVY

SARA PROTASI

University of Puget Sound

CAMBRIDGE
UNIVERSITY PRESS

Shaftesbury Road, Cambridge CB2 8EA, United Kingdom

One Liberty Plaza, 20th Floor, New York, NY 10006, USA

477 Williamstown Road, Port Melbourne, VIC 3207, Australia

314–321, 3rd Floor, Plot 3, Splendor Forum, Jasola District Centre, New Delhi – 110025, India

103 Penang Road, #05–06/07, Visioncrest Commercial, Singapore 238467

Cambridge University Press is part of Cambridge University Press & Assessment, a department of the University of Cambridge.

We share the University's mission to contribute to society through the pursuit of education, learning and research at the highest international levels of excellence.

www.cambridge.org
Information on this title: www.cambridge.org/9781009001717

DOI: 10.1017/9781009007023

First published 2021
First paperback edition 2022

A catalogue record for this publication is available from the British Library

Library of Congress Cataloging-in-Publication data
NAMES: Protasi, Sara, 1978– author.
TITLE: The philosophy of envy / Sara Protasi, University of Puget Sound, Washington.
DESCRIPTION: Cambridge ; New York : Cambridge University Press, 2021. | Includes bibliographical references and index.
IDENTIFIERS: LCCN 2020057996 (print) | LCCN 2020057997 (ebook) | ISBN 9781316519172 (hardback) | ISBN 9781009001717 (paperback) | ISBN 9781009007023 (epub)
SUBJECTS: LCSH: Envy. | Ethics. | Social psychology.
CLASSIFICATION: LCC BJ1535.E57 P76 2021 (print) | LCC BJ1535.E57 (ebook) | DDC 179/.8–DC23
LC record available at https://lccn.loc.gov/2020057996
LC ebook record available at https://lccn.loc.gov/2020057997

ISBN   978-1-316-51917-2   Hardback
ISBN   978-1-009-00171-7   Paperback

For M and m, amori della mamma: may you learn to love and envy well.

For Shen-yi, 我的寶貝: "words cannot describe."

Contents

Figures

Tables

Preface and Acknowledgments

The first memory I have of reflecting philosophically about envy is from when I was about ten years old. I remember walking in the garden of my church before Confession. That year I was preparing for my First Communion, and I was a very conscientious believer who did her spiritual homework. I must have been told about the seven deadly sins at Sunday school, and I recall marveling at how envy could be in the same list as gluttony or vanity. Envy was clearly The Worst Thing Ever. So shameful, so painful – nothing else was as bad in my eyes. Envy was both the only one of those sins worth confessing to, and the one that was hardest to confess to.

Throughout the years since I have observed a lot of envy in the different communities that I inhabit as an academic, a dancer, a parent, and a human being with decent observation and introspection skills. Since that day in the church's garden my thoughts on envy have evolved: I have a more comprehensive and, hopefully, truthful view of envy now. But I don't know if I would have become the kind of person who reflects philosophically about the same topic at ten and at forty without the guidance and example of my parents. They were both excellent students, who implicitly showed me the importance of education without ever pressuring me explicitly. I had the privilege of growing up in an apartment full of books, where reading the newspaper daily was the natural thing to do. My mother, Angela Plutino, showed me that it was possible for a woman to be educated, have a successful teaching career, and be a nurturing mother; she encouraged my writing ambitions and praised my literary attempts from an early age. My father, Marco Protasi, showed me what academic life looked like, and spent many evenings conversing with me about philosophy, theology, and literature. He also embodied an ideal of rational and thoughtful Christianity that I ultimately could not embrace, but which still affects the way I think about morality and life.

There is much more I could say, but the succinct version is that I owe thanks to both my parents that this book exists.

Philosophy is a communal enterprise, always, but this is particularly true when it is about a delicate human subject such as envy. It turns out that, even if people are reluctant to admit their envy, they all find it a fascinating subject and are much more willing to share their envious feelings and experiences once they hear that envy might not be all bad! I am grateful to all of the many people who engaged with me in candid discussions on sensitive personal matters. I enjoyed the enthusiastic responses to my defense of envy, but I particularly appreciated the many objections that pushed me to strengthen my arguments and that, sometimes, changed my positions. I acknowledge many such contributions in each chapter.[1]

But writing a book's acknowledgments is, as it turns out, a chance to think back about one's intellectual journey, and so I am going to express here gratitude toward the myriad friends and colleagues who have walked alongside me for parts or the entirety of the journey so far.

Starting with the event that divides academic life into two ages (BD and AD, Before Dissertation and After Dissertation). I was lucky to have the most wonderful dissertation committee: Tamar Szabó Gendler, advisor extraordinaire, who always strikes the perfect balance between demandingness and encouragement, rigor and care, demonstrating how to be an exceptional scholar and teacher, and also honestly and humbly disclosing the work that went into it; Steve Darwall, whose generosity I will forever be grateful for (he agreed to be not just in one but *two* dissertation committees of mine!) and whose vast knowledge of many fields relevant to my work has proved invaluable for my research through the years; June Gruber, who kept all of us philosophers on track, provided psychological expertise, and made me feel less intimidated in meetings; and finally Verity Harte, who constantly motivated me to make my arguments tighter, my historical references more careful, and my writing more exact.

Among the Yale faculty who have contributed directly or indirectly to developing the ideas in this book, I owe special mentions to three of them. Michael Della Rocca has supported me both intellectually and emotionally since I was a first-year student, and I would not have become a professional philosopher without him. Zoltán Gendler Szabó helped me see how

---

[1] It is customary to apologize in advance for one's forgetfulness, and in my case it is not at all a formality: while I did my best to write down the name of everybody who provided feedback to me, my memory is atrocious. So, if you helped me along the way, and your name does not appear in the book, please know I am truly grateful to you, too.

I thought about love and envy as two sides of the same coin – the epiphany occurred in front of beers at a dive bar in New Haven and I still remember where I was sitting! Finally, Shelly Kagan knew when to step in, and when to step back, and even though my philosophical style is pretty much the opposite of his, I learned a lot from him. But I am grateful to all of the brilliant teachers whose courses I have taken or audited at Yale, because they have all contributed to shape the philosopher I am still trying to become.

My fellow graduate students – in particular Gwen Bradford, Pamela Corcoran, Eric Guindon, Maya Gupta, Julia Jorati, Matt Lindauer, Mark Maxwell, Aaron Norby, Alex Silverman, Esther Schubert Palacios, and Mary-Beth Willard – were (and still are) inspiring, fun, and a frequent source of emulative envy and admiration. They pushed me to be my best self with their altruism, warmth, honesty, and sheer brilliance. It is thanks to such models that I applied for and was granted a completion dissertation fellowship by the American Council of Learned Societies and the Mellon Foundation, which I am very grateful for. Portions of Chapter 1 were previously published in Protasi (2016) and (2017b), Chapter 2 is a significantly revised version of Protasi (2016), and Chapter 4 is a lightly revised version of Protasi (2017c). I thank the publishers for granting me permission to reuse this material. I am also thankful to Hilary Gaskin for her precious advice and support on this project.

Before my time at Yale I was welcomed by two other wonderful communities of scholars. I was sent to the University of Michigan by my Italian advisor Tito Magri. Among the many ways in which he helped me become a professional philosopher, this was maybe the most consequential, for reasons I came to fully appreciate only years later. My young self was equal part awed and terrified by those Michigan philosophers, who all sounded like geniuses to me. Among them, I am especially grateful for their teaching, support, and friendship to Aaron Bronfman, Stephen Campbell, Vanessa Carbonell, Victor Caston, Eduardo García-Ramírez, Allan Gibbard, Lina Jansson, Molly Mahony, Eleni Manis, Ivan Mayerhofer, Alex Plakias, Ian Proops, Peter Railton, Neil Sinhababu (honorary member), Erica Stonestreet, Wendy Tng, and Ken Walton.

I was at the University of Chicago in between doctorates, as appropriate a choice for a liminal existence as there can be. I went there to study with Martha Nussbaum. I owe Martha so much more than can be expressed in a few lines. She was the first living philosopher whose book I devoured like a novel, and the only one whose influence I find in everything I write. She and Aristotle have changed my life – in that order.

Academic life is nomadic life. After Ann Arbor, Chicago, and New Haven, I have philosophized in Manhattan, KS (thank you, Amy Lara, Jim Hamilton, Kathy Karlin, Andrew Moon, Chris Remple, and Sangeeta Sangha); Leeds, UK (shout-out to the best philosophical karaoke: Elizabeth Barnes, Ross Cameron, Daniel Elstein, Gerald Lang, Heather Logue, Aaron Meskin, and Tasia Scrutton; and also thank you, Jason and Starr Turner, for shepherding us through parenting); and Singapore (*namaste*, Christina Chuang), before finding some stability in Tacoma.

The philosophy department at the University of Puget Sound has welcomed me and my family with open arms. They have supported me not only in all aspects of my job but also in my personal life, and have never made me feel like I should set aside any aspect of the latter in favor of the former. Thank you, Bill Beardsley, Doug Cannon, Justin Tiehen, and Ariela Tubert.

My department exemplifies the best of my university, whose faculty and staff have taught me what it means to be a teacher–scholar. So many of them have enriched my life in the last five years, but I am particular thankful to Nancy Bristow, Gwynne Brown, Julie Nelson Cristoph, America Chambers, Katy Curtis, Eric Orlin, Lo Sun Perry, Melvin Rouse, Renee Simms, Jason Struna, Seth Weinberger, and Heather White for their mentorship and friendship. I am grateful to the University of Puget Sound for a pre-tenure sabbatical leave grant intended to support the writing of this book.

But even with financial support and time off from teaching, this project would have never been successful without the help of several peer groups, those I formed with Isha Rajbhandari and Sarah West; Saba Fatima and Alison Reiheld; and Olivia Bailey, Mara Bollard, Alida Liberman, Alice MacLachlan, and Denise Vigani: You are all beautiful, caring, and super-smart, and I cannot believe you are my friends and colleagues!

Tyler Doggett and Neal Tognazzini were both tremendous sources of peer support as well. They are exemplars of nurturing masculinity and almost self-effacing generosity. I cannot list all of the many ways in which they supported me throughout the years, but they really went above and beyond the call of duty. I also want to thank the students enrolled in PHIL 420 Everyday Ethics at Western Washington University for their feedback on Chapters 1–3 of a previous draft of this book.

Among the men defying the male academic stereotype are also David Livingstone Smith, whose mentorship with regard to publishing and public philosophy was very appreciated, and Jens Lange and Niels van de Ven, who promptly and generously responded to my requests for references and explanations of more technical aspects of work in psychology.

But there is life outside of academia, you might be shocked to hear. In the years this book was written I was truly lucky to be gifted friendship, dance wisdom, and yummy food (among other components of *eudaimonia*) by Diana Busch, Giulia Cardillo, Jomarie Carlson, Levin Conway, Tiffany Gilkison, Jane Kenyon, Betsy Kindblade, Melanie Kirk-Stauffer, Birgitte Necessary, and Mary Ellen Sullivan. I am also grateful to my aunt, Chiara Protasi, and my brother, Davide Protasi, for their love and support from afar. Among the many beloved friends from my Roman gang (really too many to list – you know who you are!), a special mention goes to my first philosophy teacher, Sergio Cicatelli, whose initial lecture on philosophy as stemming from wonder mesmerized and bewitched me, and I have not woken up from that spell since.

Finally, the person who deserves the most important acknowledgment is my loving partner, attentive co-parent, witty friend, and gifted colleague, Shen-yi Liao. Without him, nothing that matters would be possible. He was the cutest of those Ann Arbor geniuses, and he has been there every step of the way, sustaining all of my pursuits and showing me every day what a real feminist looks like. My flourishing is intertwined with his: We love and envy each other in just the right way – blooms, weeds, and all. This book is dedicated to him and to our awe-inspiring and occasionally maddening little sprouts, Ming-li Maya and Ming-yun Mira.

Introduction
The Sidelong Gaze

You are four, and you really *really* want a big red heart-shaped lollipop. You have been staring at it for days in the candy store window. And then, today, here it is, in the hands of your classmate, who's, of course, gloating about it. You are so mad, so upset, and there's this unpleasant ache, deep down in your tummy. "NO fair!" you think. Can you really be blamed when you feel a deep satisfaction at the sight of the lollipop slipping from your friend's little hands and falling on the dirty ground?

You have grown up now, and you think back to the lollipop episode with a mixture of amusement and shame. And yet, as you retell the story to your best friend, you cannot help but notice that today they look so good, with their new fashionable haircut. Your best friend is one of the coolest people at your high school, and you are – not. That sinking feeling in your belly resurfaces. You repress a little sigh, and go on chatting, casually dropping a: "Hey, I saw Rainier making out with Sam in the cafeteria the other day. I thought you two were getting serious?"

By the time you are a first-year student in college you and your best friend from high school have grown apart. You are focused on studying and are working hard to get a scholarship. When you discover the one you had applied for has been given to your roommate, you are heartbroken. You are happy for them too, since they are nice and you respect them. You are not an insecure teenager anymore, and you know they won fair and square. But there's this gnawing awareness that they are always *a little* better than you. So, you wish them all the best, and move out.

You have become a college professor. You have spent years studying hard, looking up to people like your roommate. You applied for more scholarships, and won some of them. You got lucky, too, and landed a good job at a university near your hometown. You decide to go to your high school reunion. You are happy to see your long-lost friend, who's coming to hug you. They are sporting a smart suit, looking great. You feel a familiar pang. But you have learned to use that feeling more productively. You compliment their suit. They cheerfully answer: "Thanks. I can tell you where I got it, maybe you can get one too." "Yeah, thanks, maybe I will!" is your reply. And you smile.

Do any of these scenarios resonate with you? Chances are some of them will. Everyone feels envy at some point in their life. Some people are more aware of their envy than others; some people are prone to feel envy more than others; some people feel more malicious kinds of envy than others; and some people are crippled by their envy more than others. Still, there is no culture that is devoid of envy, even though it takes different forms in different places and times.

Notwithstanding envy's ubiquity, it is a maligned emotion. It is condemned by all religious traditions, feared in all societies, repressed by most who feel it, and often kept a secret even to oneself. Because envy is a cross-cultural emotion we have good reasons to think that it serves an important function in human psychology, and yet it has a terrible reputation. This book aims to restore the truth about envy and argues that such a reputation is at least partially undeserved. Like other slandered negative emotions, such as contempt and disgust, which have already been rehabilitated in the philosophical and psychological literature, envy has a role to play in our lives and may be essential to our flourishing. Once we can see the bright side of envy, its benefits and its reasons, then we can also better deal with its darkest features, its harms and its deceptions.

My overarching argumentative strategy is to develop an original taxonomy of envy as an emotion. Once we know what envy is and how many kinds there are, we can look more fruitfully into how to deal with envy – how to cope with, inhibit, or encourage it – and into its value or disvalue. Thus the first two chapters are devoted to laying out the *ontology* – what envy is. The remaining three chapters develop the *practical normativity* of envy – what is good and bad about envy in three main domains: ethics, love, and politics. The Conclusion tackles the *axiology* that stems from envy – the value of enviable things, which are more than you might expect. Finally, an Appendix traces the *history* of envy.

Here is a chapter-by-chapter overview of the book.

Chapter 1 can be seen largely as preliminary: it builds on established conceptual theories and empirical evidence about the nature of envy and, in particular, how it differs from jealousy. Envy and jealousy are often confused with each other, to the point that in English the very terms "envy" and "jealousy" are often used interchangeably. However, the scholarly consensus is that they are distinct emotions. It behooves any analysis of envy to start by clarifying how envy differs from jealousy: in agreement with the dominant view, I argue that envy is about being concerned with the *lack* of a valuable object, while jealousy is about being concerned with the *loss* of a valuable object. I devise several original objections to this popular way of drawing the distinction, and show how the view can respond to them. I also highlight the ways in which envy does indeed resemble jealousy. After this discussion of envy in relation to jealousy I introduce the *definition* of envy on its own. Here, too, I draw from preexisting work in both philosophy and psychology, in order to define envy as: an aversive emotional response to a perceived inferiority or disadvantage vis-à-vis a similar other with regard to a domain of self-importance, which motivates to overcome that inferiority or disadvantage.

Chapter 2 – the conceptual heart of this book – argues for the view that there are four kinds of envy. Envy is essentially a response to a perceived inferiority. Such inferiority can be overcome either by bringing oneself up to the level of the envied or by pulling them down to one's level. This double motivation has been explained in two distinct ways, one mostly proposed by psychologists, the other discernible in the philosophical tradition. I argue that these models of explanation track two variables, *focus of concern* and *obtainability of the good*, whose interplay is responsible for the variety of envy. *Emulative envy* stems from being primarily concerned with getting the good for oneself, and perceiving oneself as capable of doing so; the typical behavioral tendency is self-improvement. *Inert envy* is the sterile version of emulative envy: the envier wants to get the good for oneself, but doesn't think that they can do so; the typical behavioral tendency is self-loathing, wallowing in one's misery, and avoidance of the envied. *Aggressive envy* derives from being primarily concerned with the envied's possession of the good, rather than the good itself, and perceiving oneself as capable of taking the good away from the envied; the typical behavioral tendency is thus sabotaging and stealing the envied object. Finally, *spiteful envy* is a less productive version of aggressive envy: the envier wants to take the good from the envied, but doesn't think that they can do so; the typical behavioral tendency is spoiling the good. I illustrate a paradigmatic case for each, providing a detailed analysis of the phenomenology, situational determinants, motivational structure, and typical behavioral outputs, and I explain how they differ from nearby emotions and attitudes such as admiration, covetousness, and spite.

Chapter 3 focuses on envy's *moral* and *prudential* dimensions in the private sphere. How does envy, in all its forms, affect an agent's interactions with other people, including friends and relatives? Is it always bad to feel? Can it bring genuine advantages and is it ever adaptive, as evolutionary psychologists claim? I argue that there can be no univocal answers to these questions. Instead the answer varies for different kinds of envy. Emulative envy is neither morally nor prudentially bad; inert envy is very bad prudentially, but (mostly) not morally bad; aggressive envy is morally very bad, but may bring some genuine prudential gain; and spiteful envy is both morally and prudentially very bad. These differences have been overlooked by philosophers and psychologists, and are relevant to a variety of practical applications, especially in the fields of clinical practice and organizational studies. Controversially, I argue that emulative envy can in certain circumstances even be a *virtuous* emotion, and should be encouraged and cultivated.

Chapter 4 analyzes the relationship between envy and its apparent opposite, *love*. From Plato and the Fathers of the Christian Church to modern clinical psychologists, the received wisdom is that envy destroys love, and that love extinguishes envy. Such an opposition is plausible: envy is believed to necessarily involve malice toward the envied, while love is believed to necessarily involve concern for the beloved's welfare; envy feels bad, while (reciprocated) love feels good; envy brings with it Schadenfreude, pleasure at others' misfortune, while love brings with it what Germans call "Mitfreude," joy at others' success. Indeed, the experience of envy in loving relationships is perhaps the hardest kind of envy for people to weather. Against this received wisdom, I argue that envy and love are not incompatible opposites but two sides of the same coin. They thrive under the same psychological conditions and, as such, often accompany one another. In fact, I argue that love can benefit from emulative envy, and – if it is *wise* – love can tolerate some amount of inert, aggressive, and spiteful envy. Envy is the dark side of love, and love can illuminate envy.

Chapter 5 investigates the implications of my taxonomy for the *public* and *political* sphere. Envy is surprisingly absent in the recent revival of political emotions and this chapter aims to start remedying such lacuna. I start by reviewing a debate in distributive justice that is dominated by what I call the *Envious Egalitarianism* argument, according to which egalitarianism should be rejected because it is motivated by the vice of envy. John Rawls tackles this argument in *A Theory of Justice*, and his approach shapes the subsequent debate on envy in political philosophy. I argue that such a debate is misguided for two reasons: it uses an exceedingly narrow notion of envy – which I call *uberspiteful* envy – and it is exclusively focused on so-called "class envy" and thus on differences of socioeconomic status. Instead, I suggest a more contemporary lens which considers the role of envy in all its varieties and with regard to different kinds of differences in identity and status. In particular, I focus on racial relations and introduce the idea of *envious racial prejudice*. I apply my taxonomy to this new perspective, devoting particular attention to the case of Asian Americans, whose experience of racism is often underinvestigated at least in part – I suggest – because they are the object of envy. I conclude by acknowledging that the application of my taxonomy to the public sphere is not straightforward, and that political envy is often mingled with other emotions, such as resentment, indignation, and particularly jealousy. Thus, I end this chapter by returning and complicating the view I defended in Chapter 1.

The Conclusion is a collection of musings on what envy tells us about the structure of human value. I start with the notion of *fitting envy* and the idea that some things are worthy objects of envy. This notion implies that envy informs us not just of particular things we as individuals care about, but also of general goods that we as a species ought to care about because they are authentically good. Thus, I reject the ingrained conviction that authentic goodness is necessarily non-comparative and non-positional, and try to develop the implications of the idea that human psychology is deeply shaped by *social comparison*. I venture to suggest that there are two different but related such implications. The first is metaphysical: what is good for humans is almost entirely dependent on how we relate to and stack against one another. The second is epistemic: what is judged to be good relies almost entirely on standards that are relative and dependent on interpersonal comparison.

Because I see philosophy as a collaborative enterprise that stretches across time and place, the book contains an Appendix, in which I survey notions of envy and related emotions as they have been discussed in the ancient Greek tradition, in late antiquity and medieval thought, and in the modern era (with a quick dive into the twentieth century). The Appendix, which is limited mostly to the "Western" tradition, can be read both as a complement to the book or independently from it: it can be a starting point for the historian who has never thought about envy, or it can be a way to retrace already familiar notions in the history of thought. Rather than attempting a comprehensive review, I highlight the more interesting and influential views, and highlight connections with the contemporary debate.

CHAPTER I

What Is Envy?

O jealousy! Thou magnifier of trifles.

Friedrich von Schiller, Fiesco, or the Genoese Conspiracy

1.1 Introduction: Two Different Green-Eyed Monsters

One day I was talking to my mother about the topic of my dissertation, which was on envy, and she exclaimed, "I never feel envy, but I often feel jealousy!" Since this conversation happened in Italian, she used the terms: "invidia" and "gelosia." While the translation between Italian and English may appear straightforward, things are a bit more complicated below the surface. If an English speaker had said "I am not envious, I am just jealous!" not only the force of the distinction would have been diminished but possibly the distinction itself would have been unintelligible, or at least fuzzy. That is because, as I discuss below, in English "jealousy" is often used as a synonym for "envy." This is not an idiosyncrasy exclusive to English. French, for instance, behaves this way too, which is perhaps not surprising given that "envy" and "jealousie" derive from "envie" and "jalousie," respectively. (However, other romance languages such as Spanish and, as I said, Italian do not share this feature.)

There is a second notable linguistic phenomenon concerning envy, namely that in some languages (such as Dutch) there are *two* words that can be aptly translated as "envy" in English, one of which has a more positive connotation than the other (I come back to this linguistic practice in Chapter 2).

For helpful feedback on the final version of this chapter I would like to thank Neal Tognazzini and two anonymous reviewers for Cambridge University Press. For comments on a previous version I am grateful to William Beardsley, Douglas Cannon, Shen-yi Liao, Justin Tiehen, Ariela Tubert, and four anonymous reviewers.

In some linguistic communities, then, speakers are arguably more specific in talking about their envious experience, while in others speakers are much vaguer about it, since they also include what many people perceive as a different emotion. This is not idiosyncratic to envy: our linguistic practices are known to influence the way we think about our emotional experience, even though the extent of this influence is debatable (Prinz 2016). One could interpret these linguistic differences as reflecting deep divides in the emotional experience, or think of them as only superficial and argue that, deep down, we all feel the same emotions and only talk about them in different ways. More generally, given that language is an important component of culture,[1] one could wonder whether emotions are natural universal phenomena grounded in hardwired responses, or cultural local ones that are constructed from more primitive biological elements.[2] I do not wish to take a stand in this debate at a general level, but I do locate myself in the social constructionist camp with regard to envy in particular, albeit with a few provisos.

On the one hand, it seems that envy is present in all cultures (Foster 1972; Parrott and Mosquera 2008), and there are plausible evolutionary explanations for it (Hill and Buss 2008). Thus, I believe that *something like* the emotion that I call "envy" in English is indeed a universal human experience. At the same time, envy seems too cognitively complex and dependent on social interactions and thus cultural norms to be interestingly discussed as a universal emotion. In this book I draw from a variety of ancient, modern, and contemporary sources across different disciplines to support an account of envy that is unavoidably particular and specific to the spatiotemporal context of my likely audience: educated individuals from Westernized countries.[3]

---

[1] Note that language and culture can come apart. English and Dutch are very close linguistically (they are both West Germanic languages), and yet their envy vocabulary, so to speak, is very different. French and Italian also belong to the same linguistic family and yet they differ in whether the word for jealousy can be used to refer to envy. Vice versa, I have talked to native English speakers from very different cultural contexts (North America, the United Kingdom, Singapore, Australia) and they all confirmed they often hear envy and jealousy used as synonyms. So, on the one hand, language seems to affect emotional experience independently of culture, but, on the other hand, closely related languages can behave very differently down the line, presumably due to different cultural contexts. The relation between language, culture, and emotion is complicated indeed.

[2] See Mallon and Stich 2000 for a review of the debate, and an interesting proposal to dissolve it; see also Barrett 2006, 2017 for a more recent perspective on the construction of emotions.

[3] The empirical evidence that I rely on is mostly collected through study of contemporary "WEIRD" subjects, that is, individuals who live in Western, Educated, Industrialized, Rich, Democratic societies (Henrich et al. 2010). This is another reason why my account is culturally specific.

Overall I aim to steer clear of as many theoretical commitments as I can: I do not commit myself to any specific view about emotions in general. While I have my leanings, I hope that my analysis of envy can prove useful across different schools of thought. I try to use terminology that is as neutral as possible. This theoretical neutrality has the further advantage of making the book accessible to a wider audience, that is, readers who are not familiar with the intricacies of the debate on the ontology of emotions, or other more technical discussions in this field.

That being said, the definition of envy, and how it differs from jealousy, is a necessary preliminary for an inquiry into its nature. Too many times I find myself talking about envy in informal settings and being asked what I think about – jealousy! Therefore the bulk of this chapter is dedicated to clarifying the relation between envy and jealousy. Section 1.2 provides evidence and explanation of why they are confused with each other. Section 1.3 presents the most prominent and persuasive view of how they differ, namely that envy is about lack of a good, while jealousy is about the loss of a good. But human emotionality is messy and complications arise, so Section 1.4 is devoted to ambiguous, hybrid, and transitional cases. Last, but certainly not least, Section 1.5 introduces the definition of envy that I use throughout the book.

1.2   Envy and Jealousy as Rivalrous Emotions

Before proposing an account of the difference between envy and jealousy, let me substantiate my claim that they are often conflated and thus the claim that they are, indeed, distinct (or else there would be no "conflation").

Merriam-Webster's first definition of "jealous'" is "hostile toward a rival or one believed to enjoy an advantage: ENVIOUS," while the *OED* lists "envy" as a synonym of jealousy as its second meaning.[4] Seminal works on envy in sociology and anthropology contain discussions lamenting the presumed synonymy of these English terms (Schoeck 1969, 71–2; Foster 1972, 167–8), which is presented as an unfortunate source of confusion for scholarly investigation. Social psychologists have since cast doubt on the synonymy claim, arguing that "jealousy" encompasses a range of meanings that include those of "envy," but not vice versa (Silver and Sabini 1978). They have provided evidence that two emotions are

---

[4] www.merriam-webster.com/dictionary/jealous?show=0&t=1316726021; www.oed.com/view/Entry /100958?redirectedFrom=jealousy#eid.

phenomenologically experienced as distinct *even by English speakers*: envy is more likely to be characterized by feelings of inferiority and self-criticism, wishfulness and longing, and a motivation to self-improve; jealousy is more likely to be characterized by feelings of suspiciousness and distrust, rejection and hurt, hostility and anger at others, and fear of loss (Smith et al. 1988).

Furthermore, jealousy is almost always accompanied by some envy for the rival, but the opposite does not hold, and envy is characteristically associated with concern for public disapproval, while jealousy is associated with self-righteousness (Parrott and Smith 1993).

This second result is crucial to understanding the linguistic asymmetry: jealous people do not worry about hiding their jealousy, because jealousy, albeit condemned when excessive, is less stigmatized than envy and considered more legitimate. Consequently it makes sense for "jealousy" to incorporate some of envy's meaning, but not the opposite.

Both linguistic conflation and differentiation of the two emotions have also been proved via taxometric analysis, which not only confirms the qualitative differences between envy and jealousy but also shows that envy and jealousy are *discrete* complex affective kinds rather than different regions of the same continuous affective domain (Haslam and Bornstein 1996).

Finally, philosophers and scholars of religion also tend to agree that envy and jealousy are distinct emotions (e.g., Farrell 1980; Neu 1980; Ben-Ze'ev 1990, 2000; Schimmel 2008; Taylor 1988, 2006).

An interdisciplinary consensus of this size is hard to ignore: sociologists, anthropologists, psychologists, and philosophers all agree that envy and jealousy are distinct. But then, why are these emotions so often confused with each other?

First of all, both emotions involve a *three-party relation*. First, there is the *agent*, the person who feels the emotion: they who are jealous, or envious. Second, there is the person toward whom the emotion is directed: they who are the primary *target* of jealousy, or envied. Note the awkward way of referring to the person jealousy is directed at. That is because saying "I'm jealous of x" in common parlance is ambiguous. It may refer to the logical equivalent of the envied, or it may refer to the logical equivalent of the object of envy, the thing in virtue of which we envy the envied – which is often another person in the case of jealousy.

But in abstract terms, when thinking about the logical structure of the two emotions, let me call that object in virtue of which we feel the emotion *the good*. Different theorists will have different names for the notion I am referring to, but here I want to stick to a commonsensical view, because we are trying to understand why these emotions are so similar and so I am using a schema that enhances the similarity.

The good, in the case of jealousy, is usually a person, but it need not be. As Gabriele Taylor puts it, "[i]n both cases the person experiencing the emotion sees herself as standing in some relation to the valued good, where this good may be some material possession, a social position or position of relative power, a personal quality, or some kind of personal relationship" (Taylor 1988, 233). However, paradigmatic cases of jealousy usually involve three people. The jealous spouse's jealousy is targeted at another person who is seen as threatening one's relationship to a loved one. In my terminology, the other person is the *target* of jealousy, and the loved one is the *good*.

It is clear from this description that the target of jealousy is some sort of rival. But so is the target of envy, the envied. Both emotions are thus *rivalrous* or *adversarial* emotions. There is some sort of competition between the agent and the target, and the good is the prize, the object they both want. Even in cases of nonprototypical jealousy we can see at least an adversarial relation: the person who jealously guards their privacy is acting against someone who is seen as an enemy, even if potentially an abstract one, such as corporations or the government. Often, albeit not always in the case of jealousy, this competitive nature involves an element of *comparison*. The jealous spouse typically fears that the rival will be seen by their beloved as superior, more attractive in some way. The envious necessarily sees the envied as in a superior position, as we shall see soon. While the comparative element is not necessary in jealousy, it is common enough. Relatedly, the competition is often, albeit not necessarily in either emotion, perceived as a zero-sum game: only the agent or the target can win the prize, in the eyes of the agent, and that is what drives the competition and determines the adversarial nature of the relation.

In virtue of these features, both emotions are affectively *aversive*, in the sense that they are painful to experience, because they negatively affect the agent's self-esteem, involve the idea of a threat to one's well-being, and create a conflict with another person.

Now, note that there are many counterexamples to the picture I just drew. In fact, most of this book is devoted to showing that there are forms of envy that do not fit neatly into this description. But this is a common, if often implicit and unconscious, way of thinking about the two emotions that should help to see why they are often associated and confused with each other.

Finally, envy and jealousy frequently *co-occur* in a situation: the same agent can feel both envy and jealousy directed at the same target. The romantic rivalry situation is the more common scenario in which this occurs, but another obvious case is that of sibling rivalry: a jealous spouse is also envious of their rival, and siblings often feel both envy and jealousy toward each other. I shall come back to both of these cases later.

So, to sum up, envy and jealousy are rivalrous painful emotions involving a three-party relation, which are directed at a competitor and are concerned with a good, and which often arise together. It is in virtue of these similarities that envy and jealousy are often confused with one another in our everyday discourse and even in introspection. But how are they different? That is a slightly more complicated question, and the subject of Section 1.3.

1.3   To Lack or to Lose, That Is the Question

Shakespeare's play *Othello* may be interpreted as portraying both a paradigmatic case of envy and one of jealousy. Iago has failed to be promoted to lieutenant by Othello, who favored Cassio instead. Pained by his perceived disadvantage, Iago plots to bring both Othello and Cassio down and, in particular, endeavors to destroy Othello's happiness. He makes him believe that his wife Desdemona has an affair with Cassio. Othello falls prey to an obsessive jealousy, and eventually kills Desdemona and then himself, while Iago is sentenced to death by torture.

Now, let me acknowledge up-front that this is a simplified version of a complex work of art that has given rise to innumerable interpretations, so I am not attempting to provide a persuasive analysis of the play itself. Even a quick reading of the synopsis no doubt provides the opportunity for several different ways of looking at the emotions that the characters feel. For instance, Iago can be seen as envying Cassio, but hating or being resentful of Othello. I think this complexity is not only due to Shakespeare's artistic talent but also due to the actual complexity of the emotions that arise in the circumstances he conjures. However, let me assume a simplified version of the story in which Iago is envious of Othello, and Othello is jealous of Cassio. It is plausible enough to conceive of Iago in the following way. He looks at Othello as someone who has everything: a beautiful wife, a successful military career, the friendship and admiration of his peers, and social esteem. He probably tells himself that Othello, a Moor, does not deserve that – and we see in Chapter 2 that the perception of undeservingness often accompanies the experience of envy, even though most scholars conceive of it as a defense mechanism rather than a necessary feature of envy itself. When we envy someone, it feels better to think that the envied's superior position is due to an injustice, as opposed to a personal failure or shortcoming. Iago is a pretty despicable character who ends up being responsible for many deaths, including that of his wife and his own. It seems that Othello was right in assessing Cassio to be a superior candidate for the position.

As for Othello, he is jealousy personified: he is one of the most famous literary representations of romantic jealousy. But one should not see him as only protective of his relationship with his wife, but also of his standing in Venetian society. Desdemona and Othello married in secret because Desdemona's father, Brabantio, would not approve of her marrying a man who is Black and not Christian. Othello's privileged position in Venice is fragile, and not just because social esteem is always fickle and military honor is subject to the fortune involved in battle. Othello is not supposed to have his fortune – like all tragedies, he is bound to see a reversal of his success. So, it is understandable that Othello comes to believe that Desdemona is unfaithful, notwithstanding her desperate assurances to the contrary.

Othello, given his position as an outsider to Venetian society, is prone to protecting himself from the loss of valuable goods (social prestige, marriage to a beautiful loving wife), and he does so by striking against a perceived rival (Cassio, the target of his jealousy). Iago is prone to desiring the same goods, which he perceives himself as lacking. Since he thinks they are out of his grasp, he devotes himself to spoiling them. Both emotions are depicted in their worst possible versions and outcomes: Othello's jealousy is unjustified and misplaced, and he also acts on it in the worst possible way. Iago's envy is also misguided in several ways, which will become clearer in the next chapters of this book. Neither envy nor jealousy need always be so nefarious or unwarranted, although it is their destructive and irrational features that make for great literature. But even though these are dysfunctional manifestations of these emotions, they well exemplify the core of their difference: jealousy is fundamentally about *loss*, whereas envy is fundamentally about *lack*.[5]

---

[5] This aboutness can be cashed out in various ways: in terms of situational antecedents, of patterns of appraisal or evaluation, of fittingness conditions, etc.; it is compatible with conceiving of emotions as natural kinds or as psychological constructs. Again, in this book I attempt to remain neutral with regard to these theoretical presuppositions.

This way of thinking about envy and jealousy is widely accepted and shared across disciplinary perspectives.[6] Many philosophers defend this view (such as Taylor 1988; Ben-Ze'ev 1990; Purshouse 2004; and Konyndyk DeYoung 2009), but the earliest explicit instance I found in the literature is due to anthropologist George Foster, who writes, "[e]nvy stems from the desire to acquire something possessed by another person, while jealousy is rooted in the fear of losing something already possessed" (Foster 1972, 168) and helpfully refers to jealousy as "the normal counterpart of envy" (ibid.). He suggests as a typical example the case of a man who is jealous of a romantic rival who is, in turn, envious of him. The idea here is that envy covets what jealousy guards. An analogous case in a non-romantic context can be found in Tolkien's *The Lord of the Rings*: Frodo jealously guards the ring against Sam and Gollum's envious desires.[7]

So, while both emotions are rivalrous and competitive, the jealous sees the rival as attempting to take away what is rightfully theirs, whereas the envious sees the rival as having something they (the agent) want. While the envious may think they have a right to it, that is not a necessary feature of the emotion, and bystanders often disagree and see the envious in the negative light of an aggressor more often than not. This difference with regard to perceived entitlement and justice of the gap between the agent and the target explains the different societal attitude toward the two emotions.

Obsessive and disproportionate jealousy is condemned, but jealousy by itself is often accepted or at least excused as understandable. In a romantic context, in many cultures a bit of "healthy" jealousy is taken to be a sign of true affection and care for one's partner; moderate sibling jealousy is considered normal and developmentally appropriate (more on this topic later). In non-romantic contexts, too, jealousy can have a positive connotation. The best defense for this claim lies perhaps in the Old Testament, where divine jealousy is omnipresent and Yahweh is often described as "jealous," meaning that he expects the people of Israel to be faithful to him (Schimmel 2008, 19).[8]

This sense of righteousness characteristic of jealousy explains why jealousy is not as hidden as envy. As Solomon Schimmel, a psychologist who has studied envy in the Jewish tradition, puts it, "Jealous people will probably be

---

[6] In psychology, see, e.g., Lazarus 1991; Parrott 1991; Parrott and Smith 1993; Miceli and Castelfranchi 2007. In sociology, see Clanton 2006. In anthropology I discuss Foster 1972. Notwithstanding its popularity, the lack versus loss model is not the only view available in the literature. See Protasi 2017b for a review and critique of alternative accounts.

[7] Thanks to an anonymous reviewer for this example.

[8] Thanks to Neal Tognazzini for reminding me of this example.

more ready to take overt action to protect what they believe are rightfully theirs. Overt crimes of passion motivated by jealousy are frequent, whereas crimes of envy tend to be secretive. In general, it is shameful to be envious but more acceptable to be jealous in protecting what one rightfully possesses" (Schimmel 2008, 19). Parrott and Smith confirm in their psychological study (1993) that envy is more strongly associated with feelings of comparative inferiority and shame than envy. Admitting envy thus implies admitting one's perceived inferiority. Furthermore, in most people's conception, envy also involves a desire to deprive another person of something valuable that this other person rightfully owns: it's no surprise that people fear envy from others and deny it when they feel it. Jealousy, on the other hand, seems more excusable – an emotion we would rather not feel, nor be the target of, but understandable as a response to a perceived threat. Jealousy is on the defense, while envy is on the attack, so to speak. (In Chapter 2 I argue that not all kinds of envy imply aggressive desire. But the most visible and feared ones do.)

The lack versus loss model also explains the linguistic asymmetries introduced in Section 1.2. The linguistic asymmetry (the fact that we often say "jealous" when we mean "envious") is due to the desire to avoid social stigma: we trade on the similarities between the two emotions to admit only the one that is less shameful, even if sometimes we are actually feeling the other, whether we are aware of it or not.

Our different attitudes toward jealousy and envy also emerge in fictional representations. Try and find an envious hero, or even an envious scoundrel described in sympathetic terms – I challenge you![9] The envious are always depicted as unappealing characters, most often despicable or scary villains. The jealous, even when they commit hideous crimes such as killing their wife or their children (as in the case of Medea), are depicted as struggling with all-too-human demons and can be at least tragic heroes. We hate and fear the Iagos, while we pity and empathize with the Othellos (or, at the very least, we are more likely to excuse them. Note that I am making here a *comparative* claim, which is compatible with being wary about jealousy and its potentially devastating consequences).

Finally, the lack versus loss model also explains why envy and jealousy frequently co-occur: the lover perceives the other person not only as

---

[9] Alright, there is a counterexample to almost anything. But the envious hero is most definitely not an archetype, unlike the jealous one. Note that characters who are occasionally envious (such as the protagonist of *Lucky Jim* by Kingsley Amis), rather than being prototypically envious, are not real counterexamples.

threatening a possession (the loving relationship), but also as having something the lover does not have (a particular quality, or the capacity to attract the beloved in a way that is disruptive of the relationship, etc.).

To sum up, envy and jealousy are both unpleasant emotions targeted at another person that is conceived of as a rival or competitor of sorts, who stands in a relation to a valued good in a way that is different from the agent's: in the case of envy, the target is perceived as better off, possessing what the agent lacks; in the case of jealousy, the target is perceived as worse off, lacking what the agent possesses (at least in her perception). Consequently, the envier is motivated to overcome her comparative disadvantage, possibly by depriving the envied of the good, while the jealous is motivated to protect her comparative advantage, possibly by fending off attacks from the rival and/or locking away the good.

But, then again, things are not quite so simple. In Section 1.4 I propose some complicated cases and see if this model can handle them.

1.4 Complications: Ambiguous, Hybrid, and Transitional Scenarios

Like any theoretical model that attempts to simplify a complex and messy reality, the lack versus loss model is not going to perfectly capture every contrast between lived experiences of envy and jealousy. In this section I consider situations with which the view seems to struggle.

First, I have mentioned that envy and jealousy often co-occur. In some contexts they co-occur systemically: think of sibling rivalry. When a new child is born the older sibling usually fear that their special relationship with their parents will be affected, and this is especially common for the first born, who is used to having their parents all to themselves. Children are rightly concerned about the arrival of a competitor. Even though parents assure their children that they are loved equally, the reality is that they are not. Some children are loved more or better than others, some children receive more resources than others, and it is a truism that some children are just liked more than others.[10]

Even aside from particularly unequal circumstances, children always vie for the limited parental resources, such as time and energy, and find

---

[10] The literature, spanning several disciplines, on sibling rivalry in general and unequal allocation of parental resources in particular is too large for me to provide just a couple of quick references. One of the most striking but perhaps not surprising pieces of data is that light-skinned children are preferred to their dark-skinned siblings (Rangel 2015).

themselves behaving at the same time defensively (jealously) and proactively (enviously). If they perceive themselves to have a special relationship of some kind with a parent, they will be afraid to lose it. If they perceive the other siblings to be better off in some respect, they will want to outperform them.

Furthermore, interpersonal comparisons in general are frequent, widespread, often unconscious and immediate, and almost unavoidable in many settings (I shall talk more about this topic in Section 1.5). But siblings, in particular, are continuously, and sometimes unfairly or inappropriately, compared to each other along a variety of dimensions, not only by their parents but also by relatives, family friends, teachers, and so forth. I still remember when my little brother came home from his first day of middle school and reported back that his teacher, upon hearing his last name, told him: "Your sister was a very good student, but don't worry, we don't make comparisons."

Therefore, both envy and jealousy are likely to arise among siblings, but it may be difficult, even from a first-personal perspective, to distinguish between what is owned, but in danger of being lost, and what is lacked, but potentially attainable. Young children, especially, may not have a sufficiently articulate conception of what's at stake, and their emotional experience may be less defined as a consequence: their beliefs will be primitive, their desires inchoate, their feelings mixed, intense, and confusing. The emotion felt toward one sibling may not be easily diagnosed as one of either envy or jealousy. This kind of *epistemic ambiguity*, however, is not unusual when it comes to emotions, and it is to be expected in the case of close, frequently co-occurring emotions such as envy and jealousy.

But some cases of sibling rivalry can be construed as truly *hybrid* cases, meaning that both a loss and a lack are at stake at the same time. Imagine the following situation, inspired by the reality I mentioned above that children are lover unequally:

> Ugly Duckling never felt loved by her mother. Her sisters were always complimented, supported, looked after in material and spiritual ways, but since she was always the shiest and least "shiny" among them, she never got her mother's affections. Ugly Duckling is intensely jealous of her sisters.[11]

Notice how natural it is in this case to want to use "jealous." At the same time the emotion seems to be a mixture of envy and jealousy according to

---

[11] This is not an unusual pattern for children, and above all daughters, of narcissistic mothers (McBride 2008). Thanks to Maria Miceli for stimulating my thoughts on this kind of case.

the lack versus loss model. Ugly Duckling thinks her mother never loved her, and one cannot lose what one never had. So technically, according to our model, we would have to say that Ugly Duckling is envious. But that does not sound like the whole story: intuitively we think that Ugly Duckling deserves to be loved, or is in some sense entitled to parental love. Whether or not children have a *right* to be loved (Liao 2015) they certainly have a reasonable expectation to be loved. So, while Ugly Duckling has never had her mother's love, she perceives it as being in some important sense "due" to her. As we have seen, when we own something, we tend to think we have a right to it, and a right to protect it from threats. We interpret Ugly Duckling's emotion as jealousy because in many other counterfactually near worlds Ugly Duckling *would* have had her mother's love, and she would have every right to be protective about it. In this kind of case, then, the emotion felt by the agent is, it seems to me, truly hybrid, because the disadvantage felt by the agent is perceived as both a lack and a loss, depending on the perspective that it is entertained. However, such an example is not a paradigmatic case of either emotion, because it is *not* a standard situation, given that most parents love all of their children, even when they have preferences among them.

Another hybrid case is the following, drawn from a popular American TV series (*The Office*) (with apologies to fans of the original British one):

> Jim is in love with his coworker Pam, but Pam is already engaged to Roy. Pam does not know what she feels. She thinks of Jim as a good friend, but she is not yet ready to admit feeling more than friendly love. Roy is intensely jealous of Jim, and also envies him for being of a superior social and intellectual standing.

Roy's emotions toward Jim are pretty easy to catalogue. He soon becomes aware that he has a romantic rival. Pam is clearly attracted to Jim, and Jim is presented to the audience as a much more desirable partner for Pam: Jim makes more money and is more educated (he works in the office, while Roy is a warehouse worker), he is more good-looking in a "nice White boy" sort of way, and he is much more attentive and attuned to Pam's needs. (There are not-so-subtle classist biases at play that I cannot belabor on here.) Roy feels both jealousy and envy – again, a typical case of co-occurrence. But what does Jim feel toward Roy?[12]

---

[12] Again, remember the culturally local perspective of my analysis. In a classical Greek setting, this case is uncomplicated: both Jim and Roy would feel *phthonos*, without the need for further distinctions. See the Appendix.

Jim is *not* in a romantic relationship with Pam, but would want to be in one. He lacks what Roy has, and so we would expect him to feel envy. But this does not sound quite right, as it did not sound right in Ugly Ducking's case. While Jim might feel a tinge of envy for the man who has what he lacks, and while he might be wounded in his self-esteem because Pam does not at first acknowledge that he is a more desirable partner than Roy, it seems that Jim mostly feels jealousy.[13]

There are authors who interpret jealousy as being primarily about the need for romantic attention (Tov-Ruach 1980; Wreen 1989). For them, Jim's case is the paradigmatic case of jealousy. I critique this view in greater detail elsewhere (Protasi 2017b). Here I want to highlight that the lack versus loss view has the means to account for this case. Jim is in love with Pam. While he does not have a socially sanctioned relationship with her, he is her close friend and confidant, and he is emotionally committed to her. For a long time (until he comes to believe – erroneously – that she will never leave Roy) he does not date anyone else and he devotes her a great deal of care and attention. Thus, he *does* have an exclusive relationship with her that nobody else, not even Roy, has. So, on the one hand he is rightly concerned that Pam's marriage to Roy will extinguish their relationship; on the other hand, he, like Ugly Duckling, is emotionally warranted in expecting Pam's reciprocation, and may think of Roy, consciously or not, as an obstacle to that reciprocation. Jim's emotion is, too, a hybrid case of envy and jealousy. Note that hybrid cases are not particularly problematic. Even if emotions in general are natural kinds (a big if), socially and cognitively complex emotions such as envy and jealousy are bound to come in different varieties and flavors: even if jealousy were like H_2O (again, not an obvious assumption), we could imagine it being mixed with another substance, much like we can mix water and heavy water.

All the scenarios that I described so far could qualify as "borderline" cases of some sort, either epistemically (in the sense that the subject does not know what they are feeling) or metaphysically (in the sense that it is

---

[13] Jerome Neu analyzes a similar case: "How are we to describe the emotional state of the third party in situations where there are two lovers, one of whom is jealous over the other and fears the encroachments of the third party, while the third party has not made any advances but certainly desires to supplant the jealous lover?" (Neu 1980, 434). His verdict is that the third party feels "admiring envy." I find this response unconvincing in a case like Jim's, since there is definitely nothing like admiration in his attitude toward Roy and also because he does have a relation with Pam which grounds some sort of claim toward her, as I explain above.

ontologically unclear whether it is one or the other). But there is a final case, which is also borderline, but across time, such as the following:

> Akira realizes that their husband Brad is cheating on them with Wataru. They first become jealous and try to win their love back, but eventually realize that the betrayal has weakened their relationship and they are falling out of love for Brad. Akira and Brad split up, and Brad marries Wataru. When Akira thinks of their former rival Wataru, they find themselves envious, because they see Wataru as younger, fitter, and smarter and they fear they won't be able to find another partner.

We could call this a *transitional* case. At some point in the transition it is *metaphysically vague* what Akira is feeling, whether jealousy or envy, but at the ends of the spectrum it is clear what they feel. The in-between state might be particularly painful and ripe for practical implications: Akira is clearly in pain, but might wonder what that pain means. Is it jealousy, in which case maybe they should fight for their love with Brad? Or is it envy, in which case they should not? In addition to pain, Akira feels hostility toward Wataru, but that is not decisive either, since both jealousy and envy may involve such feelings (remember, they are both rivalrous).

Additional introspection may provide some clue: if Akira wishes they were more like Wataru, and would like to improve themselves, or feels ashamed and a failure, or is overall more focused on their personal inadequacy than on losing Brad, then they are probably feeling more envy than jealousy; if they are pained by Brad's absence and feel lonely and abandoned, but at the same time feel distrust toward him, then they are probably feeling more jealousy than envy.

The lack versus loss model nicely makes sense of this transition: Akira's emotions end up being different because their situation and focus change. They move from being concerned with guarding their relationship to Brad (a good they have, but are afraid to lose) to being concerned with their inferiority to Wataru with regard to the general valuable good of being loved by *someone like* Brad (a good they currently perceive themselves as lacking and would like to acquire again).

You may still be unconvinced about these complicated cases. That's okay: real life is complicated, and emotions are messy. No theoretical model will ever perfectly capture all possible cases of actual emotional experience. What matters is to have a sense of how envy differs from jealousy in paradigmatic cases, so that from now on we can focus on envy proper.

1.5 What Is Envy, Then? A Definition

Finally, I can propose a fuller self-standing definition of envy, which I shall use throughout this book. Recall what I said before about envy and jealousy sharing a tripartite structure. It is worth repeating this formal characterization, which will become helpful in Chapter 2 when distinguishing between different kinds of envy. Envy's three-place relation is composed by the *envier*, that is, the subject who feels the emotion; the *envied* or target, that is, the person toward whom the emotion is directed; and the *good*, that is, the object with regard to which the envier is in a disadvantageous position vis-à-vis the envied.

Envy, then, is about feeling that one is at a specific kind of disadvantage, or of inferiority, that is, a perceived *lack* of an object that is believed to be good. In what I just said there is a lot of emphasis on subjectivity: emotions are unavoidably the product of a subject's perceptions and value judgments. Envy is about *perceived* disadvantage and *perceived* goodness. Confessing one's envy is difficult not least because it is very revealing. Tell me what you envy and I will tell you who you are, or at least what you care about.

Perceptions involved in envy may of course be incorrect, either because the envier commits a factual mistake (e.g., it is false that they are disadvantaged vis-à-vis the envied), or because the envier makes an evaluative mistake (e.g., they perceive as good what is actually bad). For the time being I am going to assume that the envier is always correct in their perceptions and beliefs, but I will come back later to cases in which that is not the case.

Because envy is about a perceived lack, disadvantage, or inferiority, it alerts the agent of a problem and is thus bound to be painful. Envy is an *aversive* emotion: its affect is undoubtedly negative, even though it ranges from unpleasant to excruciating. This feature of envy is virtually undisputed. Christine de Pisan claims that the "darts and stings" of envy make it the only unpleasant sin (de Pisan 1985, as cited in La Caze 2001, 34). Descriptions of the phenomenology of envy are usually quite colorful and often involve the idea of being eaten from the inside and other metaphors of internal corruption, some of which I detail in the next chapters. Envy is notoriously associated with the color green. While this association became entrenched in the English-speaking world thanks to Shakespeare, it is present in other linguistic communities as well and is probably as old as the ancient Greeks, who considered a certain green paleness a sign of illness (Neaman and Silver 1995).

In the historical Appendix I recount how many philosophers, such as Plato, Aristotle, Hobbes, Locke, and Spinoza, consider the painful nature of envy to be its defining feature, as do some contemporary psychologists (Tai et al. 2012). But even those who do not define envy simply as a pain, but rather as another kind of mental state, or those who think about envy under the guise of a vice or a sin, often remark on its painful or unpleasant nature. The thought voiced by Pisan above – that envy is the only unpleasant sin – often recurs in the history of ideas. I should say I am actually not so sure that that is the case: wrath seems the obvious counterexample, and even sloth is not clearly pleasant. But even if other vices or sins are or can be unpleasant, it is uncontroversial that envy itself is never pleasant, even though the experience of some of its behavioral consequents may be so. (For more on envy as a deadly sin, see the Appendix.)

So, envy is an aversive response to an inferiority with regard to a good vis-à-vis another person, someone who is perceived as having what the envier lacks. But there is more. Envy necessarily involves comparing oneself to another. Both the vast psychological literature on social comparison and the history of Western philosophy tell us that envy requires two more conditions to arise.

First, there is what we can call the *similarity condition*, according to which we envy only those who are similar to us in some relevant sense. Aristotle in the *Rhetoric* already discusses this notion, which, at its core, is as old as Hesiod (cf. Sanders 2014, 34, and see Chapter 4 and the Appendix for more on Aristotle's views on similarity and envy). Among the many philosophers who follow Aristotle in discussing this condition, Hume in the *Treatise* analyzes the way in which similarity makes comparison both possible and informative (again, see Appendix).

Contemporary psychology has confirmed these philosophical intuitions (Miceli and Castelfranchi 2007; Smith and Kim 2007), and it has also uncovered the extent to which social comparison in general affects our cognitive and emotional processing. Susan Fiske vividly describes human beings as "comparison machines" (Fiske 2011, 13), by which she means that we continuously and often inadvertently compare ourselves to people who are like us in capabilities, endowments, values, and aspirations. Empirical evidence shows that social comparison is an essential element of human cognition, and it is both habitual (Corcoran et al. 2011; Mussweiler 2003) and automatic (Mussweiler et al. 2004). Social comparison serves three crucial functions in human psychology (Fiske 2011): it provides information needed to evaluate and improve ourselves, it protects our self-esteem, and it helps us fit into our groups.

I will come back to the important role of social comparison throughout the book. For now, what I want to highlight is that envy is essentially comparative but, unlike jealousy or admiration, is specifically targeted at people whom we perceive as in the same comparison class as we are. We do not envy people out of our league, so to speak. This is one way in which envy is revealing. A philosopher I know once told me that they are envious of Plato. Assuming they are right about their own feelings, that tells me this philosopher is a pretty self-confident person who has a quite high opinion of their philosophical talents! (I should say I envy both those talents and their confidence!)

Now, of course, people can misjudge their own capabilities and status. Some people are very insecure and badly underestimate themselves, while others are presumptuous and make the opposite mistake. But a fascinating fact is that, for most people, social comparison tends to always be *slightly upward*: we compare to those who, from an impartial perspective, are slightly better than us. That is, most of us are *systematically* shooting a bit high. This tendency may serve a variety of purposes, such as positive self-evaluation, self-improvement, and self-enhancement, but it is also a risky business: if we compare ourselves to someone whom we perceive as similar, and find out that they outperform us in something important to us, then we are painfully disappointed. And, indeed, we are likely to find ourselves in this situation if we are always shooting a little higher than we realize (see Miceli and Castelfranchi 2007, 453–4 for a detailed discussion of all these issues).

The similarity condition is an established empirical finding, but philosophers are often dissatisfied by it because what counts as "similar" is heavily context-dependent, even though psychologists tend to focus on seemingly objective (and easy to quantify and measure) variables such as gender, sex, and age. For instance, when we envy someone for their athletic fitness, age and gender are relevant and salient features, while more specific personal features may be unimportant. But in other contexts being similar means sharing the same level of skills and interests, such as two professors in the same department who work in the same field and compete for the same award. However, again, remember that Aristotle and Hume, among many others, remark on this feature of envy extensively, and this is why I include similarity in the very definition of envy.

There is a second necessary condition for envy's arousal, which I shall call the *self-relevance condition*. This condition can be best understood by thinking of envy as part of the process by which we cope with threats to our self-esteem (Salovey and Rothman 1991). The most widely cited model in this context is Abraham Tesser's "self-evaluation maintenance" (SEM) theory, which he and his colleagues developed in the 1980s. This theory concerns the ways in which feedback stemming from social comparison impacts our self-evaluation.[14] The model predicts that we are motivated to maintain a positive evaluation of the self. When we are outperformed by a similar other, the feedback we receive in terms of self-evaluation depends on *how important to our sense of identity* the domain of comparison is.

Suppose I strongly identify with being a philosopher: if I perceive myself inferior to another early-career woman philosopher teaching at a liberal arts college (that is, someone similar to me), this comparison will affect me negatively and I am likely to feel envy.

But now suppose I compare myself to another colleague, who is similar to me in age, gender, and fitness level, *with regard to our soccer skills*. She happens to be a decent soccer player, while I am mediocre, and yet this inferiority does not bother me. Quite the contrary: when she scores a goal, I rejoice in her accomplishment and tell everyone that she is in my department. What is happening here? Instead of a process of *comparison*, a process of *reflection* has taken place: because I do not identify with being a soccer player, her superiority does not make me feel threatened. Instead, my self-esteem is boosted by the fact that we are similar and I "bask in reflected glory" (Cialdini et al. 1976). Again, remember that social comparison happens all the time, and one of its functions is to protect our self-esteem. While one protective mechanism is to compare downward, and being reassured that we are better than others (this is one of scorn's and contempt's functions), basking in reflected glory is an example of the protective functions of upward comparison. But it is premised on the fact that the superiority of the similar other is not about an ability or achievement that is relevant to who I perceive myself to be.

The importance of the self-relevance condition in envy is also shown by research on child envy. Very young children (3–5 years), who have not developed specific interests and a sense of "who they are," experience envy across *all* domains, whereas older children (5–11 years) feel envy only in areas that they rate as self-defining (Bers and Rodin 1984. Children between 0 and 2 probably do not experience envy a defined here, insofar

---

[14] See Tesser and Collins 1988; Tesser et al. 1988. See Salovey and Rodin 1984 and Salovey and Rothman 1991 among others for an application of this model to envy.

as they do not sense themselves as separate individuals).[15] In my experience, children also may not have a well-defined notion of comparison
classes. I am always bewildered by how my daughters compare their
drawing ability to mine or that of other adults: they get frustrated, and
sometimes envious, of the fact that people much older than them can do
things better, with seemingly no understanding that the comparison is not
really diagnostic due to the age gap. I am not that good at drawing, but
I am more talented than even the most precocious 4-year-old child, for
obvious reasons. Their self-esteem is threatened even though from an adult
perspective it should not be. Sibling rivalry is exacerbated by this inability
to understand comparison classes: my 4-year-old daughter expected to be
praised for her ability to walk as much as her 1-year-old sister who was just
starting to take her first steps. The fact that I didn't compliment her on a
skill she had already mastered was a source of pain for her, because she saw
her sibling as similar notwithstanding the age gap.

   The self-relevance condition is widely acknowledged in the empirical
literature, but in my experience philosophers, again, tend to be frustrated
by a perceived vagueness, as with the similarity condition. This is not
surprising, because the two conditions are related and perhaps versions of
the same thing: they both identify whether the target's superiority is in
some way informative about the subject's own standing. In the social
comparison literature, "similarity is measured by the individual's evalua-
tions of his or her similarity with the more successful other, either on
dimensions that pertain directly to the comparison [...] or dimensions
that [...] partially define one's self-image" (Schaubroeck and Lam 2004,
34). The idea of self-image or self-identity are bound to be complex and
subject to philosophical scrutiny, and this is admittedly lacking in the
empirical investigations on social comparison and envy. I will not attempt
to fill this lacuna here, but let me say that under definitions of self-image or
self-identity one would have to include what we care about, what we aspire
to be, and what we perceive ourselves as being. Thus, it ought to include
our temporal selves as well: we can imaginatively put ourselves in counterfactual scenarios and compare our past or future selves to people we are
not currently similar to. For instance, I might envy a graduate student who
outperforms my past self; or a more senior colleague, because I forecast
being inferior to them once I reach their career stage. As one can see in the
Appendix, Hume also analyzes scenarios in which the target is currently

---

[15] For an influential psychoanalytic perspective on envy in infants, which is very different from mine,
see Klein 1957.

perceived as inferior but approaching at a worryingly fast pace – that is the kind of envy felt by the teacher who sees that their pupil is about to surpass them. All these cases put pressure on the two conditions I have highlighted here, but not in a problematic way. The empirical research focuses on paradigmatic cases and on the general population; there are always going to be unusual situations or idiosyncratic individuals. The definition of envy I am about to propose is not meant to characterize all possible cases of envy, nor to account for all positions in the logical space. It is derived by overlapping prominent accounts in philosophy and in the social sciences, which in turn are grounded in anecdotal observations, empirical evidence, and intuitions.[16]

According to this definition, envy is an aversive response to a perceived inferiority or disadvantage vis-à-vis a similar other, with regard to a good that is relevant to the sense of identity of the envier.

This definition does not yet tell us what envy motivates one to do, which may be seen as a further way of discriminating between emotions. Envy is usually perceived as necessarily malicious, aggressively bent toward the envied. However, envy's motivational tendency is actually disjunctive. In order to overcome one's perceived inferiority, the envier can either bring oneself up to the level of the envied or pull the envied down to one's level. There are several ways this can happen, as we shall see in Chapter 2.

---

[16] Two very comprehensive reviews of the psychological literature on envy are Miceli and Castelfranchi 2007 and Smith and Kim 2007. Crusius and Lange 2014 define envy as I do here at the very beginning of their article (284). For a review of philosophical accounts of envy, in addition to the Appendix of this book, see D'Arms 2017. In the next chapters I provide further reviews on the specific topic of benign envy.

CHAPTER 2

Varieties of Envy

Calamities are of two kinds: misfortune to ourselves, and good fortune to others.

Ambrose Bierce, *The Devil's Dictionary*

2.1 Introduction: Envy Is Said in Many Ways

A friend of mine, whom I shall call Happy Californian, one day posted on Facebook the following status update:

> Woke up this morning and it really hit me:
> It's November 12th.
> It's 81 degrees outside.
> I spent five minutes luxuriating over the choice of wearing shorts or a short skirt.
> I don't think I can ever leave L.A.

I, and many of her friends, "liked" that post, of course, as we were socially expected to do: aren't we happy that our friend is so happy? We should

For comments on the latest versions of this chapter, I am grateful to Jens Lange and Neal Tognazzini. I am also grateful to the plethora of interested readers and listeners with whom I discussed my taxonomy throughout the years. I cannot possibly recall them all, but here is a hopefully not-too-incomplete list: Holly Andersen, Endre Begby, William Beardsley, Stephen Campbell, Douglas Cannon, Devon Cass, Myisha Cherry, Pamela Corcoran, Stephen Darwall, Thomas Feeney, Nicolas Fillion, Axel Gelfert, June Gruber, Eric Guindon, Maya Gupta, Martin Hahn, Verity Harte, Dai Heide, John Holbo, Hud Hudson, Lina Jansson, Julia Jorati, Matthew V. Lindauer, Yena Lee, Shen-yi Liao, Andres Luco, Michaela Manson, Nicholas Martin, Cameron McCulloch, Aaron Meskin, Maria Miceli, Daniel Putnam, Evan Rodriguez, Lisa Shapiro, Neil Sinhababu, Tamar Szabó Gendler, Weng Hong Tang, Evan Tiffany, Neal Tognazzini, Justin Tiehen, Ariela Tubert, Matthew Walker, Dennis Whitcomb, two anonymous reviewers, and audience members at talks and colloquia at University of Puget Sound, Davidson College, Simon Fraser University, Nanyang Technological University, University of California San Diego, National University of Singapore, the *Piece of Mind* Graduate Conference at University of Missouri-St. Louis, APA Eastern Division Meeting in Baltimore, and the *Hostile Emotions: Perspectives from Philosophy and Psychology* conference at University of Bielefeld.

rejoice of her fortune, even those of us living in much colder and grimmer climates, should we not?

As it turns out, many of us struggle to rejoice of the good fortune of our friends, and this phenomenon is amplified by social media use.[1] Empirical studies show that Facebook, for instance, can be a powerful source of painful feelings and aversive reactions such as envy, depression, sense of unfairness, and Schadenfreude (e.g., Krasnova et al. 2013; Johnson and Knobloch-Westerwick 2014; Tandoc et al. 2015; Verduyn et al. 2015; Appel et al. 2015).[2] But people tend to hide these negative responses, especially envy, as we saw in Chapter 1.

As Smith and Kim put it:

> Despite envy's capacity to cause discontent and despite its assumed presence in many human interactions, most scholars claim that people deny feeling it. People's tendencies to misreport or be mistaken about their emotions are a general feature of many emotions (Platman, Plutchik, & Weinstein, 1971; Plutchik, 2002; Watson, 2000), but the nature of envy may amplify such tendencies. Many scholars claim that people not only avoid admitting the feeling to others but that they are also loathe to acknowledge the feeling in private as well (e.g., Foster, 1972; Schoeck, 1969; Silver & Sabini, 1978). These presumed tendencies may largely be because envy is so painful and self-threatening (e.g., Foster, 1972) and because societal norms reinforce its repugnant nature (e.g., Silver & Sabini, 1978). (Smith and Kim 2007: 54)[3]

In this quote you can see the many references cited by Smith and Kim. The evidence concerning people's reluctance to admit envy is very robust. However, when I present these findings to philosophers they often propose counterexamples, including from their own personal life: "*I* have no problem admitting I am envious!" I am happy to grant that some individuals may be atypical or unconventional (a few anecdotes are not data, after all), but I also invite the skeptics to pay attention to *how* people admit their envy: it is rarely done without qualifications or euphemisms, in all seriousness, or without fretting to add some explanation or justification. It is rare to hear someone say, "I am envious," full stop, dead serious.

---

[1] The COVID-19 pandemic has exacerbated these dynamics, and I plan to examine its effects in future research.

[2] Lin and Utz 2015 presents some interesting qualifications.

[3] The whole discussion on pp. 54–6 is worth reading in full, especially with regard to the methodological difficulty of investigating envy based on self-reports The phenomenon is observable even in classical Greek culture (cf. Sanders 2014, 36) and it is a common refrain in early modern philosophy.

The responses provoked by Happy Californian's post did align with the empirical evidence. Many people "liked" the post and expressed appreciation and happiness for their friend's good fortune. Nobody expressed outright envy or displeasure. However, some comments stated: "Can I be a little jealous? No envious?" "Feeling 'envy'!" and "Let others feel positive jealousy!"

We saw in Chapter 1 that it is common to say "jealous" in lieu of "envious," the reason being that confessing jealousy, a protective response toward what we own, is more acceptable than confessing envy, a proactive response toward what we lack that is usually interpreted as necessarily aggressive. But the responses highlighted here suggest that people often use "jealous" to refer to a *specific kind of envy*, one that implicitly reassures the target that we do not mean ill, that we do not intend to deprive them of their enviable object. "Jealousy" is co-opted this way because English lacks a term that denotes a *benign* kind of envy, as other languages do.

Dutch, Thai, Polish, and Arabic (and probably others) have two terms that refer to envy.[4] One term refers to what in English we would just call "envy," which some authors consider the only real envy or envy proper (but I will argue against this position later on). The other refers to a kind of envy that is free of malice, and thus less shameful to admit.

There are languages that are somewhat intermediate between those that have one term for envy and those that have two. Spanish, for instance, uses the standard locution "sana invidia" to refer to benign envy, and the corresponding Italian expression may be "invidia buona."

The idea that there are two kinds of envy is supported by many contemporary psychologists and can be traced back to some ancient philosophies as well, such as Aristotle's view in the *Rhetoric* (see below,

---

[4] Van de Ven et al. 2009 (420) lists words in Dutch, Polish, and Thai. I further researched these words (consulting both dictionaries and native speakers), and here is what I believe are the best transliterations and translations: Dutch: "benijden" and "afgunst" (both of which usually translated as "envy" in English, but the first one refers to benign envy – van de Ven has researched this extensively on Dutch speakers, and I rely on his work and testimony); Polish: "zazdrość" (usually translated in English as "jealousy") and "zawiść" (translated as "envy" or "jealousy," defined as "a feeling of discontent at another's good fortune or success" in the *Cambridge Dictionary* online); Thai: ความอิจฉา (phonetically: "kwaam ìt-chǎa" translated as "jealousy, envy" on thai2english.com and "envy" on Google Translate) and ความริษยา (phonetically: "kwaam rít-sà-yǎa," translated as "envy, jealousy, covetousness" on thai2english.com and "envy" on Google Translate) (note: kwaam is a prefix that converts verbs or adjectives into abstract nouns). Classical Arabic also has analogous terms (thanks to Matteo Di Giovanni and Hadi Jorati for help with meaning and transliteration): غبط ("ġabṭ," phonetically), usually translated with "emulation"; حسد (phonetically: "ḥasad," usually translated as "envy"). Van de Ven (2016) claims that also German and Turkish have two words for envy: "beniden" and "misgönnen," and "imrenme" and "haste," respectively. I have not further investigated this claim.

and the Appendix). This chapter is devoted to showing that this dichotomy, however, is too simplistic and does not adequately capture all of our experiences of envy. Understanding the nuanced nature of envy will allow us to see the many different ways in which envy can be bad or good.

I start by discussing the recurring distinction between behavioral tendencies of envy: envy can either motivate to push oneself up to the level of the envied, or to pull the envied down to one's own level ("level up" or "level down" for short). This leveling orientation has previously been explained in two distinct ways. The first model of explanation, mostly proposed by psychologists, focuses on the role of *perceived control* over the outcome: roughly, when the envier thinks they can level up, they will feel benign envy; when they think they cannot can level up, they will feel malicious envy. The second model of explanation is discernible in the philosophical tradition and is grounded in the notion of *focus of concern*: roughly, when the envier is concerned about the envied good, they are motivated to get it, and thus to level up; when they are concerned about their inferiority with the envied rival, they are motivated to take them down, and thus to level down. I show that these models of explanation need not be incompatible alternatives. The variables at play are independent and their intersection is responsible for the existence of *four kinds of envy*. I illustrate a paradigmatic case for each, providing a detailed analysis of the phenomenology, situational determinants, motivational structure, and typical behavioral outputs, and I explain how they differ from nearby emotions and attitudes such as admiration, covetousness, and spite.

2.2   What Does Envy Do? Leveling Up and Leveling Down

As defined in Chapter 1, envy is an aversive response to a perceived inferiority or disadvantage vis-à-vis a similar other, with regard to a good that is relevant to the sense of identity of the envier. Envy's unpleasantness motivates the envier to do something about their situation. As Dorothy Sayers put it: "Envy is the great leveler: if it cannot level things up, it will level them down" (Sayers 1999, 80). Out of metaphor, in order to overcome their inferiority, the envier can either pull themselves up to the level of the envied, or pull the envied down to their level.

There is a *third* option not mentioned by Sayers. Rather than trying to close the gap with the envied, thus trying to deal with envy directly, one can cope with envy *indirectly*. Envy is seen by many psychologists as fundamentally aiming at regulating social status (e.g., Crusius and Lange 2017).[5] When one's situation cannot be changed, the pain of inferiority associated with envy, and the related wounds to one's self-esteem, can still be alleviated.

A common coping strategy is to reevaluate the object of envy and come to see it as not good for oneself. This is sometimes referred to as the "sour grapes" strategy, from the famous Aesop's fable in which a fox, being unable to reach some grapes hanging from a vine, remarks that the fruit is not ripe enough. Rather than admitting defeat she pretends that she was not really interested in the enterprise in the first place.

This kind of rationalization is considered an exemplary form of cognitive dissonance (Festinger 1962) and of adaptive preferences (Elster 1983), both phenomena which are usually considered as irrational, harmful to the subject, or otherwise suboptimal (e.g., Nussbaum 2001b; Khader 2011). I cannot address this complex topic here, but it seems to me that when it comes to coping with envy there can be a healthy reassessment of one's values and priorities, whether conscious or unconscious, that need not involve self-deception or a detrimental or skewed value system.[6] In many cases in which envy arises, and especially when the kind of envy in question is malicious, as we will see, it is rational and appropriate to bring oneself to not desire the envied good by changing one's evaluation of it.

This is because the envied good may make only a minimal or indirect contribution to one's own well-being, and the envier might do better to focus on more substantive or enriching objects. For instance, imagine one is envious of their friend's good looks. Clearly, the friend's physical features are exclusive to them. The envier, however, may come to realize that what they truly prize and desire is the associated self-confidence, which they can actually work on obtaining via psychotherapy, for instance. Or perhaps they can improve their appearance, but in a way that is congruent with the way their body is: part of what the body positivity movement is about is that

---

[5] I have some qualms about this way of thinking about envy. It does not seem to easily account for cases such as envying someone for their superior moral virtue (although these may be explained away as parasitical or non-typical) and it does not differentiate envy from other emotions concerned with the regulation of social status such as pride. More generally, functionalist explanations do not tell the whole story of an emotion.

[6] There is a huge literature on adaptive references and surely more than one author must have made a point similar to mine. Elizabeth Barnes (2016) talks about the rationality of developing preferences that are compatible with one's embodiment in relation to the claim that disabled people's preferences are necessarily adaptive and thus irrational. Most discussions of adaptive preferences take place in political philosophy, where the concept is expected to do the "political work" (Terlazzo 2016, 207) of "explaining both why some preferences deserve suspicion and what role suspicion should play in determining what is owed to those who hold them" (208).

different body shapes and sizes can be equally beautiful, and that one should develop a grooming style that fits their unique embodiment.[7] Another common case is envy for wealth: the envier might realize that having lots of money, while making some contribution to happiness, is far from guaranteeing it, and they should rather focus on friendships, experiences, and achievements. (I complicate this picture a bit in the Conclusion.)

Sometimes the envied good is genuinely valuable, but is a scarce or exclusive resource, and the envier might do better to focus on analogous goods that are more readily available, or that are shareable. For instance, one might envy their colleague's unique role in the firm. Since the position is not shareable, the envier has an interest in coming to desire an analogous role instead. This reconfiguration of the envier's desires might not eliminate envy altogether, but transform it, as we shall see when talking about emulative envy below.

Finally, reassessing one's values might have a useful diagnostic function: the envier might come to realize that in fact what they thought was good is not good at all. For instance, adolescents might envy their more popular peers, but then realize that their coolness is based on shallow values that they do not reflectively endorse.[8]

Note that in some of these cases envy turns out to be objectively unfitting, that is, an *inappropriate* reaction to the circumstances. If an emotion is fitting, that means that anyone in the right context has a reason to feel it, independently of their emotional propensities and values. If we adopt D'Arms and Jacobson's (2000) language of the *shape* and *size* of an emotion, envy may be inappropriate when the envier's perceptions of the situation are inaccurate (shape) or when it is excessive or not sufficiently intense (size).[9] Some of the cases discussed above fall under the first category: if the envied object is not good but bad, envy is misplaced (the same holds if the envier is not in fact in a position of inferiority vis-à-vis the envied). When envy is inappropriate with regard to shape ideally the envier should come to see that, and their envy should, in time, subside.

In the remainder of the chapter I focus on *appropriate envy*, that is, an emotion that is fitting to the circumstances giving rise to it.[10] When envy

---

[7] I reflect on what it means for everybody, and every body, to be beautiful in Protasi 2017a.

[8] See Exline and Zell 2008 for a clinical psychology perspective on this issue.

[9] In later work they additionally talk of variances in *depth* (how hard it is psychologically to eradicate an emotional tendency and its related value-laden concern) and *width* (wide concerns are "firmly enmeshed in our web of psychological responses," D'Arms and Jacobson 2005, 116).

[10] For a defense of the claim that envy is at least some times fitting, see D'Arms and Jacobson 2005, and the Conclusion.

is appropriate, the envier's *direct* motivational tendency, either leveling up or leveling down, is also fitting and thus the envier has a reason to act on it without trying to get rid of their envy indirectly. That is, if the envier is actually in a position of inferiority with regard to an actually valuable good, it is fitting (albeit not necessarily advantageous or morally permissible) that they should try and remedy the situation.

This idea of *leveling orientation* is intuitive, and present in virtually all accounts of envy, in one version or another. But there are two main ways of explaining why someone would be inclined to level up or down, one that we mostly find in the psychological literature, and the other one that has been proposed or at least considered by philosophers.

2.2.1   Leveling Orientation and Focus

Aristotle's account of envy provides a notion that is crucial to my own account. He distinguishes between two emotions: *phthonos* and *zēlos*. (The Greek terms are best left untranslated, for reasons explained in the Appendix.) Both are aversive reactions to a perceived inferiority to someone who is similar to us with regard to some valued good. Their main differentiating feature is that when feeling *phthonos* we feel pain at the thought that another person has something, while when feeling *zēlos* the distress is caused by the thought of not having the object. The motivational consequence of this different focus is that "[*zēlos*] makes us take steps to secure the good things in question, [*phthonos*] makes us take steps to stop our neighbor having them" (*Rhet.* 1388a34–5, tr. by W. Rhys Roberts). That is, one motivates to pull the envied down to one's level, whereas the other motivates to push oneself up to theirs. It is possible, then, to interpret Aristotle as saying that there are two kinds of envy: one is characterized by a focus on the envied, which motivates to level down and is thus malicious and morally reproachable, and the other is characterized by a focus on the good, which motivates to level up and is thus morally laudable. (For a defense of this interpretation, and a more detailed presentation of Aristotle's views on envy, see the Appendix.)

Aristotle thus sets the stage of the development of the notion of *focus of concern*. In the contemporary philosophical literature Aaron Ben-Ze'ev (1990, 2000, 2002) talks about this notion in his general theory of emotions, and argues that in envy the agent's focus of concern is personal underserved inferiority. However, Ben-Ze'ev does not refer to the notion when drawing the distinction between malicious and nonmalicious envy, even though he does define these two kinds of envy on the basis of their different leveling orientation (Ben-Ze'ev 2000, 289).

Gabriele Taylor (1988, 2006) also has a notion of "focus" and she does use it to distinguish between kinds of envy, albeit in a way that is different from Aristotle's and mine. She argues that there are *three* kinds of envy. Envy characterized by a focus on the good is *admiring envy*. Envy characterized by a focus on the envied can be of two kinds: *emulative* or *destructive*. Emulative envy motivates to level up, while destructive envy motivates to level down. (I critique her taxonomy in Section 2.4.1.1.)

Other philosophers who talk about envy use the notion in yet other ways. Jerome Neu (1980, 433–4), for instance, mentions "focus of concern" in his distinction between jealousy (where the focus is on the valued object) and envy (where the focus is on the rival), and not between what he calls *admiring envy* and *malicious envy*, which differ in leveling orientation: admiring envy motivates to level up, while malicious envy motivates to level down.[11] Justin D'Arms and Allison Kerr (2008) reject the proposal that focus plays a crucial role in differentiating between kinds of envy, and I come back to D'Arms' argument as to why in Section 2.4.1.4.

2.2.2 Leveling Orientation and Control

Philosophers, then, have investigated the ways in which our values and concerns with the good affect what becomes salient to us: whether we are more bothered by our lack of the envied object, or whether we are more bothered by the fact that the envied has it.

In psychology we do not find a similar interest. Jan Crusius and Jens Lange (2014) discuss the correlation between malicious and benign envy and "focus of attention." But this notion is different from the kind of focus we find in the philosophical discussion, insofar as the term refers not to a *determinant* of envy that concerns the agent's *values*, but rather to a *consequent* of envy that concerns what the agent *pays attention to*. The authors found that when agents feel benign envy they tend to focus their attention on the envied good, and when they feel malicious envy they tend to focus on the envied. This empirical finding is compatible with the philosophical insight concerning focus of concern as a variable about

---

[11] Daniel Farrell also uses the notion of "focus of attention" to distinguish between envy, where the focus is on what the target has and that the agent wants, and jealousy, where the focus is on the amorous or sexual triangle, that is, the relations and the allocation of favors between the three parties (Farrell 1980, 532).

values, insight which to my knowledge has not been tested so far, and which may prove hard to test empirically, given that people may lack epistemic access to what they truly care about.[12]

So how do psychologists explain leveling orientation, that is, why we are sometimes motivated to level down and sometimes motivated to level up? Studies in social comparison show that the way we react to informative social comparison depends on perception of control over the outcome. If we believe that we have no control over our poor performance and that there are scarce possibilities of improvement, we react aggressively toward those who outperform us, and we feel worse about it (Testa and Major 1990; Lockwood and Kunda 1997).

Therefore, psychologists working on envy think that *perception of control* is the crucial determinant of leveling orientation, responsible for whether we experience benign or malicious envy.[13] This is true not only for episodic or occurrent envy, but even for dispositional envy: dispositional benign envy is correlated with hope for success, while dispositional malicious envy is correlated with fear of failure (Lange and Crusius 2015). Once again, as was the case with philosophy, in psychology we find different approaches and ways of drawing distinctions between different kinds of envy. Maria Miceli and Cristiano Castelfranchi (2007), for instance, argue that envy proper is always malicious, while Niels van de Ven spearheaded the view that benign envy is envy proper (van de Ven et al. 2009, 2012; van de Ven 2016). But there seems to be a consensus about the fact that when we feel in control and hopeful we can improve our standing and we are more inclined to level up, and when we feel hopeless and helpless with regard to improving our standing we are more inclined to level down (e.g., Miceli and Castelfranchi 2007; Smith and Kim 2007; van de Ven et al. 2009, 2012).

2.2.3   *Perceived Deservingness as a Third Factor?*

In Section 2.2.4 I define two variables of envy that are derived by the two paradigms described above. But before moving on I ought to address a third potential factor that has been proposed as a possible explanation for the existence of malicious and benign envy: perceived desert or

---

[12] Van de Ven (2016, 341) suggests that we could think of focus of attention as an antecedent, but still interprets it as a psychological, not a normative, notion: what the agent pays attention to, as opposed to what they value or are concerned with.

[13] Also a few philosophers (e.g., Francis Bacon and Rawls) explain leveling orientation this way. See Appendix.

deservingness. (This is a fairly technical section that can be skipped by those already convinced that envy is not a moral emotion at its core.)

Philosophers have fairly consistently rejected the notion that envy is a moral emotion, that is, that it necessarily involves a perception that the envied's advantage is unjust or undeserved (see Appendix for details). In recent years, however, that view has been challenged. Marguerite La Caze (2001) has defended the view that at least some forms of envy are moral, namely those that "are directed at undeserved success and beneficiaries of unjust circumstances" (La Caze 2001, 32). She thinks that envy focuses on *objects* that the envied possesses, whereas resentment focuses on *wrongs* that have been done to us and others, and indignation is focused only on the undesirability and wrongness of *states of affairs*. La Caze's view, however, remains idiosyncratic in the literature. I find Aaron Ben-Ze'ev's detailed critique of her account persuasive. He argues that envy fails to satisfy what he thinks are two criteria for assessing an emotion as moral: the "core evaluative concern of the emotion is moral" (Ben-Ze'ev 2002, 148), and the emotions' effects or consequences tend to be morally positive.

With regard to the latter, Ben-Ze'ev highlights how envy's effects can be harmful or beneficial depending on many other factors. With regard to the former, he claims that envy's core concern is negative assessment of the subject's *undeserved* inferiority, where desert is, however, interpreted as a specific personal concern which has nothing to do with justice or impartial morality (Ben-Ze'ev 1992, 2002). It is the kind of unfairness a child might appeal to when they are told that it is time to go to sleep, or they cannot have more candy; or the feeling we feel when contemplating premature baldness, or the lack of a convenient parking spot when it rains (Parrott 1991 calls this element of envy "global resentment"). Ben-Ze'ev concedes that envy is *normative*, insofar as "it argues something about how situations of fortunes ought to be," (Ben-Ze'ev 2002: 152) but is not moral (but rather amoral).

I agree with Ben-Ze'ev that envy always involves a normative element (focus of concern is about what the envier values), even though I do not think that envy *necessarily* involves the sort of entitlement Ben-Ze'ev describes. However, entitlement may be present because of the rationalizing and coping mechanisms that frequently accompany envy: we come to envision the situation in a way that protects our wounded ego and that often brings us to reconceive the situation as one that warrants resentment and indignation, or perhaps jealousy (Schaubroeck and Lam 2004; Miceli and Castelfranchi 2007).

The idea that envy may be at some level a moral emotion enjoys some support in psychology. Richard Smith, one of the most authoritative voices on envy, has defended the view that envy necessarily involves a perception of *subjective injustice* (Smith 1991; Smith et al. 1999). Miceli and Castelfranchi (2007) offer a detailed critique of the evidence that allegedly stems from these studies. It is actually not fully clear to me to what extent "subjective injustice" differs from perceptions of "global resentment," which Miceli and Castelfranchi consider to be frequently associated, but neither necessary nor sufficient, components of envy. I agree, however, with Miceli and Castelfranchi on the fact that the best way to settle this matter may not be empirical, but rather a question of conceptual clarity or usefulness.

More recently, Niels van de Ven, Marcel Zeelenberg, and Rik Pieters have analyzed the role of perceived deservingness of the outcome as determining kinds of envy (van de Ven et al. 2012). This study is directly relevant to my claim that the different kinds of envy stem from the two factors of focus of concern and perceived control, since they purport to show that there is a correlation between perceived deservingness and kinds of envy: when enviers perceive the superior situation of the envied as deserved, they tend to feel benign envy, and when they perceive it as undeserved, they feel malicious envy.

Again, this research seems to show that there is a necessary moral component in envy. But it seems to me that there are a few reasons to think that deservingness is not an independent variable.

First, when I perceive the envied's superior position as deserved, given our similarity I am likely to see their result as attainable also by myself, and thus I am likely to be more focused on the good and more motivated to self-improve. At the same time I will not be bothered as much by the fact that *they* are in that position – that is, I will not focus on them.

Second, van de Ven and collaborators showed that benign envy correlates with liking the envied, while malicious envy correlates with disliking the envied. While it is not clear how perceived deservingness interacts with like or dislike of the envied, they speculate that when we do not like the envied we tend to consider their fortune as less deserved, and vice versa. But disliking the envied correlates with an adversarial attitude toward the envied, and thus with being more focused on the envied than on the good.

Third, subsequent studies (Lange and Crusius 2015; Lange et al. 2016) have shown that while malicious envy correlates with perceived undeservingness, benign envy is *unrelated* to appraisals of deservingness.[14] Once again the correlation between deservingness and malicious envy is in itself easily explained by malicious envy's well-known defensive mechanisms and capacity to mask resentment: conceiving the envied's advantage as undeserved may well be a post hoc rationalization and a way to assuage guilt and shame caused by one's malicious envy and sense of inferiority. But that benign envy appeared in these subsequent studies to not correlate with undeservingness one way or the other confirms that envy, by itself, need not involve appraisal of deservingness.

Finally, most of the studies on envy, by methodological design, focus on correlation rather than causation, which leaves open the possibility that appraisal of deservingness be a systematic effect of other variables, such as perceived control and focus of concern.

To sum up: if appraisal of desert was systematically involved in envy that would make envy a moral emotion. But given what we know about envy's power to induce confabulation and post hoc rationalization, and given that envy has traditionally been conceptualized as a nonmoral emotion (and is experienced as such by impartial bystanders, who often see through the envier's claims of desert), in the absence of robust and uncontroversial empirical evidence to the contrary it is best to exclude perceived deservingness from the determinants of kinds of envy.

2.3 The Variables of Envy: Focus of Concern and Perceived Obtainability of the Good

The psychological consensus is that perception of control matters in determining what kind of envy one feels. Similarly, the philosophical consensus (insofar as philosophers agree on anything) is that attribution of value plays a role. I propose we join the two paradigms. If we postulate that both focus and perceived control affect whether we level up or down, and if we think of them as independent variables, we obtain *four* kinds of envy instead of the traditional two. In this section I discuss the two variables, whereas in Section 2.4 I describe in detail the four kinds of envy that result from them. I aim to show that this taxonomy well accounts for our varied experience of envy, and can reconcile different intuitions and apparently contrasting views about this emotion.

---

[14] In one study benign envy was said to be "marginally positively correlated with benign envy" (Lange et al. 2016, 178), even though by conventional standards the result was not significant (p < 0.10).

When feeling envy the agent is involved in a triadic relation with an object (the envied good, something that the agent perceives to be lacking) and a target (the envied person, who is perceived as having the good, thus standing in a superior position vis-à-vis the envier).

As Aristotle first intuited, the relation between these three parties can look quite different, insofar as the envier can either be focused on the good or focused on the envied. *Focus of concern* is the first variable that affects the kind of envy we come to feel.

2.3.1   *Focus of Concern*

As stated earlier, focus of concern ought to be distinguished from focus of attention, which is different in two ways. First, I might be concerned with something without being attentive to, or even conscious of, it. This is particularly the case with an emotion as socially stigmatized and uncomfortable as envy: it is often the case that mere observers can see through the real motives of our envious attitudes in a way involved parties cannot.

Second, attention is non-normative, while concern is value-laden: what the envier focuses on is what she cares about. The kind of valuing I have in mind here is prudential: the envier values the object as good from the point of view of her well-being.[15]

The envier focuses on the good when she values the good *for its own sake*, by which I mean: independently from the fact that the envied has it. Thus, I am using the expression "for its own sake" somewhat technically, and not in opposition to "instrumentally." For instance, I might envy my friend for their money, not because I care about money for its own sake, but because I want the things that money can buy. Even though money is desired as an instrumental good, I can still be more focused on the good than on the envied.[16]

But this would not be envy without a comparative element (van de Ven et al. 2009, 2012): the pain that results from the lack of the good is exacerbated by the fact that the envied possesses the good. Envy is not the same as *covetousness*, defined as the desire to have what someone else has. When I covet someone's partner or possession, the fact that the other person has what I want only occasions or triggers the desire for the good, and does not exacerbates the pain, because it does not impact on one's self-judgment. (More on covetousness below.)

---

[15] I am thankful to Stephen Campbell for help in formulating this point.
[16] I am in debt to Aaron Meskin for a discussion on this.

The envier focuses on the target when they are pained by the unfavorable comparison to the envied. The good is not valued independently from the fact that the envier has it, but rather *as a means to overcoming one's inferiority vis-à-vis the envied.* Sometimes we experience envy with regard to objects that we previously did not even particularly desire or assess as good, only because it is possessed by someone toward whom we are competitive, or whom we are disposed to envy. This attitude may be particularly common in younger individuals, who are still in the process of shaping their set of values and are more amenable to peer pressure and emulation.

Focus of concern is an *exhaustive* variable, meaning that there is no third alternative: I am either focused on the good or on the envied, in the relevant sense. To some extent I am also always concerned with myself, but this focus on the self does not vary in different kinds of envy, and thus we can set it aside.[17]

It is also practically *exclusive*: even though it is theoretically possible for the envier to be exactly equally focused on the object and the envied, such a perfect balance is unlikely to take place. If it did, the resulting emotion would be a borderline case.

However, this variable should not be interpreted as dichotomous, that is, non-continuous. Focus of concern is better understood as a *continuum*: enviers are either more focused on the good or more focused on the envied (or else, again, we would not have the triadic structure that typically characterizes envy as a rivalrous emotion).

An example might help to understand in which sense focus of concern is a continuous variable. Imagine a case of sibling envy that stems from the

---

[17] An authoritative tradition in psychology discriminates between social comparison emotions by distinguishing between *focus of attention on the self* and *focus of attention on the other* (Master and Keil 1987; Smith 2000; in philosophy see also Solomon 1976). This distinction seems problematic to me. Most emotions are self-focused in a trivial sense: the subject experiences the emotion as involving herself in some crucial way (surprise and awe are exceptions). Smith 2000 mentions anger and resentment as other-focused emotions, but this strikes me as inexact: they are both emotions that involve the self in important ways. If we were not focused on the self, why would we care about slights or wrongdoings perpetrated against us? *Social* emotions, in particular, are self-focused also in the sense that they involve a relation between the self and a community and are concerned with the way the community recognizes or judges the self. This holds also for an emotion like shame, which is mentioned by Smith as an example of self-focused emotion. It is clear that shame is focused more inwardly than resentment, not as a matter of attention, but rather with respect to *targets*. Shame is directed toward oneself: when I am ashamed, not only my flaws, *as seen by another*, are the object of my shame, but I direct this sense of failure toward myself. When I resent someone, I am focused on what *they* did to *me*, but I direct my anger toward *them*. Envy is focused on the self and targeted toward another. But what determines interesting variations in envy is focus of concern, rather than focus of attention.

fact that one is envious of their sibling's easier relation with their parents: the sibling has an easier time talking to them, feeling supported and understood, can better express their emotions, is less hesitant in making their needs clear, etc.

A possible characterization of the envier's focus of concern is that the envier independently values having a good relation with their parents, but they are also bothered that it is their sibling who is better than them in this regard: their relation and shared life experiences provide simply a background against which the lack of this good strikes the envier as particularly painful. If that were the case the envier would be more focused on the good than on the envied, but they would still also be a little concerned with the sibling's superior standing. Hence their feeling envy rather than merely wishing they had a better relationship with their parents.

Now envision a different scenario: suppose the envier is particularly prone to compete with their sibling, because their relatives make explicit comparisons between them and often remark on the sibling's greater success. Their relationship is competitive as a norm. In that case the envier may be more focused on the envied, even though they will still be a little focused on the good as well.

Furthermore, the agent's focus may shift from good to envied and vice versa even within the same case of envy, due to changed circumstances. For instance, after a fight with their parents in which the envier felt deeply misunderstood, they may be more focused on the good even in the context of an overall stronger focus on the envied. Focus of concern therefore needs to be conceived of as a continuum and as a *dynamic* variable.

What is the motivational consequent of this evaluative component of envy? Arguably, when one is more focused on the good, one is more inclined to get the good itself, and less concerned with depriving the envied of it. The envier in the first scenario above wants to have an easier relation with their parents, and values that good independently from the fact that their sibling has it, so presumably their efforts go in the direction of pursuing the good for themselves rather than depriving the sibling of it. In this context the envier's gain need not mean the envied's loss.

But there are situations in which leveling up and leveling down amount to the same thing. In a *zero-sum game* a person's gain is exactly balanced by the other person's loss, and so if the envier levels up then automatically the envied is leveled down.

Think of situations like running a race, or competing for a specific job, or wanting the last ice-cream in the freezer. In all those situations the envier cannot obtain the good without the envied losing it. However, it matters under what description the envier conceives of and relates to her situation: when the envier is more focused on the good than on the envied, their intention is not so much to deprive the envied of the good, but mostly to get it for herself, and the undesirable outcome for the envied is only a side effect.[18]

Vice versa, when one is more focused on the envied than on the good, one is more inclined to deprive them of the good. What bothers the envier is precisely that the envied has the good, so the envier's primary aim is to take the good away from the envied. Getting the good for oneself at the same time, however, as a result of the envied's deprivation, is not simply an undesired side effect, as in the previous case: getting the good is *instrumental* to overcoming one's disadvantage, even though it may not be considered valuable independently from the fact that the envied has it.

2.3.2 *Perceived Obtainability of the Good*

But there is a further specification with regard to leveling down that requires introducing a second variable: *perceived obtainability of the good*.[19] This is also a continuous variable, since individuals have varying degrees of self-confidence at different times, depending on circumstances being more or less favorable, on personality, and so forth. What "obtaining the good" amounts to depends on whether the envier is (more) focused on the good or on the envied. If the envier is focused on the good, obtaining the good means just that – getting the good for oneself – but if they are focused on the envied, obtaining the good primarily means *taking it away* from the envied, and only secondarily, and when possible, also obtaining it for oneself.

Obtainability of the good is a more nuanced variable than the psychological notion of perceived control over the outcome, because it includes the notion of the good, which is in turn affected by the notion of focus of concern.[20] Thus, we can characterize leveling orientation much more precisely than in either the philosophical or the psychological paradigm alone. In particular, leveling down, as I indicated earlier, is one motivational tendency that can produce *two* different typical behaviors,

---

[18] This is not a particularly idiosyncratic point: the doctrine of double effect is also based on the idea that we can distinguish between the content of our intended action and a foreseeable but contingently related side effect of our intended action. See McIntyre 2019 for a review.

[19] Henceforth, for concision, I will omit "perceived."

[20] I suppose this notion comes first in the order of explanation, thus making my account unavoidably normative and philosophical, by my own characterization.

depending on perceived obtainability: if I perceive myself as capable of taking away the good and acquire it myself, then I will try to *steal* (either literally or figuratively) the good; but if I perceive myself as incapable of doing so, I will try to *spoil* the good.

There are many factors that determine whether a good is perceived as obtainable or not. Some depend on the subject, such as self-esteem or other personality traits: a self-confident or an optimistic agent will be more disposed than an insecure or a pessimistic one to see the good as obtainable, quite independently from what is actually the case. Other factors are more objective, such as the nature of the good at stake: some goods may be exclusive or non-shareable, so that their acquisition is simply not possible (think of envying someone's unique material property, or properties necessarily tied to someone's identity). There are also circumstantial or psychological features that may be thought of as intersubjective or social: for instance, individuals from privileged backgrounds are likely to be more hopeful with regard to the possibility of overcoming their disadvantage (and they might be warranted in feeling that way).

While I am not aware of any empirical evidence on the possible interactions between these two variables, one can speculate about some occasional reciprocal causal influence. For instance, it is possible that, when we are really desirous of something, we perceive it as more likely obtainable, thus engaging in some kind of wishful thinking. But, in general, it does not seem to me that being more or less concerned with the good systematically affects whether we perceive it as more or less obtainable. Instead, whether one perceives the good as obtainable may have some recurring effect on focus of concern. For instance, perceiving an envied good as easily obtainable may make one more focused on it, and vice versa. The phenomenon of "sour grapes" seems to suggest this much. However, many other factors seem to influence what enviers focus on and more generally what agents care about: their value system, their preferences, their history, and so forth. Given the wealth of factors that influence this variable, it does not seem likely that we can find any *systematic* causal effect of obtainability of the good on focus of concern.

The two variables, then, do not correlate, but are rather independent. If we intersect them, four distinct kinds of envy arise, as exemplified in Figure 2.1.

The emotions occupying the quadrants on the right-hand side roughly correspond to the more traditional notions of benign (upper quadrant) and malicious (lower quadrant) envy. The emotions occupying the quadrants on the left-hand side can be seen as the *unproductive* versions of the first

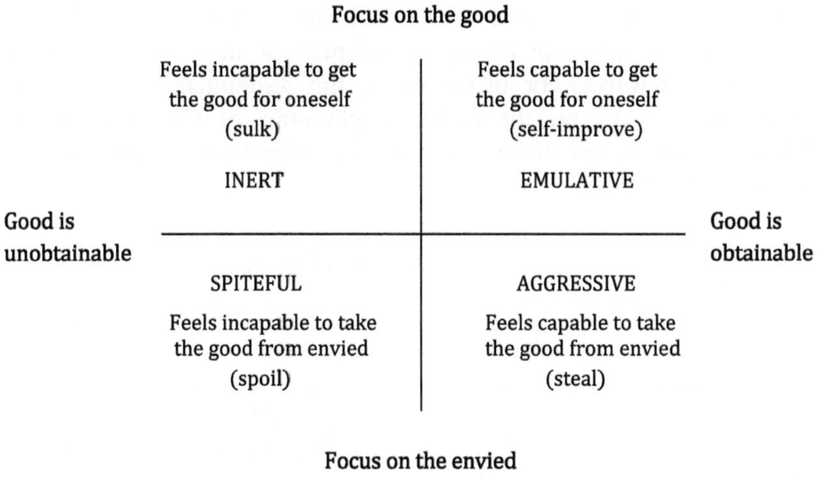

Focus on the good

Feels incapable to get the good for oneself (sulk)	Feels capable to get the good for oneself (self-improve)
INERT	EMULATIVE

Good is unobtainable ———————————————————— Good is obtainable

SPITEFUL	AGGRESSIVE
Feels incapable to take the good from envied (spoil)	Feels capable to take the good from envied (steal)

Focus on the envied

Figure 2.1   Varieties of envy.

two, and they account for features of the experience of envy that are familiar and yet often neglected by the literature, especially in the case of inert envy.

Like any theoretical model, simplifications are unavoidable. Figure 2.1 gives the appearance of clear-cut, easy to differentiate, paradigmatic, and static emotional occurrences. Real-life cases, however, are more indefinite, difficult to identify, idiosyncratic, and dynamic, and may involve dispositions. Some cases will be vague, either epistemically (meaning we cannot know whether one is, say, experiencing inert or emulative envy) or metaphysically (meaning one is really in an in-between state[21]). Some agents might tend to experience only some kinds but not others, depending on their personal traits and tendencies. For almost any agent, chances are that one's envy might evolve or devolve in another kind.

Furthermore, the axes of the diagram are only artificial boundaries. Thus, two cases of envy that are in different quadrants may be more similar to each other than two cases that are in the same quadrant: what matters is their relative distance.

Notwithstanding these limitations, the model is explanatorily very powerful. It accounts for quite different behaviors that are thought to stem from envy, such as emulation of the envied and spoiling the good; for

---

[21] Namely, their envy may fall on the 0,0 point of the graph, or 0 on the x or y axis. Any taxonomy of emotion conceptually implies borderline cases.

quite different attitudes toward the envied, ranging from esteem to hatred; and, finally, for quite different moral judgment of the envier, who can be seen as praiseworthy, or blameworthy, but also pitiable and morally excusable. I focus on the ethical implications of the taxonomy in Chapter 3. In the remainder of this one I provide a more detailed picture of each kind of envy.

2.4   The Varieties of Envy

I now present an exemplary case for each kind of envy. By exemplary I mean most realistic and plausible characterization, rather than average or median. Therefore, the exemplary cases may be located in a different position in each quadrant, rather than being equidistant.

Each kind is presented through an imagined, but empirically plausible, case study. Each differs in phenomenology, in how the envier sees and relates to the envied, in motivational tendencies, and in typical behavioral outcomes. All these characteristics result from the interaction of focus of concern and perceived obtainability of the good. The envier's name always starts with the first syllable of the corresponding kind of envy.

2.4.1   Emulative Envy

> Emma is a philosophy professor. She envies her colleague Diotima, because she perceives Diotima to be always a tad more productive or successful than she is. Emma values being an excellent philosophy professor for its own sake: being a philosopher is a defining part of her identity. Diotima is a role model for her: Emma can see how Diotima's achievements depend on hard work, not on some innate or mysterious talents. So Diotima becomes a constant spur to do better, to improve herself. Their relationship is cordial, even friendly, and Emma is happy that Diotima is in her department. Diotima provides a sort of moving target that keeps Emma on track. Emma's envy is emulative.

Emulative envy is the result of being more focused on the good than on the target, and believing oneself to be more capable of getting the good for oneself than not.

The envier is motivated to level up, that is, to obtain the lacked and valued good, thus bridging the gap with the envied, and is confident that she can achieve her goal.[22] The envied is there not as a rival to beat for its

---

[22] For the correlation between motivation to self-improve and upward comparison in conditions of high similarity, see Schaubroeck and Lam 2004, who review and describe a variety of relevant

own sake, but as a model to look up to: Diotima represents what Emma believes she can become. Because Emma perceives herself as not that far off from Diotima, she is motivated to improve herself. In particular, she is spurred to set up specific, concrete short-term goals (Lange and Crusius 2015; van de Ven 2017).

Because of its hopeful and non-adversarial character, emulative envy is the least unpleasant kind of envy. The envier is confident that she can achieve the good, differently from inert envy, and is not as bothered by the envier's better position as in aggressive and spiteful envy. However, emulative envy is not a pleasant emotion, given that it still involves the pain of perceiving oneself as worse off than a similar other with regard to a self-defining and self-relevant good. It is still, after all, envy, and envy is no fun. Psychological studies on benign envy, which is sufficiently close to emulative envy for this purpose, confirm that it is experienced as unpleasant by the subjects (van de Ven et al. 2009; Crusius and Lange 2014; Lange and Crusius 2015; Falcon 2015).

The typical behavioral tendency of emulative envy is, as already stated, to try to improve one's standing. Emulative envy is not only non-malicious, insofar as it does not motivate the envier to pull the envied down, but it may be prudentially good, if the attempt to pull oneself up is successful. If the envied object is actually good, emulative envy may even be a fully virtuous emotion. (I explore these normative implications in greater depth in Chapter 3.)

To sum up, this is how I define emulative envy: qua envy, it is an unpleasant reaction to the perceived superior standing of a similar other in a domain of self-relevance. It feels less painful than any other kind of envy because it involves the hope to improve one's situation and the confidence that one may be able to do so. The envier looks at the target like a model, someone to emulate rather than defeat or bring down. Consequently, emulative envy is completely void of malice or ill will.

Emulative envy resembles Aristotelian *zēlos*, but is not quite the same. For one, they are both culturally specific, and thus their referents are different. Second, as we shall see later, emulative envy need not be virtuous (even though it is the only kind of envy that *can* be virtuous), whereas *zēlos* is always virtuous by definition. (See also the Appendix.)

---

findings on p. 37. For the more specific correlation between benign envy and self-improvement, see again Schaubroeck and Lam 2004; van de Ven et al. 2009, 2012; Crusius and Mussweiler 2012; Crusius and Lange 2014; Lange and Crusius 2015.

Emulative envy only *partially* corresponds to what psychologists conceptualize as benign envy, because the notion of benign envy omits the normative variable of focus of concern, and because it only involves a thin notion of self-improvement, which may not qualify as genuine by philosophical standards. But there is a significant overlap between the two notions, which is why I can use much of the relevant evidence concerning benign envy to support the existence of emulative envy. Even though such evidence is quite robust, many philosophical objections still arise. Facing these objections will allow me to clarify further what emulative envy is, and is not, in my view.

In the remainder of the section, I will (1) contrast my account with two alternative philosophical accounts, (2) distinguish emulative envy from admiration, and (3) show that, contrary to frequently raised objections, emulative envy is a kind of envy proper.

2.4.1.1   Alternative Accounts of Emulative Envy

In the philosophical literature there are at least two other accounts of emulative envy that are sufficiently similar to mine to be worth addressing: one by John Rawls and the other by Gabriele Taylor.

John Rawls briefly mentions "emulative envy" in section 80 of *A Theory of Justice*. I discuss Rawls' overall treatment of envy in Chapter 5 and in the Appendix. For now, suffice it to say that he defines emulative envy as a form of envy "which leads us to try to achieve what others have. The sight of their greater good moves us to strive in socially beneficial ways for similar things for ourselves" (Rawls 1999, 467). He seems to think that emulative envy thus defined differs from what he calls "benign envy," which he explicitly sets apart both from emulative envy and from envy "proper," that is, malicious. "Benign envy" is basically no envy at all, it is just a way of "affirming the value of certain things that others have" (ibid.). Of malicious envy or envy proper, he says that it is connected to a sense of defeat and failure – thus implicitly individuating the importance of perceived low control – but he does not articulate this intuition. While Rawls' notion of emulative envy is underdescribed, it seems to me that it shares with mine an emphasis on the potentially positive aspect of envy when it is experienced in a context of hopefulness and focus on the good.

Taylor's account (Taylor 1988, 2006), which I briefly mentioned earlier, is much more detailed, and I find it the most compelling alternative to my own. Let me anticipate that I find its main flaw to be the lack of empirical grounding, which I believe leads Taylor to overlook the importance of perceived control and perceived obtainability of the good.

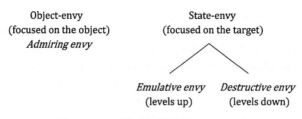

Figure 2.2   Gabriele Taylor's taxonomy.

Taylor's taxonomy includes three kinds of envy: admiring, emulative, and destructive envy. She starts by distinguishing between two kinds of envy: object-envy and state-envy. *Object-envy*, which she also calls *admiring envy*, focuses on the object, the thing that we envy. The envied "plays a relatively minor role as being merely the occasion for the envious person's realization of her deficiencies" (Taylor 2006, 43). This kind of envy is not vicious, and it may be beneficial to the envier if the object is actually good. In this respect Taylor's admiring envy is similar to my emulative envy.

However, what she calls emulative envy is a subspecies of *state-envy*. State-envy focuses on the target, the person whom we envy, who is seen as a rival or competitor. In this kind of envy the envier feels deprived by comparison to the other and wishes they could remove their disadvantage. How the envier chooses to do so determines a further distinction. If the envier is motivated to level down they feel *destructive envy*, which is the worst and more malicious kind of envy. If the envier is motivated to level up they feel *emulative envy*. Figure 2.2 illustrates Taylor's taxonomy.

Taylor explicitly refers to Rawls when presenting this kind of envy. She is less sanguine than him in her normative assessment, though, for two reasons. First, she thinks that emulative envy's social benefits depend on the goodness of the envied object: "The envied person may, for all we know, be the chief of a group of gangsters" (Taylor 2006, 45). Second, and more importantly, she correctly sees in "emulation" the notion of competition and rivalry. Emulation is necessarily comparative, and she believes that in comparison always lies the potential for vice. I come back to this normative point in Chapter 3, but for now let me just remark on the structural problem of Taylor's distinction.

Taylor does not provide an explanation for why enviers who are *equally* focused on the target come to have such *different* wishes and behavioral tendencies. In this respect Aristotle's taxonomy is explanatorily superior: those who decide to level down are importantly different from those who decide to level up, insofar as they are focused on different things. She is

also seemingly unaware of the rich contemporary social psychology literature on the topic, and her only empirical references are to psychoanalysis,
and in particular to Melanie Klein's work (1957), whose understanding of
envy is quite idiosyncratic and disconnected from current psychological
research. As a consequence Taylor does not realize the importance of
perceived control over the outcome, which in my own account is crucial
in explaining different motivational tendencies.

Taylor's account also fails to clearly distinguish what she calls admiring
envy from admiration. That is the task awaiting anyone who wants to
defend a positive kind of envy, and to which I turn next.

2.4.1.2 *Emulative Envy and Admiration*

It is unsurprising that emulative envy and admiration are confused with
each other, for they have much in common.[23] They are both complex,
value-laden responses to upward social comparison: both the admired and
the envied are perceived as superior to the self. Thus, the agent "looks up"
to the target of the emotion in both cases. However, the admiring gaze is
only superficially analogous to the envious one. The two emotions differ in
affect, appraisal, situational antecedents, and motivational tendencies.

First of all, they feel quite different from the inside: psychologists have
shown time and again that emulative envy is painful while admiration is
pleasant (Crusius and Lange 2014; Lange et al. 2016; van de Ven et al.
2009, 2011, 2012). As Søren Kierkegaard put it, "admiration is happy self-
surrender; envy is unhappy self-assertion" (Kierkegaard 1941, 139). That is
compatible with the experience of either being somewhat mixed: emulative
envy's pain may be tempered by hope, which is pleasant, while admiration
may be accompanied by awe, which is never wholly pleasant. But overall
their affective component is quite distinct.

The phenomenological difference seems connected to the fact that
emulative envy is focused both on the self and the other, with the focus
on the self being quite crucial, while admiration is mostly focused on the
other person. Admiration, like its close cousins awe, wonder, and
adoration,[24] is an emotion whose appraisal concerns an object of exceptional value, as assessed on its own grounds. When the admired is a person
there is an implicit, comparative component, but it not as salient as with
envy, and it is absent when admiration is not directed at a person but at an

---

[23] This section borrows content from Protasi 2019.
[24] See Archer and Grahle 2019 for a collection of recent articles on admiration.

object.[25] Emulative envy, even when it has a strong focus of concern on the envied good, necessarily involves comparison to the envied.

Such a difference in appraisal corresponds to a difference in the circumstances that give rise to the emotion: emulative envy arises when comparison is toward someone who is similar in status or ability, and with regard to a self-important domain. Admiration, instead, typically arises toward people who are perceived as much superior to the agent and its "stimulus events [...] are not directly relevant to the individual's current goal pursuits" (Schindler et al. 2013, 90).

Relatedly, the relation between the agent and the target looks quite different as well. Admiration is affiliative: it motivates the agent to become close to the target. Emulative envy is competitive (like any other envy), even if not adversarial: it motivates the agent to become like the target but not necessarily to like them.

Finally, with regard to their motivational tendencies, the emerging consensus in psychology is that admiration and benign envy serve two different functions (Schindler et al. 2015; van de Ven 2016, 2017). Earlier studies (van de Ven et al. 2011) showed that benign envy outperforms admiration in the effectiveness to motivate the agent to self-improve. Admiration was not shown to motivate agents to emulate the admired. But these results were contradicted by subsequent research by Ines Schindler and her collaborators (Schindler et al. 2013, 2015), which showed that admiration is in fact linked to the tendency to emulate the admired other. This apparent contradiction has been seemingly dissolved with further studies and the current most plausible hypothesis is that both emotions motivate improvement albeit in distinct ways (van de Ven 2017). Admiration is linked to a specific way of emulating the admired person: admiration *broadens* cognitive processing (Harmon-Jones et al. 2012; Schindler et al. 2015), and inspires the agent to develop a commitment to abstract ideals, thus motivating them to *long-term improvement*. Envy *narrows* cognitive processing (Harmon-Jones et al. 2012), and spurs the agent to pursue the goal of obtaining the lacked good in a more immediate way, thus motivating to *short-term improvement*. (These empirical findings nicely dovetail with envy's iconography and cultural tropes of the envious gaze as one that comes through squinted eyes, which well represents the envier's focus on the lacked good.)

---

[25] One could even argue that even when we admire a person we in fact admire her qualities, or achievements, and there is no interpersonal comparison at all.

To summarize, admiration is a pleasant emotional response to the perceived excellence of an object (often but not necessarily a person), whose primary function may be to "enhance one's own agency in upholding ideals" (Schindler et al. 2013, 86). Emulative envy, qua envy, is an unpleasant emotional response to the perceived superiority or advantage of a similar other in a self-important domain, which may be the most adaptive and less harmful response to being outperformed in evolutionarily important domains of resource competition (Hill and Buss 2008).

2.4.1.3 *Emulative Envy and Emulation*

Emulative envy is sometimes confused with emulation. A notion of emulation that may seem to fit the bill particularly well is the Cartesian notion of emulation, which Descartes describes in par. 172, book 3 of *The Passions of the Soul* (Descartes 1985). According to Descartes, emulation is a form of courage that involves hope: seeing that someone else has achieved a certain goal makes the agent believe that it is indeed possible to achieve that goal. It is an energetic disposition to pursue objectives that one hopes to be within reach. Such a hope stems from the fact that others, those one intends to emulate, have succeeded.

Emulation's affect is not mentioned by Descartes, but he says hope is caused by a combination of joy and desire (book 3, 165), and thus we can infer that it is overall pleasant (especially given that anxiety is its opposite, and is said to impede the body to act). Emulation, consequently, is also likely to have an overall positive affect. Thus, it is phenomenologically different from emulative envy, which, as I said above, is overall unpleasant.

In general I agree with Descartes that emulation is more like an "energy": it's a disposition to engage in certain actions, rather than an emotion per se, and one that is often motivated by the emotion of hope. Thus, emulative envy differs from Cartesian emulation.

Are there other notions of emulation that we might consider? When we talk of emulation in everyday conversations we use it in a variety of contexts where one need not be similar to the model: in religious contexts one's model could be a prophet, or even God (as in the case of wanting to emulate Jesus Christ); in educational contexts one's model could be one's parent. While it is possible to perceive one's parent as similar (and thus to envy them), it is also common to want to relate to one's parents in a non-comparative way. These non-comparative notions also differ from emulative envy.

2.4.1.4 Is Emulative Envy Really Envy?

At this point one may be convinced that emulative envy exists, that it has the characteristics I attribute to it, and that is different from admiration and emulation, but doubt that it is a kind of *envy proper*. I address three versions of this objection: that emulative envy is not envy proper because it is not wholly unpleasant, that emulative envy is not envy proper because it is not difficult to confess, and that emulative envy is not envy proper because it is not malicious.

First, consider the following argument: envy proper is necessarily unpleasant; but emulative envy is not unpleasant; therefore, emulative envy is not envy proper.[26]

Above I showed that the second premise of this argument is false: I have explained why we should expect emulative envy to still be overall painful (it is a response to perceived inferiority) and I showed the empirical evidence that confirms this expectation (to reiterate: Crusius and Lange 2014; Lange et al. 2016; van de Ven et al. 2009, 2011, 2012).

So, if one keeps denying that emulative envy is unpleasant, they are ignoring the empirical evidence and/or confusing emulative envy with emulation or admiration.

The second objection is analogous to the one raised by Miceli and Castelfranchi (2007, 456) against benign envy. The argument is the following: envy proper is necessarily difficult to confess; but emulative envy is not difficult to confess; therefore, emulative envy is not envy proper.

However, once again the available empirical evidence casts doubt on the notion that emulative or benign envy are readily admitted: van de Ven et al. (2009), in their comparison between malicious and benign envy, have found that they are both associated with feelings of shame and negative feelings about oneself. This is not surprising given that both kinds of envy involve inferiority in a self-important domain, hence they affect one's perception of the self in the eyes of others. But notice that this result is compatible with a comparative difference that I foreshadowed in

---

[26] This objection has been raised by many. A recent occurrence is in Salice and Montes Sánchez 2019, where the authors move this objection in particular against my account, and combine it with the third objection (that emulative envy cannot be envy insofar as it is not malicious). I do not have the space here to attempt a point-by-point rebuttal, which might also be of scarce interest to a larger audience. Overall, it seems to me that I approach the issue from a fairly different perspective from the authors. For instance, I rely more heavily than them on the wealth of empirical evidence concerning both emulative/benign envy and admiration. I also completely disagree with their way of understanding admiration, which they claim, in agreement with Ben-Ze'ev 2000, to be equivalent to "being happy for."

the introduction: namely, emulative envy is probably *easier* to admit than the other kinds. (Recall also that benign forms of envy are often admitted under the description of "jealousy," thus showing an often unconscious need to "temper" the gravity of the confession.)

Finally, the most common objection to any notion of non-malicious envy takes the form of the following argument: envy proper is necessarily malicious; but emulative envy is not malicious; therefore, emulative envy is not envy proper.

Given that there are many historical and contemporary, psychological and philosophical, accounts of envy as not necessarily malicious, the argument risks being question-begging: the truth of the first premise is exactly what is being disputed. Therefore the objector needs to appeal to some kind of evidence to back up premise one. But throughout the chapter I have referred to the ample psychological, linguistic, and anecdotal evidence supporting the existence of a non-malicious kind of envy.

However, Justin D'Arms has defended a subtler interpretation of the objection, such that it does not require empirical support.[27] According to him the proponent of the view that envy is necessarily malicious is "best understood as holding a disjunctive view of envy's constitutive desires" (D'Arms 2009, 5). In other words, "[e]nvy is a distinctive kind of psychological state that is essentially competitive" (D'Arms 2017, 8) and "the characteristic dissatisfaction of envy supplies or embodies some level of motivation toward whatever would ameliorate the situation; in other words, envy involves a desire that would be satisfied either by outdoing or by undoing the rival's advantage" (D'Arms and Kerr 2008, 48).

Now, up to here I agree with D'Arms. He goes on to say:

> Which of those motivations will emerge in action depends on many factors. It depends on what the situation affords, including the probabilities and expected costs and benefits of success at either option. And it depends on other attitudes and desires of the subject, including how much he likes the rival, whether he thinks it would be wrong to deprive him of the good, and how much that wrongness matters to him. (D'Arms 2017, 8)

In my view, instead, the crucial variables are only two – focus of concern and perceived obtainability of the goal – to which all the other antecedents can be reduced, which makes my model more parsimonious.

---

[27] See D'Arms 2009, 2017 (note: these are both Stanford encyclopedia entries, the latter is a revised version of the former); D'Arms and Jacobson 2000; D'Arms and Kerr 2008. Given that D'Arms is the common denominator in these works, I refer to the view as *his*, even though it is shared with Dan Jacobson and Alison Duncan Kerr.

More importantly, genuine envy, for him, involves a subterraneous and implicit maliciousness even in what only *appears to be* benign envy: if the target's advantage is undone, then one's envy would be satisfied. He suggests that it is only a matter of moral conscience whether enviers opt for leveling up or down (enviers who level up are "decent enviers" (D'Arms 2017, 8)). He and Alison Duncan Kerr (2008) suggest that enviers might not be aware of their implicit desire for the rival to lose the good, and might not act on it, but that desire is there nonetheless. Of course, once we get in the domain of unconscious and implicit desire, finding evidence becomes harder. But if benign envy was necessarily implicitly malicious it would be difficult to explain the evidence supporting its positive motivational power, that is, the fact that people, both in experimental and real-life settings, seem motivated by it to self-improve. That people are thus motivated is best explained by the idea that their focus of concern lies in a concern for the good rather than in a concern for the rival.

What Emma cares about, in our initial description, is to become as excellent philosopher (to the level personified by Diotima, but not because Diotima has it) and such a good requires autonomous development of philosophical skills. Since stealing such talents is not possible the only leveling-down option is spoiling Diotima's philosophical talents (maybe by causing Diotima a brain injury). But such an outcome would not appeal to Emma, and not primarily because of Emma's moral conscience, as D'Arms speculates. Even if Diotima happened to lose her philosophical talent on her own, Emma's envy would not be extinguished because its constitutive desire of obtaining the good for herself would not be satisfied but rather emptied of its object: Emma cannot feel emulative envy toward Diotima if Diotima is not worthy of being emulated anymore. But Emma would still want to get to the level where Diotima had been.

Justin D'Arms addresses my view by asking "what role the perceived inferiority to the rival can be playing in emulative envy, if the envier is held to care *only* about the good, and not the inferiority as such" (my emphasis, D'Arms 2017, 7). This question, however, ignores my specification that focus of concern be not a dichotomous, but rather a *continuous* variable: the envier always cares about both the rival and the good, in different measures. I attempted to provide here a clarification as to how emulative envy's concern for the inferiority does not imply a manifest desire to bring down the envied.

Now, in replying to D'Arms through Emma's case I am operating at a conceptual level, like he is, and thinking in terms of desire and envy's "satisfaction." It is worth noting that this language never appears in the empirical literature. Emotions and desires can persist or fade for all sorts of reason, so whether envy is satisfied or not need not be evidence for its nature, components, or motivations. (This is why, even though I adopted D'Arms' language of satisfaction in a previous discussion of my taxonomy (Protasi 2016), I dropped it here.)

In order to account for some of the empirical and linguistic evidence that seems to support the existence of benign envy, D'Arms has introduced the notion of "emulative desire" (D'Arms 2017, 7), which is a mental state felt in "cases in which people want to have skills or other traits that are possessed by another person, and are pained by their lack, but in which they have no desire at all for the other person to lose those traits" (ibid.). He claims that what I and others (such as van de Ven et al. 2009) consider terms for "benign envy" in other languages are best translated as "emulative desire." D'Arms makes the point that:

> it is not clear that anything in van de Ven et al.'s interesting experiments motivates translating the relevant terms as "benign envy" rather than as "emulative desire," or understanding the benign and malicious phenomena they distinguish as two variants of one emotion. (D'Arms 2017, 22–3)

But while D'Arms only refers to the seminal work by van de Ven and et al. from 2009, there is now a large empirical literature on this topic, and many more studies, experiments, and models that support conceptualizing benign envy as a distinct kind of envy proper.[28]

Ultimately, D'Arms concludes that whether one opts for one view or the other depends on the explanatory advantages of considering benign envy as genuine envy, and I hope that such advantages will emerge throughout this book.

In conclusion, I argued that emulative envy is not even implicitly malevolent, and yet it is a kind of envy proper. But coming to feel emulative envy as opposed to other kinds of envy is not always within the agent's control. For instance, it is a matter of moral luck whether the good is beyond reach, or the agent lacks confidence in her abilities. When either is the case, the envier may come to feel inert envy.

---

[28] See Lange, Blatz, and Crusius 2018 and van de Ven 2016 for reviews; Falcon 2015 presents a taxometric analysis approach that supports a categorial distinction between two kinds of envy. For a critique of the distinction and a defense of a unitary approach in psychology, see Cohen-Charash and Larson 2017.

2.4.2 Inert Envy

Indrani has been struggling with infertility for years. Indrani values having a biological child for its own sake, and she is motivated to have one. However, she has tried unsuccessfully to conceive for years. One day her dear friend Priya tells her excitedly that she is pregnant. Indrani congratulates her, faking enthusiasm, holding back tears. She feels an intense envy that she cannot confess, and even though she would never wish Priya ill, she cannot bring herself to see her as much as she usually does. She invents excuses, does not go to her baby shower and overall withdraws from the relationship. She cannot genuinely rejoice for Priya's happiness, and she hates herself for that. Only when she finally gets pregnant herself is Indrani able to reconnect with her friend.[29]

Inert envy is the result of being focused on the good, but believing oneself to be incapable of getting the good for herself. Since she perceives (let us assume correctly) the good as unobtainable, the motivation to improve her situation is frustrated.

I speculate that inert envy is very painful in unique ways. While there is no direct empirical evidence supporting my claim, given that inert envy is not conceptualized as such in the psychological literature, my hunch is that the inert envier experiences more despair, frustration, self-loathing, and shame than any other kind of envy. Perceiving oneself as incapable of obtaining the good is likely to correlate with frustration and low self-esteem, which in turn correlates with self-loathing and shame. Hopelessness is conceptually tied to inert envy because of the envier's perception that obtaining something very valuable is not possible or unlikely – whether it becomes despair proper will depend on circumstances and intensity of feelings. Inert envy's feelings are thus decidedly unpleasant and peculiarly inward-looking, and they turn the person into a despondent, sulky, sullen agent – or, rather, patient.

Thus, inert enviers are not motivated to self-improve because they feel hopeless about the possibility of overcoming their disadvantage; consequently the envied cannot function as a model as in emulative envy.

[29] A Google search on "baby envy" leads to dozens of articles and blog posts reporting stories analogous to the one I tell here: see for instance http://parenting.blogs.nytimes.com/2013/08/07/fertility-diary-baby-envy/. Some of the commenters talking about their baby envy also recount emulative envy (when one finds other people's pregnancies encouraging and promising for one's situation) or more spiteful kinds (as when one wishes another woman to have a miscarriage, or feels the need to harm pregnant women). A case of aggressive envy in this domain could motivate the envier to kidnap another woman's baby, a rare, albeit not wholly unheard of, occurrence: see for instance www.theguardian.com/us-news/2017/may/04/baby-snatcher-bronx-new-york-kidnapping-true-crime.

Priya, the target of Indrani's envy, is only a standard of self-assessment, a sort of litmus test, and a disappointing one at that: it shows to Indrani, *and to others*, that Indrani is lacking in some respect that she perceives as self-defining.

If the envied's advantage were to be undone by fate the envier might feel some relief. Imagine that Priya had a miscarriage. Indrani might feel a transient relief, which would immediately be followed by guilt, shame, and sadness for her friend. Such relief is different from Schadenfreude proper, that is, pleasure at another's misfortune, which typically accompanies malicious kinds of envy (van de Ven et al. 2015). Rather than pleasure proper, Indrani's pain is assuaged because her inferiority is made less salient to her. But Indrani wants to have her own baby; that desire is still there.

It is precisely for these features that I suspect inert envy is often accompanied by guilt: inert enviers are more focused on the good than on the envied, and thus are not prone to see the target with explicit and conscious hostility; at the same time, they will find themselves experiencing mixed feelings toward them, including relief if the envied loses the good, and desire to be away from them. It is natural, then, to expect shame and guilt to follow, especially when the target is a loved one.

The behavioral outputs of inert envy are subtle, mostly inwardly focused, and sometimes hard to decipher. They can be best characterized negatively, by what they are not: as I said, they do not involve self-improvement; but neither do they involve active malice or aggression. The envier will then mostly wallow in their misery.

In previous work (Protasi 2016) I argued that being in the presence of the envied may trigger in the inert envier unconscious or unintended mildly hostile reactions, such as gossiping and backbiting. I used to think that gossiping and backbiting was a behavioral tendency of aggressive envy only when the good at stake was reputation.

However, I now think that when we spread negative gossip because of envious feelings we, consciously or not, feel hostility toward the envied and we intend to harm their status. If status is directly involved that means we are focused more on the rival than on the good, and thus envy is either aggressive or spiteful.[30] I should reiterate that these are educated guesses, since the empirical literature tends to mention gossiping and backbiting

---

[30] I owe this change of heart to the many conversations I had throughout the years. I cannot think of a particular person I ought to acknowledge, but I hope this note counts as a collective thank you to all who made this point.

only in relation to envy in general, without distinguishing between subtypes.[31]

But there are some typical expressions of inert envy that are in the vicinity of backbiting: half-hearted compliments, unenthusiastic congratulations, faint praise, and the like. Compliments, congratulations, and praise have two components.[32] Their content is a positive value judgment: the target possesses some nice trait ("you have such nice hair!"), or has achieved or has been befallen something good ("great job on that project!" "congratulations on your baby!"). But that is not all: there is an affective component, which can be interpreted both as a sincerity condition and as a performance condition.[33] An envier fails to meet the first one when they lack a sympathetic and warm appreciation toward the complimented/congratulated/praised target. Inert enviers typically engage in these expressive acts only superficially, thus insincerely, without feeling the affective component, because they are pained by their lack of the trait or object. In turn, that lack of feelings will cause the envier to fail the second condition: they will perform the speech act somewhat inappropriately, in the wrong tone, with a forced facial expression, and so forth. So their act is not felicitous.

In some cases the content will be affected as well, in that they may add a clause that explicitly reflect this pain (e.g., "You're such a good painter! I will never be able to paint like that" "Congratulations on your baby! Adoptions agencies keep rejecting me"), and thus the compliment or praise may be unpleasant or embarrassing to receive for the target.

In contrast, the emulative envier will express praise such as: "You are such a good painter! I really need to work more on my skills. Would you teach me?" Such a compliment still contains a comparative judgment and an admission of inferiority, but the optimism and lack of self-pity outweigh the frustration, and the compliment is quite pleasant to receive.

---

[31] See for instance Wert and Salovey 2004 and Smith and Kim 2007. An exception is van de Ven et al. 2012, who use gossiping as a way to assess whether someone feels malicious envy.

[32] Compliments, congratulations, and praise are a subset of speech acts that express reactive attitudes broadly construed, that is, both in the technical, narrower sense that they imply understanding of the targets qua moral agents (as in the case of moral praise or congratulations) and in the sense that they express a reaction to *non-moral* features of targets that are still, however, subject to normative assessment (as with complimenting nice hair). Even in a non-moral domain, these acts are performed with the expectation of a response on the part of the target, most often one of gratitude, which, in the context of envy and lack of wholeheartedness, creates some awkwardness to say the least. The envied person can perceive the lack of enthusiasm and endorsement, and react with embarrassment or even resentment.

[33] In am in debt to Trip Glazer for this suggestion.

Anthropologists have long been aware of the complicated relation envy bears to compliments and congratulations: in so-called peasant societies, which have very limited resources and where most contexts are interpreted as zero-sum, the implicit assumption is that *any* such expressive act implies some degree of malicious envy, therefore compliments and praise are feared and etiquette rules prohibit making them. In the same societies, not only does one avoid boasting about one's good fortune, but one goes as far as hiding it (cf. soiling the newborn babies' faces with mud, minimizing or denying the qualities of one's children, hiding one's wealth behind walls, and so forth), in order to avoid the scary and dangerous "evil eye" of the enviers (Foster 1972; Aquaro 2004; Lindholm 2008).

Dehumanizing praise can also be a behavioral output of inert envy: "You are so good at pulling all-nighters, you are a robot, not a person!" Such praise is a defensive mechanism, a way of explaining why the envied could achieve what the envier could not.[34] Backhanded compliments, instead, seem to be straightforward expressions of poorly disguised hostility and do not necessarily imply appreciation of the envied good. Miceli (2012, 40) provides some funny examples of backhanded compliments. She does not, however, discuss their implications for the structure of envy.

Some recent empirical research by Jens Lange and Jan Crusius discusses some possible behavioral patterns that they attribute to malicious envy, but that seem to me more likely to stem from inert envy. They say:

> For instance, people prone to malicious envy may often actively deny the goal to get good grades in an educational situation, or disidentify with the goal to pursue a better position in the company. They may also be more likely to switch to other comparison domains to bolster their self-esteem, or they may engage in self-handicapping. This reflects a pattern of a self-protection strategy (rather than a self-enhancement strategy) in responding to self-esteem threat evoked by upward social comparisons. (Lange and Crusius 2015, 292)

It seems to me that inert enviers will be more prone both to a "sour grapes" strategy and to self-handicapping, given that they are not focused on bringing the envied down, while at the same time they don't believe they

---

[34] Studies on ingroup/outgroup relations in the United States reveal that envied groups are often perceived as high in competence but low in warmth: a typical example is the way many White Americans see Asian Americans, the "model minority": they are often depicted as unlikeable, cold, scientific, uncreative, efficient, etc. In particular, the Chinese both were and are dehumanized in ways that are quite different from how other, less envied, racial groups are: they are represented as a multitude of all-identical individuals. I discuss this kind of envious prejudice in Chapter 5.

can self-improve. This is one of those cases where I think psychologists could benefit from more fine-grained distinctions, and from investigating inert envy in particular.

Self-handicapping is a defining feature of inert envy. Its structure is, in other words, *self-defeating*: it aims to achieve something that it presupposes to be unachievable. This feature is unique to inert envy: even spiteful envy, as we will see, can bring some meager satisfaction to the envier. Thus, one can cease feeling it only by changing one's goals or perception of self. Of the normative consequences of inert envy, however, I will talk more in Chapter 3.

To sum up, this is how I define inert envy: qua envy, it is an unpleasant reaction to the perceived superior standing of a similar other in a domain of self-relevance. It feels much more painful than any other kind of envy because it is self-defeating. The relative focus on the good induces the envier to feel inadequate compared to the target in an unproductive and self-loathing way. No productive behavior stems from inert envy, which motivates to be sullen and sulky, and at most to direct to the envied half-hearted congratulations, dehumanizing praise, and lukewarm compliments. Therefore, inert envy is neither actively malicious nor benign; it is a rather passive and self-defeating emotion.

In the remainder of the section I further clarify my account of inert envy by differentiating it from covetousness.

2.4.2.1 Inert Envy and Covetousness

Explaining how inert envy differs from covetousness requires us to define covetousness. It is not a notion or term usually found in the psychological literature on envy. The reason is that it is a primarily *moral* term, and one that does not seem to refer to an emotion but rather to a conative attitude, a species of (immoral) desire. But inert envy, as I defined it, is neither immoral not a desire.

But, lest you accuse me of glibly dismissing an interesting possibility, let us analyze two philosophical accounts of covetousness, by Robert C. Roberts and Rebecca Konyndyk DeYoung, which do bear some resemblance to inert envy. (Neither author provides an explicit definition of covetousness, but I think they would agree on the characterization above in terms of immoral desire.)

Roberts claims that covetousness implies the awareness that the desired object belongs to another person, without any rivalry or competitiveness. Rather, "the focus may overwhelmingly on the thing desired" (Roberts 2003, 262). Roberts' notion of covetousness, however, does not include perceived control over the outcome, which is responsible for inert envy's "sulking" tendency and ultimately self-defeating character.

A glimpse of the unproductive nature of inert envy may be found in the characterization of covetousness provided by Konyndyk DeYoung. In her book on the seven deadly sins she does not define covetousness, but provides two examples of it. One is the biblical story of Ahab and Naboth (Konyndyk DeYoung 2009, 43). As said in 1 Kings 2–4 (NIV): "Ahab said to Naboth, 'Let me have your vineyard to use for a vegetable garden, since it is close to my palace. In exchange I will give you a better vineyard or, if you prefer, I will pay you whatever it is worth.' But Naboth replied, 'The Lord forbid that I should give you the inheritance of my ancestors.' So, Ahab went home, sullen and angry ... He lay on his bed sulking and refused to eat." This case might indeed be interpreted as one of inert envy.

However, her second example of covetousness is that of Kind David, who covets Uriah's wife, Bathsheba. David sends Uriah to die, so he can have Bathsheba. Now, it is not clear to me that this action is motivated by envy rather than sheer lust. But if this were a case of envy then it would have to be either aggressive envy or emulative envy (depending on what David's focus is and what his perception of the good is) because there is nothing inert in David's behavior.

More generally, Konyndyk DeYoung employs an explicitly religious and prescriptive lens which suits the discussion of covetousness as a sin or vicious character trait. But that is not the approach that I adopt here. While there might be cases in which both covetousness and inert envy are appropriately invoked, the two notions are not at all synonymous, nor do their referents overlap that much.

In conclusion, inert envy, notwithstanding its neglect in most discussions on the nature of envy, is a familiar emotional experience that my taxonomy best accounts for. It showcases a fascinating combination of morally valuable elements, such as caring for a good for its own sake and wishing to be able to obtain it, and morally suspicious ones, such as feeling relief at someone's misfortune. It is also likely to be a gateway to more malicious, and downright immoral, kinds of envy. Thus, thinking about inert envy alerts us to the gap between our best intentions and the incapacity to realize them, and of the effects of such a gap on our moral character. It also brings to light the role of moral luck: the same person might find themselves sliding from emulative to inert envy, or, vice versa, ascending from inert to emulative envy, just in virtue of a change in circumstances outside of their control. Inert envy reveals the psychological and moral complexity of a multifaceted emotion such as envy. This complexity is lost in the simplistic distinction between benign and malicious envy that is popular in psychology, and even in more sophisticated taxonomies like Gabriele Taylor's.

It is now time to look at the decidedly rotten apples in the family of envy.

2.4.3 Aggressive Envy

Agrippine is a science fiction writer. She envies Ursula, who is her main rival. They are very close in fame and book sales, but Ursula has so far succeeded in selling more books, and in receiving more awards, critical praises, and interviews. Agrippine believes that winning the Hugo Award would turn the tables. They are both in the final list, but Agrippine knows that the jury is leaning toward awarding it to Ursula. She bribes two of the jurors, and as a consequence she wins the prize. Even if she did not win because of her artistic merit, Agrippine is happy because she defeated her rival. However, she still sees Ursula as an enemy to beat.

Aggressive envy is the result of being focused on the envied, and believing oneself to be capable of taking the good away from them. When I am more focused on the envied, what matters to me more than getting the good per se is outperforming the other person. Therefore I will be more inclined to bring the envied down. But there will be different behavioral outputs depending on perceived obtainability of the good.

If I perceive myself to be able to deprive the envied of the good, even if I care more about beating the envied than getting the good in itself, I will not be motivated to spoil the good or to engage in behaviors so destructive that my chances to obtain the good decrease. That is, I will be motivated to sabotage the envied only. What sabotaging the envied means depends on the good at stake, as it was for self-improvement, and it may not always be an obtainable goal. For instance, if the envied object is "having won a prestigious fellowship" there is not much that the envier can do to deprive the envied of it. The envier may try to spoil the envied's happiness, or spread rumors that the fellowship was undeserved, and so forth, but it is unclear whether these attempts at bringing the envied down count as "leveling down" in a case such as this. Notice also that, in labeling envy, intent matters: if the envier finds herself unwittingly muttering under her breath unpleasant remarks about the envied, and then regretting this immediately after because she realizes that her attitude is unfair toward the envied, then she probably feels inert envy. If she purposively spreads damaging rumors with the hope that the fellowship be taken away from the envied, then she feels aggressive envy. There are likely to be cases in between.

In zero-sum contexts, as we have seen in the case of emulative envy, leveling down equates to leveling up. In the case of a race, sabotaging the envied may mean tripping the envied, which may also result in the envier winning the race if they are right behind. The good is pursued as a way to bring down the envied, but is also a nice bonus, something the envier will appreciate rather than regret (as it was in the case of emulative envy, where the envied's loss of the good might have caused regret and pity in the envier).

Thus, aggressive envy is actively malevolent. The envied, much like a rival in a duel, has to be attacked and defeated. Because of the rivalry that develops between the envier and the envied, in addition to the behaviors aimed at taking the good away from the rival, the aggressive envier might try to harm the rival out of sheer malice (we could call this uber-aggressive envy). Furthermore, aggressive envy implies confidence in one's own ability to level one's disadvantage. As a consequence, aggressive envy is painful, qua envy, but also involves the pleasant anticipation of getting even. These feelings are likely to be highly motivating, although motivating toward morally reproachable results.

Aggressive envy is not the same as malice or Schadenfreude. Malice is the desire to inflict harm, which is a component of, but not reducible to, aggressive envy. Malice is also present in other emotions, most obviously hatred. Schadenfreude is a pleasant affect, and again it is associated with different emotions, not just aggressive envy but also resentment and *ressentiment.*[35]

To sum up, aggressive envy, like the other kinds of envy, is unpleasant, but it can be mixed with the anticipatory pleasure of revenge. Such a pleasure is presumably absent when aggressive envy is not acted upon. If it is acted upon it might be mitigated by possible feelings of guilt and shame in agents who are morally conscientious, or at least sensitive to social disapprobation. If the envier succeeds in stealing the good from the envied their envy might either cease or temporarily subside, depending on how strong and longstanding is the rivalry with the target.

---

[35] See Feather and Sherman 2002 for evidence that Schadenfreude is more closely associated with resentment than envy; see Smith et al. 1996, 2009, for the association with envy (but notice that Smith conceives of envy in ways that do not clearly distinguish it from resentment, so these results may not contradict those of Feather and Sherman); van de Ven et al. 2015 seek to reconcile these and other seemingly conflicting findings by arguing that only malicious envy predicts Schadenfreude.

In Chapter 3 I discuss in greater detail aggressive envy's potential for evil. For now I just want to stress that my model has the theoretical advantage of accurately distinguishing between different kinds of badness that stem from envy: aggressive envy is different from its timid and frustrated relative, inert envy, on the one hand, and from its most ferocious one, which we are about to meet.

2.4.4 Spiteful Envy

> Spike envies his long-time rival Angel, because Angel is loved by an attractive and cool girl named Buffy. Spike does not love Buffy, but he desires her as a status symbol. He cannot take Buffy away from Angel: even if he kidnapped her, she would never love him. So he kills her. If he can't be Buffy's beloved, neither can Angel.[36]

Spiteful envy is the result of being focused on the envied, and believing oneself to be incapable of taking the good away from them. If I perceive myself to be incapable of ever getting the good, even by sabotaging the target, then my frustration and aggression toward the envied will give rise to full-blown, swiping destruction: both the envied and the good will be affected. Spike knows that even if he gets Angel out of the way, Buffy will not love him, and so the only way to find relief from his pain is to kill Buffy. There are, of course, more mundane examples, like the child who is not allowed to take the toy another child is enjoying and breaks it in response, or subtler ones, like someone who organizes a surprise party to celebrate a friend's nomination for an award despite the fact that the friend is deeply superstitious about such events.[37]

In spiteful envy the envied is not even a rival to be deprived of the good and thus defeated in a productive way, because the envier does not believe that can be done. Nor is the good perceived as something that can be stolen. Both the envied and the good thus become targets of destruction. It is in spiteful envy that we find the truth of the dictum: "Envy spoils the good it covets."

---

[36] The vignette is loosely inspired by the TV show *Buffy The Vampire Slayer*.

[37] We will see in Chapter 5 how egalitarians have been accused of spiteful envy, because they are charged with wanting to take away social goods from the most advantaged classes even when that does not bring any advantage to the least advantaged classes. The accusation becomes even more serious if envy is defined in a uberspiteful way, such that the envier is even willing to pay an additional cost for the sake of leveling down (John Rawls defines envy along those lines; see Chapter 5 and Appendix).

Spiteful envy, insofar as it does not motivate the envier to get the good and contains elements of frustration, is similar to inert envy. But it differs from it because destroying the good is *one way* of leveling down. Spiteful envy, therefore, is not self-defeating in the same way inert envy is. Another obvious difference is that spiteful envy is also much more malicious than inert envy.

Spiteful envy is arguably the most malicious of all kinds, since it harms both the envied and the good; it is closest to what Chaucer describes in *The Parson's Tale*: "envy is against all virtues and all goodness. For it is sorry for all the goodness of one's neighbor, making it different from all other sins. There is scarcely any sin that doesn't have within it some delight, but Envy has within it only anguish and sorrow" (Chaucer 2011, 475). Spiteful envy is also the source of the very first murder in the biblical tradition: Cain kills Abel out of envy because God (from Cain's perspective) has favored Abel's gift and despised Cain's. Nothing good and much evil stems from that act.

Spiteful envy feels pretty bad since it lacks the pleasant hope of stealing the good. Contra Chaucer, however, there might be pleasure in spoiling the good, even though such a pleasure may be short-lived: Spike and Cain are left empty-handed after their acts of spiteful revenge. Spiteful envy does not motivate enviers toward behaviors that could improve their well-being, not even in immoral ways as in aggressive envy. Differentiating spiteful envy from aggressive envy allows us to see that moral considerations should be separated from prudential ones. Aggressive envy can bring long-lasting, albeit immoral, advantages to the envier. Spiteful envy cannot do so.

One might wonder how spiteful envy differs from spite proper. The difference between the two is analogous to the difference between emulative envy and emulation. The former is an emotion, the latter is better characterized as a behavioral tendency that can be associated with different emotions. I can act spitefully out of hatred, resentment, or anger. In its less serious forms it can also be a component of playfully competitive interactions.

You might notice that the sections on aggressive and spiteful envy are quite short. That is not surprising, because together they correspond to the traditional picture of envy as a deadly sin. Even though we personally may have not experienced them (of course we haven't), we all know what this envy looks like. And yet the distinction between spiteful and aggressive allows us to draw useful normative distinctions, as we will see in Chapter 3.

Summing up the content of this chapter, the Table 2.1 shows the main characteristics of the four kinds of envy.

Table 2.1. *The four kinds of envy*

	Emulative	**Inert**	**Aggressive**	**Spiteful**
Phenomenology: does it come with painful feelings?	Yes, but assuaged by hope of self-improving and obtaining the good; possibly accompanied by shame for inferiority	Yes, and intensified by self-loathing and despair; possible relief if envied happens to lose the good	Yes, but assuaged by hope of stealing the good; possibly accompanied by shame and guilt	Yes, with short-term pleasure if agent succeeds in destroying the good; possibly accompanied by shame and guilt
Envied seen as:	Model	Litmus test	Rival	Shooting target
Characterizing action tendency:	Self-improve	Sulk	Steal	Spoil

Chapter 3 is entirely devoted to discussing the moral and prudential value of these kinds of envy in the context of personal relationships. Envy has traditionally been assessed as bad; more recently, psychologists have been keen on defending "benign" envy. My taxonomy engenders a much more nuanced normative assessment.

CHAPTER 3

The Value of Envy

We can often be vain of our passions, even the guiltiest ones;

but envy is so sneaking and shameful that we never dare confess it.
Francois de la Rochefoucauld, *Maxims*

3.1 Introduction: Is Envy Guilty as Charged?

Given the outcome of Chapter 2 it will be completely unsurprising that my answer to the question whether envy is guilty as charged is a decisive "no." However, some readers may still be unpersuaded by the argument. I shall attempt, then, to produce a new argument, which derives from, instead of ending with, normative claims about envy.

As we have seen in Chapters 1 and 2, the near-universal reluctance people feel to admit their envy in a non-jocular and unqualified way has often been taken as proof of its viciousness. This is perhaps the most resilient *topos* about envy (see Appendix for further textual evidence). However, psychologists have found empirical confirmation that *both* malicious and benign envy are hard to confess, a fact which constitutes an impediment to empirical studies because it causes envy to be underreported. (Thus, researchers often have to resort to alternative ways of questioning the subjects or eliciting their envy.)

For extensive feedback on this chapter I am very grateful to Olivia Bailey, Mara Bollard, Alida Liberman, Alice MacLachlan, and Denise Vigani. I am also very grateful to the many who read previous versions or were audience members at the talks I gave on this material, among whom I especially thank: Stephen Darwall, June Gruber, Verity Harte, Amy Lara, Shen-yi Liao, Tamar Szabó Gendler, Dustin Tucker, several anonymous reviewers, and audience members at the Society for Applied Philosophy Annual Conference, Oxford, the Emotions and Emotionality conference at Georgetown University, and colloquia at the University of California San Diego, and Nanyang Technological University in Singapore.

I encourage the reader to try this yourself. Ask your friends, deadpan, in a situation in which they are seemingly feeling envy: "Are you envious?" Chances are that you will get an evasive or qualified response ("Yes, I am envious, but ... "), an embarrassed joke, or an angry denial.[1] Almost nobody admits to envy in a straightforward way, without qualification or defensiveness. This reluctance to confess envy has *two* main sources: the moral stigma attached to envy's perceived badness and the prudential embarrassment of implicitly admitting perceived inferiority.

But in this chapter I show that the varieties of envy differ with regard to how much perception of inferiority they involve and how potentially immoral their consequences are.

Here is how my argument proceeds. In Section 3.2 I make some preliminary considerations and clarify my assumptions. In Section 3.3 I present a paradigmatic case of envy as a vice, which involves both moral and prudential badness. Such a case satisfies, on the one hand, an intuitive understanding of envy, and, on the other, the definition of envy as an emotion. In the following sections I alter the example, changing the details relevant for the *normative* assessment without modifying the core *psychological* features. In Section 3.4 I present a case of envy that is morally bad but not prudentially bad. In Section 3.5 I present an opposite case of envy that is prudentially bad but not morally bad. In both these cases I argue that pretheoretical intuitions still track them as authentic cases of envy, and that they both still satisfy the psychological definition of envy as an emotion. In Section 3.6 I present the case that diverges most radically from the initial one at a normative level: it is a case of envy that is neither prudentially nor morally bad. While it might not appear to some as a case of envy pretheoretically, I show that the emotional episode satisfies all the conditions set out in the definition of envy, and thus should be recognized as such. In Section 3.7 I highlight the connections between the ontological and the normative dimensions of envy. In Section 3.8 I consider the question: "Can emulative envy be a virtuous emotion?" and I answer positively. Finally, I conclude, with Section 3.9, by briefly addressing the topic of how to respond to envy.

---

[1] Verity Harte pointed out to me that it is much easier to admit occasional and fleeting bouts of envy than being an envious person. This is true, but even admitting envy occasionally, without qualification and in all seriousness, is quite rare. Furthermore, admitting to being an envious person is often a mark of being, or wanting to appear, disdainful of conventional morality.

3.2   Preliminaries

Envy slays itself by its own arrows.

Greek proverb

Wrath is cruel and anger is outrageous, but who can stand before envy?

Prov. 27:4

Let me make four clarifications before delving into the analysis of envy's badness.

First, I assume a widely shared distinction between moral and prudential badness. A classical way of making this distinction can be found in Henry Sidgwick's classical contrast between *rational prudence*, which prescribes that one aim at one's personal good, and *rational benevolence*, which prescribes that one take into account the good of everyone else as much as one's own. Moral badness, in this picture, is thus assessed from "the point of view [. . .] of the universe" (Sidgwick 1967, 382).

Accepting such a distinction at the conceptual level does not require one to accept it at the extensional one. A relatively popular position is to think of prudence as a subset of morality. For instance, contemporary virtue ethicists such as John McDowell (1979) and Rosalind Hursthouse (1999) would argue that, for the virtuous agent, if something is morally bad then it is also prudentially bad. But even for theories such as those, distinguishing the moral badness from prudential badness of envy proves useful. One of the aims of this chapter is to show how different kinds of envy require different strategies for the moral educator. Moral education is not targeted toward the fully virtuous person, and a distinction between moral and prudential considerations tracks concerns that are perceived as different by the average person.

In order to see how the two dimensions may come apart we can apply the distinction to other dispositions or vices first. Gluttony, for example, is bad primarily from a self-interested, *prudential* point of view.[2] In contrast, cruelty is primarily bad from an impartial, *moral* point of view. Envy has traditionally been considered bad from *both* normative perspectives. On the one hand, envy is assessed as prudentially bad because it is self-defeating, as the Greek saying in the epigraph vividly portrays.

---

[2] At least, that is the contemporary perception. Gluttony belongs to the list of capital sins, and as such it is expected to produce other immoralities, some of which may harm others. Contemporary discussions in philosophy of food come to mind (think of the weak-willed ethical vegetarian).

On the other hand, envy also has a reputation for being morally bad, due to the malice and ill will that are alleged to be its necessary components.

It is possible to resist the conceptual distinction between morality and prudence that I am appealing to here. Stoic ethics, both ancient and modern, is the most authoritative representative of this position, given that it considers moral virtue to be the only truly good object. The ancient Stoic, however, is already the least sympathetic of my readers, because for him all emotions are unfitting and should not be felt by the sage. Contemporary Stoics often depart from their historical predecessors with regard to the role and value of emotions in practical deliberation. Martha Nussbaum, for instance, advocates a neo-Stoic view of emotions, according to which they are of crucial importance to the ethical life (Nussbaum 2001a). While contemporary Stoics may not be persuaded by the conceptual distinction between moral and prudential goodness, they might nevertheless be open to the possibility of a non-bad kind of envy. The neo-Stoic, then, might reject that there can be envy that is either only morally or only prudentially bad (which I present in Sections 3.4 and 3.5), but they might agree with my diagnosis of the example in Section 3.6, which I take to be neither morally nor prudentially bad.[3]

A second clarification concerns what it means to say that envy is bad. I think we actually refer to at least two distinct phenomena: envy may be bad to *feel* or to *act upon*. This distinction may appear to correspond with prudential and moral badness: envy is often bad to feel in the sense that it is painful, and it is bad to act upon because it leads to the harm of innocent others. But actions motivated by envy can also be self-defeating and self-harmful, and envy that is unpleasant to feel might still motivate behavior advantageous to the agent, so the two distinctions do not perfectly align.

Furthermore, when speaking about actions motivated by envy we can distinguish between intended and unintended behaviors.[4] This distinction is particularly important when talking about envy given that much envy is felt below the level of awareness, and given that, even when the agent is aware of feeling envy, they might try to hide or repress it. Thus, envy may often give rise to behaviors that are not intended: blunders, slips of the tongue, or even uncontrollable facial and bodily expressions such as blushing, grimacing, frowning, and the like. Throughout the chapter I thus talk about how envy may be bad to act on, express, and feel.

---

[3] I am indebted to Amy Lara for a discussion on some of these issues.
[4] I am grateful to Neal Tognazzini for input on this formulation.

Third, I assume throughout the chapter that the envied object, which is perceived as desirable by the envier, is *actually* good. Were the object to be bad, then some notions discussed here would be reversed: self-improvement would become self-worsening, for instance. But other considerations would remain unchanged: for instance, independent of whether what I envy is good or bad, expressing envy has a certain social cost (even though the cost may be higher in the case of an object that is deemed bad by the community). For reasons of simplicity I keep the actual goodness of the object constant in every case I analyze. I come back to the topic of goodness in the conclusion of the book.

Finally, here is a reminder of my definition of envy: envy is an aversive reaction to a perceived inferiority vis-à-vis a similar other, with regard to a good that is relevant to the sense of identity of the envier, and which motivates to overcome such an inferiority either by bringing oneself up to the level of the envied or by pulling them down to one's own level.

Let us now look at four experiences of envy. In each case I ask whether feeling or acting upon envy is good or bad from both a moral and a prudential point of view.

3.3 "It Should Have Been Me!"

> Envy is a moth to the heart, a canker to the thought, and a rust to the soul.
>
> Anonymous

Livia is a graduating student at the La Scala Theater Ballet School, and she is consumed by bitter, resentful, malicious envy for her classmate Carla.[5] Carla is an exceptionally talented dancer, with a rigorous, versatile technique and rare interpretive qualities. Livia is painfully aware that she is not as good as her, even though they started at the same time, practiced in the same classes, and sacrificed everything to dance for the same number of years. The graduation performance approaches, and while Carla is going to be the prima ballerina, Livia is in the corps. Again. "It should have been me" is Livia's mental refrain while she watches Carla rehearsing.[6]

---

[5] I use the name Livia for the envier due to its assonance with "lividus," which means, among other things, envious. The name Carla is an homage to Italian ballerina Carla Fracci.

[6] In all examples I use counterfactual thought as a rhetorical device, in order to illustrate how I conceive of the envier's overall mental state. This formulation was inspired by research conducted by van de Ven and Zeelenberg (2015), who tested the thought "it could have been me" and found a correlation with envy in general. More recent studies seem to suggest that there may also be a correlation between certain kinds of counterfactual thinking and certain kinds of envy.

Livia is obsessed by destructive fantasies. She daydreams about cutting Carla's pointe shoe ribbons, or hiding her costume at the last minute. But even that would not be enough to satisfy her raging ambitions and appease her envious feelings. The hell with everybody: the other dancers, the teachers, the director of the school with all his speeches about hard work. She gave up her youth, and here she is, holding the same pose for an eternity, while Carla wows the audience with her thirty-two perfect *fouetté* turns. Livia is going to burn the whole darn theater down!

There are two features of Livia's envy that deserve attention. First, Livia is more *bothered by her inferiority* to Carla, whom she sees as a long-time rival, than by the fact she is not an excellent dancer. As a consequence she is more motivated to worsen Carla's position than to improve hers. Second, she feels *hopeless*: she does not think she can become a better dancer, nor does she think that she can come to occupy Carla's superior position in other ways. Thus, her only option is to *act* spitefully. Her envy "spoils the good it covets": if she acts on her spiteful inclination and actually burns the theater down, nobody will be prima ballerina, including herself. Her inclination to bring the envied down is so intense that it becomes self-destructive and all-destructive.

Livia's envy, as you might have guessed, is *spiteful envy*. Certainly the description I gave of Livia's emotion counts as one of envy: Livia is pained by the (correct) perception that Carla, a similar other, outperforms her in a domain of self-relevance. This case satisfies the definition of envy. It also matches with the traditional portrait of envy as an irredeemable capital vice. I have already mentioned Iago as a literary example of spiteful envy. Another one may be Bette, the protagonist of Honoré de Balzac's novel *Cousin Bette*, who conspires against her whole extended family. Bette is depicted as a demonic, beast-like creature who succeeds in ravaging the life of many without, however, bettering her own.

Spiteful envy is thus bad both from a prudential and a moral point of view. It is morally bad because it is extremely malicious, but it is also prudentially bad because it "shoots at others but hits itself," as a saying goes.

Benign forms of envy are characterized by upward self-focused thoughts, namely, thoughts about past actions that one could have undertaken to improve one's situation, whereas malicious forms of envy are associated with more other-focused counterfactuals, that is, thoughts about what others could have done to improve one's personal outcome. Interestingly, there seems to also be a causal mechanism at play, such that inducing one type of counterfactual thinking can induce or increase the corresponding type of envy (see Crusius and Lange MS; at the time of writing this article had not been peer reviewed).

Spiteful envy is bad even if the envier, out of conscience or cowardice, refrains from engaging in the most destructive behaviors mentioned above, but simply unconsciously *expresses* her envious feelings or lets them slip through less than amicable behavior.

As mentioned earlier, envy often provokes unintentional actions. Suppose that spiteful Livia does not engage in any sort of dramatic endeavor. Nonetheless, she might be prone to making bitter remarks about Carla, gossiping and speaking behind her back. She will be hypocritical, sour, and petty, all characteristics that are likely to backfire: Livia will come to be despised and possibly feared, if perceived as a threat to others. Livia will then become isolated: her classmates will not want to include her in group studies, because of her lack of team spirit and cooperativeness (Hill and Buss 2008), nor will they invite her to social events, because of her pettiness and sourness. If she had a friendly relationship with Carla that would become strained and eventually dissolve, either by Carla's initiative or by hers: Livia will not be able to rejoice at Carla's success and Carla will be saddened and scared by Livia's envy (Hill and Buss 2008; Parrott and Mosquera 2008). Furthermore, expressions of spiteful envy may upset bystanders, thus exacerbating Carla's social isolation.[7] Expressing spiteful envy is therefore very bad both prudentially and morally.

But so is even merely *feeling* it. Envy is sometimes described as an acidic, burning sensation that gnaws at the envier from the inside. Since there is no evidence that envy is associated with a unique set of feelings or physiological changes, this image should be taken more as a metaphor of its effects on the agent than a phenomenologically accurate description.[8] Indeed, there is evidence that (some kind of) envy is correlated with poor physical and mental health (Smith and Kim 2007, 58–60; see also the discussion in Section 3.4). Both imagery and evidence apply particularly well to the case of spiteful envy. As a Spanish proverb says: "Envy is thin because it bites but never eats." Livia may not actually burn the theater down, but if she does she won't feel much better once the ashes are

---

[7] There is an aesthetic component to this that I cannot develop here, but that is worth mentioning in passing: spiteful envy in particular, but perhaps most envy, is *ugly* in a way that might be literal. It is not a coincidence that Greek tragic heroes, to take but one exemplary context, can be jealous (Othello, Medea), ashamed (Ajax), raging and indignant (Achilles), even disgusting (Philoctetes), but not envious. Greek tragedy does not shy away from human imperfection and makes a spectacle of it, but envy never appears as a characterizing feature of its main characters.

[8] We often find this phenomenology associated with moral condemnation of the vice of envy, where it is also often described as a disease of the soul. See Appendix.

cold: she will be left empty-handed and with rust in the soul, as the anonymous author of the epigraph of this section puts it.

That anonymous person is likely to have been a moralist, however. From an exclusively descriptive, functional perspective (Crusius and Lange 2017) spiteful envy might serve some purpose: temporarily advancing one's social status, and assuaging wounds of self-esteem, since it may also help one focus on the envied instead of on one's own failures. This cannot be a stable gain (and psychologists are well aware of the ill effects of malicious envy on the agent's psychological well-being), but it is worth noting the discrepancy between a normative outlook and a purely descriptive one.[9] Such a discrepancy will be even smaller for the next scenario.

3.4   "It Should Be Me!"

> Plots have I laid, inductions dangerous,
> By drunken prophecies, libels and dreams,
> To set my brother Clarence and the king
> In deadly hate the one against the other.
> Shakespeare, *Richard III*

> The envious man thinks that he will be able to walk better if his neighbor breaks a leg.
> Israeli proverb

Let us tweak the initial case just a little and make Livia a less clumsy and ineffective envier. In this new scenario Livia does not engage in foolish pyromaniac fantasies. When she looks at Carla, rather than thinking in counterfactual terms ("That should have been me!") she thinks in indicative ones: "That should be me!" – a voice inside her head roars. Livia is now more optimistic and forward looking. Even though she is aware she is not as good as Carla, she has an idea about how to get Carla's role. She persuades the choreographer to choose her as Carla's understudy. One day, when Carla looks particularly tired, she pushes her down the stairs. Carla loses her balance, falls, and breaks a leg. Livia (who manages to not be discovered) gets to dance in her place.[10]

---

[9] The detrimental effects on one's health might even be *increased* when one is actively suppressing expression and action, since emotional suppression is energetically costly. I thank Denise Vigani for this suggestion.

[10] There are several real-life examples of this scenario. A recent one involves skater Mariah Bell, who was accused to intentionally injure rival Lim Eun-soo (https://en.yna.co.kr/view/AEN20190321000800315?section=news). The accusation might be false in this case, but we can easily imagine a close possible world in which it is true.

Like before, Livia is more bothered by her inferiority to Carla than by the fact she is not an excellent dancer. But this time she feels *hopeful* about her chances of beating her long-time rival and taking the coveted good (being a prima ballerina) away from her. In Chapter 2 I called this envy *aggressive*. As we have seen, aggressive and spiteful envy are usually not distinguished in either the philosophical or psychological literature, and this is problematic not only for the sake of conceptual clarity but for the purpose of finding remedies for what is usually simply called "malicious" envy.

Spiteful envy tends to be bad not only for its target but for the agent: spiteful enviers are damaged by their envy both morally and prudentially. But it is not obviously the case for aggressive envy.

Because being prima ballerina is a scarce good, if Livia succeeds in stealing the role from Carla she has gained something valuable for herself. She has succeeded in her intent to bring the envied down and she has also gained an actual good. While moralists may argue that getting the role this way is not objectively valuable (and I agree with them), from Livia's perspective that is not relevant (because she is more focused on the target than the good). Assuming that Livia won't feel any pangs of guilt and will sleep soundly at night, it seems that *acting* on her envy has increased her well-being.

Again, one could resist this conclusion on various philosophical grounds, for instance from a neo-Stoic or neo-Aristotelian perspective, but in the context of moral education and envy prevention it matters that the agent perceives herself to have gained from her envy. Aggressive envy is more intractable than spiteful envy because the educator cannot always point to obvious disadvantages *from the perspective of an unscrupulous agent*. Spiteful Livia might be brought to reason when facing the incinerated ruins she caused. Most of the time spiteful envy can be addressed before such dramatic endings: a child who broke the toy in order not to share it with their sibling can learn from the experience. But a child who stole their sibling's candy and happily ate it might not be sensitive to the parent's scolding, nor to their sibling's tears. And they might become the student who cheats on their exams, and then the corporate manager who sabotages their coworkers to get a promotion.[11]

---

[11] Denise Vigani points out that the difference between aggressive and spiteful envy may be minimal, since unscrupulous people might get a real kick out of destroying the good, especially since they have, in fact, removed the disadvantage, if temporarily. Questions of moral education are largely empirical and I don't think there is any literature investigating these questions, so at this stage it is a matter of contrasting intuitions.

Now, for this kind of strategic envious behavior to be effective it needs to be secretive. Openly *expressing* aggressive envy would be morally bad, but more importantly it would be prudentially bad. The aggressive envier's confident intention to bring down the envied is a counterproductive signal, one that is most likely to damage the envier in most contexts (the exception being the very powerful). It is therefore particularly important that Livia hide her envy.

Feeling aggressive envy is still painful, but it is a productive kind of pain that motivates Livia to bring Carla down. As mentioned before, if the agent is morally conscientious then she might feel very ashamed and guilty, both unpleasant emotions which would motivate her to not act on her envy (in which case her pain would end up being ineffective). On the other hand, acting on one's envy not only increases the chances of getting the coveted good but also "discharges" the painful feeling, making the agent feel a whole lot better.[12]

Note that this modus operandi has proved quite effective at the level of international relations. Countries and populations have often fought for access to coveted resources that were seen as exclusive. Wars and inter-group conflicts can be seen as caused, among other factors, by aggressive envy.[13] If the aggressive envier cannot be secretive about their intentions, they can try to mask their envy under the guise of resentment and indignation, a strategy well known to warring nations. Adam Smith observed in his *Theory of Moral Sentiments* that rivalry between nations is due to malicious envy.[14]

Aggressive envy is obviously morally bad, but from a prudential point of view it might be not so bad to feel and act on it. Functionally speaking aggressive envy gets the job done: it accomplishes its goal of leveling down. It takes away the advantage from the envied, even though it does so illicitly. This feature makes aggressive envy particularly difficult for the moral educator to prevent: while it is easy to show to children that spiteful

---

[12] It may be fruitful to think of the successful aggressive envier according to Nietzschean paradigms. Cf. Nietzsche on the contrast between the "noble man" vs. the weak "man of *ressentiment.*" The former's *ressentiment* is "consumed and exhausted in an immediate action," while the other cannot discharge his envious anger and turns it inward in self-hatred (Nietzsche 1994, 23). While *ressentiment* is not the same as envy, but rather a personality trait that characterizes a range of actions and attitudes, envy seems a crucial component of it. I am indebted to Stephen Darwall for this suggestion.

[13] A recurring suggestion is that anti-Semitism is partially fueled by group envy (see for instance Glick 2002). See Chapter 5.

[14] "The love of our own nation often disposes us to view, with the most malignant jealousy and envy, the prosperity and aggrandisement of any other neighbouring nation" (TMS, VI. II. 28) Such envy, according to him, should be replaced by emulation.

envy does not really pay off, since it spoils the good it covets, it is not so with aggressive envy. In some circumstances it is indeed the case that breaking the competitor's leg will allow one to "walk better," or at least to get to the finish line first. The moral educator will thus have to appeal to moral principles, explaining that we ought not to try to bring an envied other down because it constitutes gratuitous harm to an innocent.[15] Note that, with both aggressive and spiteful envy, one central intervention is to render the agent sensitive to the harm wished to the envied; in both cases, that is, the envier has to be made more sympathetic so that they find the malicious motivations associated with aggressive and spiteful envy repulsive. That is, of course, hard work, especially with subjects that are not already naturally predisposed to sympathetic feelings (which in turn may correlate with dispositional malicious envy).[16] Such emotional reeducation will be harder to promote, I think, with aggressive enviers, since the prospect of gaining the good will be more salient and will obscure the harm done to the envied, or motivate the envier to come up with rationalizations of various kinds.[17]

One might object that aggressive envy brings about no genuine self-improvement, and is thus also prudentially disadvantageous. The success of this objection relies on substantive conceptions of moral and prudential badness and what counts as genuine self-improvement. I will go back to such issues at the end of the chapter. However, it is worth noticing that even if leveling down were never genuinely advantageous the difficulties for the moral educator would remain, since most children would be inclined to consider getting the coveted object as a genuine prudential advantage.

3.5 "It Could Have Been Me!"

> Envy gives a paranoid flavour to existence. Instead of desiring life, the envier comes to fear it.
>
> Joseph Berke[18]

Aggressive envy is therefore morally bad but may not be prudentially bad. Is it possible for envy to be, vice versa, prudentially but not morally bad?

---

[15] I am assuming the good or advantage has been obtained justly. If that were not the case, resentment and indignation would be legitimate responses, and the targeted person would be an appropriate object of corrective measurements or punishments.

[16] For evidence that malicious envy correlates with a tendency to manipulative and psychopathic behavior, see Lange et al. 2018, and also discussion below in Section 3.8.

[17] Thanks to Denise Vigani for pressing me on this difference.   [18] Berke 2012.

Suppose Livia is still the hopeless person we saw when we discussed spiteful envy, but *she is not focused on bringing Carla down*. What Livia would like in this new scenario is to level up, and to become an exceptional dancer. However, suppose also that she has no hope that she can make it happen, because she believes to have exhausted her potential for improvement. Since Carla's demise would *not* contribute to her goal to become a better dancer, she does not have any ill will toward Carla. But even if she does not wish any harm to fall upon Carla, she does feel relief when Carla makes a mistake. Moreover, she does not really like to watch her rehearse, she prefers to not spend time around her, and shows a generally avoidant behavior around her.

Livia is "stuck" in the very painful, hopeless, and frustrating emotion that I call *inert envy*. This envy is passive, in two senses. First, as we have already discussed, Livia cannot actualize her emulative intentions because she does not believe she can succeed at emulating Carla. Livia does not act in ways that would help to close the gap between her and Carla because she does not believe that it is possible. "That could have been me" – inert envy whines – "if the world had turned out to be just a tiny bit different." Livia went to the same school, practiced for the same long hours, and endured the same demanding physical routine and dietary restrictions as Carla, but – Livia thinks – Carla was just naturally more talented, and Livia sees this outcome as ineluctable.

Second, inert envy is not *malicious* like aggressive or spiteful envy: Livia does not engage in aggressive or harmful behaviors. However, she may be relieved when the perceived gap is temporarily reduced by Carla's occasional mistakes. Such a transient relief is different from the kind of glee, or from Schadenfreude proper, which typically accompanies malicious kinds of envy (van de Ven et al. 2015).[19] If Carla got seriously injured Livia would feel bad for her. The pleasure that Livia feels because of Carla's mishaps is caused by the fact that her inferiority is lessened, or is less salient, rather than caused by the envied's misfortune per se. Recall the scenario in Chapter 2 where Indrani envied Priya for her pregnancy. Indrani had to implement self-protective measures such as not seeing her friend until she got pregnant herself. Similarly, Livia here might need to stop attending the same classes as Carla, or might even want to change

---

[19] Even though Schadenfreude can be associated to envy, it is not the same thing as envy because it is a pleasant emotion. Furthermore, it is also felt in association with different emotions, for instance with hatred, resentment, and indignation. Van Dijk et al. 2006 stress that Schadenfreude is a multidetermined emotion. Miceli and Castelfranchi 2007, 468 plausibly hypothesize that envious Schadenfreude evokes more guilt than resentful Schadenfreude.

school. Attempting to reduce contact with the envied might be another typical behavioral output of inert envy – a slightly more active one – which, however, does not harm the envied, or at any rate reduces potentially greater harms. While envied friends might be saddened by the envier's behavior, separation is better than being on the receiving end of hostility.

We have seen, however, that inert envy is also typically accompanied by half-hearted praise and backhanded compliments. These acts can be hurtful, and do represent a mild harm, even though they are not intentional. Even though Livia may be fully convinced that Carla is not *responsible* for her pain, she might still come to see her (consciously or not) as the *cause* of it. If Livia were to develop feelings of anger and resentment, either as a way to mask and excuse her envy, and/or as a consequence of thinking of her situation as unfair, then her envy might turn spiteful or aggressive because she would come to see Livia in a hostile way. Therefore, also for this reason enviers might be better off severing their relations with, or decreasing their proximity to, the envied.

Feeling inert envy, with its despair, frustration, self-loathing, shame, and guilt, is likely to be very painful, since inert envy is a self-defeating attitude: it does not motivate self-improvement, but leaves the envier stuck thinking about a highly valued good that she cannot reach.

Expressing inert envy is also quite damaging at the social and relational level. If Livia talks about her envy she will sound insecure and sullen. People will not think very highly of her, and even if they might ultimately think she is wrong in perceiving herself as disadvantaged they might condemn her incapacity to rejoice for others' fortune, and the subsequent behaviors stemming from it.

Inert envy is, therefore, prudentially bad. However, there might be a silver lining even here. From a functional perspective inert envy's avoidant tendency might at least help the envier to lick their wounds, so to speak, and avoid worse damage to their self-esteem, by motivating the envier to stay away from the envied. But these defensive responses are effective only in the short term, and do not seem conducive to long-term self-improvement and emotional growth.

Is inert envy morally bad? That depends on one's normative commitments. For instance, if one thinks that there exist duties to self then inert envy may be assessed as morally bad. If one is an Aristotelian virtue ethicist one will reject a distinction between prudence and morality, and, once again, will assess inert envy as morally bad, albeit less bad than aggressive and spiteful envy. If one is a Stoic in the historical sense – well, they will have stopped listening to me a while ago. What I think may be defensible from a variety of normative perspectives are *three* comparative claims: first, that inert envy is, at least, less morally bad than the malicious kinds; second, that it is more prudentially than morally bad; third, that inert envy is much less morally bad if the envier inhibits it, that is, avoids acting upon it or expressing it (this last claim applying also to spiteful and aggressive envy).

3.6 "It Could Be Me!"

Of envy one could say that it is an homage that inferiority renders to superior talents.

Madeleine de Puixieux[20]

We have seen a confident but malicious Livia, and a desperate but non-malicious one. Now let us imagine a confident and non-malicious Livia. What if she looked up to Carla and proclaimed, "That could be me!" and this thought made her work even harder? In this final scenario Livia is focused on becoming an exceptional dancer, and believes that goal to be possible. She thus looks up to Carla as model for self-improvement. Her emotion is thus emulative envy.

Emulative envy's forward-looking, hopeful, and confident attitude is crucial to its nature. Even though it shares it with aggressive envy, its focus on the good makes the envier lack any ill will or Schadenfreude toward the envied (van de Ven et al. 2015). Thus, emulative envy is not morally bad by most standards (Stoics, again, excepted). But is it morally *good*? I argue in Section 3.8 that emulative envy can be a virtuous emotion, but in this section I will remain neutral with regard to specific normative frameworks and will limit myself to the claim that it is not morally bad. Remember, I assumed that the lacked good is actually good, so the envier is motivated to genuine self-improvement.

---

[20] De Puixieux 1750–1. The original French reads: "on pourroit dire de l'envie, que c'est un homage que l'infériorité rend à des talens supérieurs" (*Les caractères*, p. 143 – this is the second part of a sentence that paraphrases a maxim by La Rochefoucauld (maxim 218), according to which "hypocrisy is the tribute vice pays to virtue"). The quote is often translated more loosely as: "Jealousy is an awkward homage which inferiority renders to merit." The adjective "awkward" is an appropriate addition, I think, because even benign envy cannot be a straightforward tribute, given the social stigma surrounding envy. It is also interesting that whoever translated the quote decided to use "jealousy" in lieu of envy, thus showcasing the euphemistic use of "jealousy" as a synonym for benign envy.

Emulative envy is also not morally bad for the community: emulative enviers are templates of fair competition and, if they succeed in achieving the good by improving themselves, they move the whole society forward. In fact, the envier benefits from emulative envy as well. Even though it is painful, it spurs the agent to improve the self with regard to a valuable and important goal. I detailed at length in Chapter 2 how emulative envy is superior to admiration with regard to short-term improvement, and how the evidence concerning its motivation to self-improve has been found both inside and outside the lab. Thus, emulative envy is not just not prudentially bad: it seems positively good for the envier.

One might worry that such evidence is in tension with the consistent correlations between envy and poor mental and physical health that I mentioned earlier (Smith and Kim 2007). But *what kind of envy* is investigated in the studies that provide such evidence? Unsurprisingly most of these studies do not distinguish between different kinds of envy because they are prior to the very recent research on benign envy. Those who do make this distinction provide evidence supporting the claim that emulative envy is not bad for the envier. Furthermore, the study that is most often cited for the correlation between envy and poor health outcomes only focuses on *dispositional envy*.[21] But, as Kenneth Tai and collaborators observe, the Dispositional Envy Scale is construed so as to investigate the most negative aspects of envy, and thus it is unsurprising that it ends up tracking only negative outcomes associated with envy.[22] Now that a more comprehensive scale is available (Lange and Crusius 2015) we may see new studies reveal a more complex picture.

The typical motivations and behavioral consequences of emulative envy are thus not prudentially bad. One might still worry about sheer *expression*: showing that we feel emulative envy, either by declaring it verbally or through behavioral manifestations, may be risky for three potential reasons that emulative envy shares with other kinds of envy. First, and most importantly, expressing envy manifests perceived inferiority vis-à-vis a

---

[21] Smith et al. 1999. Remember also that Richard Smith's notion of envy is quite substantive and far from neutral between different accounts in social psychology: not only does he reject the possibility that envy is not malicious, but he also considers perception of deservingness and subjective injustice as a necessary component of envy, thus conflating envy with resentment, a move commonly opposed by philosophers as previously discussed (cf. D'Arms 2017, 9–10). For a critique of his view from a psychological perspective, see Miceli and Castelfranchi 2007, 466–7.

[22] Tai et al. 2012, 108. They further suggest that "the close coupling of envy with hostile action tendencies and consequences may be obscuring from view the underlying psychological processes through which envy influences behavior, as well as the individual and situational factors that moderate envy's effects on behavior" (108–9).

similar other, which may be prudentially bad: the agent may be bringing attention to a flaw of hers that might have gone unnoticed otherwise. Furthermore, she might even be wrong in her self-assessment. She might not in fact be worse off than the envied, but with her manifest envy she might lead others to believe that she indeed is worse off. Second, expressing envy reveals that the agent cares about a certain goal or good. This too may hurt the agent, since conceivably others might not see the good in the same positive light. Third, and relatedly, envy reveals also the agent's concern for inferiority[23] with regard to that good or goal, which might not be seen as a valuable character trait or attitude.

All these worries, however, are relatively insignificant in the case of emulative envy. First, expressing inferiority in emulative envy is necessarily tied to expressing hope to overcome it. Whether or not the perceived disadvantage is real, the observer can also see that the envier is planning to act so as to close the gap. The stronger signal that emulative envy sends with regard to the envier is self-confidence and forward-lookingness, an ultimately positive character trait.

Second, I assumed from the beginning that the envied object at stake is actually good, so whether or not the community shares this judgment is not as important to the envier. It is possible that her social reputation will be damaged, but this seems a minor concern in the face of the possibly successful pursuit of an actual good. Furthermore, realistically such disconnection is not frequent: many of the goods we routinely envy others for possessing are considered valuable by at least a good portion of the people among whom we live. Similarly (and thirdly), barring peculiar circumstances, showing concern for inferiority is not particularly damaging if the good in question is actually good – and perceived as such by most others – and if such concern is accompanied by self-confidence. Minding one's inferiority or disadvantage with regard to something good is just human, and most of us are aware of that. What we do not condone easily is a concern for inferiority that causes one to experience harmful or detrimental kinds of envy, or a concern for inferiority with regard to something that is not actually a good. For instance, if Livia were concerned with a very superficial understanding of beauty that might not play in her favor. But a very superficial understanding of beauty is excluded as a good in my initial assumptions.

In conclusion, in its paradigmatic instances emulative envy is not bad either morally or prudentially.

---

[23] I owe this suggestion to Steven Darwall.

At this point one may concede that emulative envy is a possible human experience, but argue that it is too rare to deserve as much attention as I am giving it. My answer is that it might appear to be rare, at least in part, because many of us speak languages that do not refer to it by the name of "envy," as we have seen. Once we think of the many alternative names emulative envy goes by, we might realize that emulative envy is a lot more common than it seemed at first.

Furthermore, there is empirical evidence in support of the claim that emulative envy is far from uncommon: "about half the participants in the United States and one in three participants in Spain spontaneously thought of an experience of benign envy when prompted for envy" (van de Ven et al. 2009, 426). Of course, these findings need to be taken with a grain of salt because people tend to give what is perceived as a more socially acceptable answer, as the authors themselves remark. On the other hand, the numbers are high enough that, even discounting some of it, we are still confronted with a frequently reported emotion.

Finally, let me address for the last time any reader that might still be skeptical about the genuinely envious nature of emulative envy. Consider again the definition of envy given at the beginning ("an aversive response to a perceived disadvantage to another person who is similar to us, with regard to a self-important domain"). Note that I presented an exemplary case of envy at the beginning, and I then proceeded to alter the variables of focus of concern and perception of control, features which are external to this definition.

Is Livia's emotion an "aversive response"? It is: Livia is pained by the fact that she is not capable of doing those thirty-two *fouettés*, notwithstanding the hours of practice and the years of sacrifice. That she does not have resentful or malicious sentiments for Carla does not change the fact that she suffers for her comparative inferiority.

Is Livia's perceived disadvantage to a person who is relevantly similar to her? I haven't changed Livia's skill level or the fact that she has been Carla's classmate for all these years, so the answer is yes: Carla is in the same comparison class as she is (and it is clear from the example that she perceives herself as disadvantaged).

Is the domain at stake a self-important one? Once again, that part of the example has not changed: our fourth version of Livia, like the previous three, deeply cares about dance. It is what she has devoted her entire life to.

Therefore Livia's emulative envy qualifies as envy as much as spiteful envy. One might object that the definition I adopted does not include a necessary feature of envy – the desire to level down – which is, in their

Table 3.1. *Kinds of envy in relation to their badness*

	Not prudentially bad	Prudentially bad
Not morally bad	Emulative envy	Inert envy
Morally bad	Aggressive envy	Spiteful envy

eyes, *the* single defining feature of envy. But this move would be question-begging and insensitive to the wealth of empirical evidence (psychological, sociological, and linguistic) that points to the existence of other forms of envy. This is one of those cases where moral psychology greatly benefits from integrating scientific evidence.

3.7   Ontology and Normativity Coming Together

Table 3.1 summarizes my conclusions concerning envy's badness, or lack thereof.

My model is not the only possible conceptualization of such a complex emotion, but it accounts very well for most of our shared intuitions and experiences, and it illuminates questions of value in an original and at the same time familiar way.

The ontological and normative dimensions of envy are inextricably connected. The argument presented here is meant to complement the one presented in Chapter 2.

Even though all kinds of envy, qua envy, have a competitive nature, emulative and inert envy are not adversarial insofar as the envier is more focused on the lack of the good than on the fact the envied possesses it. Remember that envy comes from the Latin *invideo*, which literally means to look obliquely and attentively. If all envy involves a metaphorical gaze of some sort the gaze involved in emulative and inert envy is directed at the lacked good, whereas the gaze involved in aggressive and spiteful envy is directed at the target, the adversary. That emulative and inert envy are not morally bad directly derives from their focus on the good, much like for Aristotle *zēlos*, and conversely aggressive and spiteful envy's moral badness derives from their hostile nature, their seeing the target as an enemy.

Note that, at the beginning of the chapter, I made an important assumption, namely that the good at stake is actually good, as opposed to bad. Naturally, if Livia was actually a torturer who envies a more capable torturer, acting on her emulative envy would be quite bad. So, the moral assessment of the four kinds of envy is conditional on the nature of the envied good and the fittingness of one's envy more generally.

Thus, focus on the good is not sufficient for envy to be morally good, nor it is necessary if one espouses a consequentialist framework, since we can easily conjure cases where one's aggressive or even spiteful envy fortuitously leads to good outcomes (imagine again the case of torturing abilities: perhaps Livia out of spiteful envy helps the prisoner to escape). Of course, there is nothing special about envy in this regard.

So, the connection between focus of concern and moral value of envy is weaker than a necessary condition, but is rather like a reliable explanatory condition of the general goodness of emulative and inert envy compared to that which is aggressive and spiteful.

What differentiates emulative and inert envy on the one hand, and aggressive and spiteful envy on the other, is, as we know, the second variable, obtainability of the goal, the goal in question being to overcome the disadvantage, either by leveling up or down.

Now, actual obtainability of the good, that is, how likely the envier is to actually overcome their advantage, might be in a similar relation with prudential goodness as focus of concern is with moral goodness. Again, being capable of overcoming the disadvantage is neither necessary nor sufficient for one's envy to lead to prudentially good outcomes: it is not sufficient because, if the envied good is a bad one, attempting to either self-improve or steal the good is not in fact prudentially good; it is not necessary for the same reason – if I am not capable of overcoming my disadvantage and the good is bad then I end up being better off. So, the relation between ontology and normativity is weaker than a conditional one.

But there is a further issue here: obtainability of the good is not the same as perceived obtainability of the good, which is the variable at stake in envy. While perceived and actual obtainability often coincide, some enviers might be systematically incorrect in their assessment of their situation.[24] Perceived obtainability is thus only an imperfect proxy for actual control over one's goals; however, it still reliably tracks the

---

[24] Denise Vigani reminded me of the tendency most people have to overestimate themselves in statistical terms, that is, to think of themselves as above average. I do not know of any study connecting this and related cognitive biases with dispositional envy, even though it would be interesting to see whether those who are more prone to this bias feel more unfitting envy as a result. It is difficult to speculate on this, since the relation between this bias and self-esteem is not clear or straightforward. A good list of references on the "above-average" bias can be found here: https://en .wikipedia.org/wiki/Illusory_superiority#cite_note-hoorens-1.

Table 3.2. *Kinds of envy in relation to both their badness and the variables that determine them*

	Greater confidence in obtaining the goal/not prudentially bad	Lesser confidence in obtaining the goal/ prudentially bad
Greater focus on the good/not morally bad	Emulative envy	Inert envy
Greater focus on the envied/morally bad	Aggressive envy	Spiteful envy

comparatively more effective and productive nature of emulative and aggressive envy. That is because with inert envy the envier is stuck in the paradox of wanting something they believe they cannot achieve, and in spiteful envy the envier is focused on the very short-term strategy of spoiling the good.

In sum, Table 3.2 shows what the four emotions look like if we consider both the variables that give rise to them and the prudential and moral outcomes.

3.8 Emulative Envy as a Virtuous Emotion

So far I have implicitly assumed a consequentialist standpoint, broadly construed: does feeling, expressing, or acting on the four kinds of envy bring about morally or prudentially good outcomes? What I consider now is the narrower question of whether emulative envy can be a *virtuous emotion*, that is, an emotion that a fully virtuous agent is not just permitted to occasionally feel, but ought to be disposed to.[25]

I find the question worth addressing not only due to my own personal attraction to virtue ethics, but also because of envy's long history as a vice and a capital sin. After all, I have drawn much of my understanding of emulative envy from Aristotle's distinction between *zēlos* and *phthonos*. Even though, as I explained in Chapter 2, *zēlos* does not exactly correspond to emulative envy, it is still the case that Aristotle himself talks about a painful emotional response to a similar other's comparative success as "good and characteristic of good people" (*epieikes estin o zēlos kai*

---

[25] Whether virtue ethics as a normative theory is a genuine alternative to consequentialism (see, e.g., Hursthouse and Pettigrove 2018), or compatible with it (see, e.g., Kagan 1992, 1998; Driver 2001; Bradley 2005), is an issue with regard to which I remain neutral.

epiekōn, *Rhet.* 1388a35). Thus, the question concerning emulative envy's potential virtuousness arises naturally. It is also a more difficult question than the "what is good about envy" one, given that extrinsic goodness comes by somewhat cheaply, especially once we have shown that not all envy need be as self-detrimental as it has been portrayed by moralists. Intrinsic goodness, however, is another matter.[26]

I shall define virtuous emotions as rationally justified and ethically appropriate stable emotional traits that are constitutive of the good life. I am not going to argue for this definition, but I take it to be a sufficiently uncontroversial understanding of what a virtuous emotion is within a traditional virtue ethics framework.

Virtue ethicists often adopt an Aristotelian framework, which some-times includes an understanding of virtue as a medial state between two contrary vices.[27]

Given that I have appealed to Aristotle as a precursor of my under-standing of emulative envy, one might expect me to adopt his conception of virtue as a mean as well. However, his treatment of envy is inconsistent with regard to this very issue. *Phthonos* as a base emotion is contrasted with the noble emotion of *zēlos* in the *Rhetoric*, whereas in the two Ethics (*Nicomachean* and *Eudemian*) he does not mention *zēlos* and attempts instead to situate *phthonos* as a vice of deficiency opposite to an unnamed vice of excess, with righteous indignation (*nemesis*) being the virtuous mean. But, as most authoritative commentators (Stevens 1948; Konstan 2003; Sanders 2014) have already remarked, this attempt is unsuccessful: explicating complex emotions such as envy in terms of a unidimensional scale of excess and defect feels artificial and forced, insofar as it flattens the rich appraisal dimension of these emotions, and it cannot account for the many ways in which they can be felt inappropriately (see also Appendix). Thus, I do not think that culturally rich and socially complex emotions such as envy, admiration, and cognate emotions are best understood as medial states between two extremes.

Another way to show that no variety of envy can be understood fruitfully as a mean between two extremes is to think about the many contraries that have been attributed to envy (unlike, for instance, courage):

---

[26] Krista Thomason (2015) also defends the intrinsic moral value of envy, on the grounds that envy helps moral agents maintain their commitments to crucial human values. I talk more about envy and human values in the Conclusion.

[27] A recent example of this approach is Kristján Kristjánsson's *Virtuous Emotions* (2018), in which the author argues that gratitude, pity, jealousy, grief, and awe may qualify as virtuous emotions (provided some conditions are satisfied).

admiration, jealousy, love, scorn/contempt, and pity/compassion all qualify as the opposite of envy, along different dimensions.[28] For instance, love is often considered to be the opposite of envy in the same way in which an antidote is the opposite of a poison (see Chapter 4 and Appendix). Scorn or contempt involves a "looking down" upon a target in a hostile way, and is thus often opposed to envy's (allegedly) hostile "looking up" (as in the title of a 2011 book by Susan Fiske: *Envy Up, Scorn Down*). Jealousy, as we saw in Chapter 1, has also been presented as the counterpart emotion of envy, which is a form of contrariety: the jealous person guards what the envious covets. I detailed at length in Chapter 2 the many ways in which admiration may be seen as contrary to emulative envy, notwithstanding the superficial similarities. Pity or compassion (*eleos*) is opposed to envy (*phthonos*) by Aristotle himself (*Rhet.* II.9 1386b16).[29] Aristotle also mentions the view that *phthonos* is the opposite of *nemesis*, even though he does not agree with that view in the *Rhetoric* (but upholds a version of it in the *Ethics* – again, see the Appendix for more details). Now, of course some of these emotions do not qualify as vicious. But my point is just that the traditional Aristotelian tripartition of two vices and one intermediate vice is not useful with regard to envy, as his own inconsistent analysis of *phthonos* and *zēlos*, across different works, shows.

However, Aristotle's metaphor of achieving virtue being akin to hitting the bull's-eye, the center of a shooting target, is helpful here: being disposed to envy virtuously is very difficult. First of all, it matters what kind of envy one feels. Even though all kinds of envy can be rationally justified, only emulative envy is ethically appropriate: if one is disposed to feel inert, aggressive, or spiteful envy then one is disposed to feel vicious emotions. From a perspective that does not differentiate between moral and prudential considerations in the modern sense, inert envy may be as vicious as aggressive envy.

Furthermore, even if one is in general disposed to feel emulative envy, they may err in single instances. There are many ways for a specific episode of emulative envy to be unfitting: it may involve an incorrect evaluation of the agent's position vis-à-vis the envied (that is, the agent might not in fact be disadvantaged or inferior to the target), or of the similarity between

---

[28] Here I use "opposite" as interchangeable with "contrary," which for Aristotle denotes states at the end of a spectrum that are mutually inconsistent, but not exhaustive, in that they admit of intermediate states and can both be false.

[29] More precisely, there are three emotions that Aristotle opposes to *eleos* – *phthonos*, *nemesis*, and *epichairekakia* – thus again showing that Aristotle's treatment of emotions in the *Rhetoric* does not neatly match his theory of virtue in the ethical works.

envied and envier (the envied might be in a different comparison class), or of the goodness of the object (the object might actually be bad).

It could also be the case that the agent is feeling the wrong kind of envy given objective features of the circumstances. For instance, one might feel unjustified emulative envy because they cannot actually overcome their disadvantage. While from certain consequentialist perspectives such a misperception might be desirable (perhaps it leads the agent to work harder even if they ultimately fail to achieve their objective), it is problematic from an Aristotelian perspective. Ethical virtue requires *phronesis*, and the wise person does not, by definition, misjudge a situation. Of course, inert envy is not an option either (*a fortiori*, neither are aggressive or spiteful envy). In these situations the wise option is to behave in a way that prevents envy from arising in the first place, for instance by reassessing one's priorities and goals. The *continent* person (*enkratic*), or, in general, someone who is on their way to virtue but has not achieved it, might occasionally find themselves feeling inert, aggressive, or spiteful envy but immediately recoil from that feeling and be moved to cope with it in the aforementioned ways (which goes to show that indirect coping is not the same as sour grapes syndrome, which is by definition irrational).[30]

No one who is *disposed* to feel aggressive and spiteful envy can count as being on a path to virtue, however, since they are systematically misguided with regard to how one ought to focus one's concerns. Part of what virtue requires is to be primarily concerned with one's lack of a good (and with the right kinds of goods), rather than someone else's possession.[31]

Thus, the wise person also cultivates states of mind that predispose them to feel emulative envy as opposed to any other kind of envy. Recall that emulative envy's characteristic tendency to self-improvement *relies upon, and in turn encourages*, the tendency to look at the situation as a non-zero-sum context, even in cases in which it objectively is.[32] Imagine that Carla has been promoted to principal dancer of the company, and assume that only one such position was available at the time. Livia would be able to feel emulative envy if she could conceive of this situation as admitting of leveling up via self-improvement, for instance by focusing on the future: "I am going to work so hard that I'll get the promotion next time!" Alternatively she might focus on analogous goods: even if she didn't become principal she

[30] I thank Denise Vigani for pressing me on this point.
[31] In this respect, Aristotle is not far from those thinkers who have been suspicious of external and positional goods.
[32] I am thankful to Tamar Szabó Gendler for encouraging me to develop this point.

might get the same role for shows in which Carla is not dancing. Being disposed to feel emulative envy characteristically involves an optimistic, mature, and proactive attitude. Such an attitude is opposite to the pessimistic, immature, and reactive thinking that is typical, in different ways, of the other kinds of dispositional envy, which all share to some extent the "magical," that is, irrational and causally misguided, outlook on reality characteristic of the evil eye. In people disposed to feel inert envy this outlook may take the form of attributing, more or less consciously, the responsibility of one's disadvantage to the envied. In dispositional aggressive envy this thinking is responsible for encouraging the envier to frame any context as zero-sum, even when it is not. This is a case where assessing one's situation in exclusively zero-sum terms is dysfunctional, even though it might be effective in single instances: there might be cases where breaking another person's leg gives an objective advantage (for instance, if one is being chased by a predator), but overall, as a stable disposition and in a society where resources are not exceedingly limited, it is misguided to think that diminishing another person's advantage make us any better.[33] Finally, if one is disposed to feel spiteful envy regularly, one is also prone to destroying valuable goods, which, again, in the kind of environment we are currently analyzing, is not rational.

There is a further condition that needs to be satisfied for emulative envy to count as a virtuous emotion: the agent has to *act upon* it in the right way. Aristotle argues that every ethical virtue requires *phronesis*, that is, practical wisdom. The wise agent is capable of correctly deliberating the course of action required in each circumstance. In our context, acting wisely for the emulatively envious agent means not just trying to self-improve and thus overcome their disadvantage vis-à-vis the envied by leveling up, but doing so in the right way. In this respect emulative envy, as I have characterized it, importantly differs from how benign envy is defined by psychologists. The main determinant of benign envy is that the envier feels in control over the situation and perceives themselves to be capable of leveling up. But emulative enviers are also focused on the good. In Livia's case that means being focused on becoming a dancer as good as Carla, and deliberating correctly about how to achieve that goal (so, for instance, developing an appropriate training regimen or working with Carla herself during class). This clarification is important in light of some very recent studies by Jens Lange and collaborators that investigate the

---

[33] There are reasonable objections to this, the most natural being that in many societies lots of resources are exceedingly limited because they are very unequally distributed. See Chapter 5.

relation between malicious and benign envy and two members of the so-called dark triad of personality traits, namely: narcissism, Machiavellianism, and psychopathy. Their most recent studies (Lange, Paulhus, and Crusius 2018) show a positive correlation between Machiavellianism and benign envy, and a positive correlation between both Machiavellianism and psychopathy and malicious envy. Clearly, this kind of "benign" envy is not virtuous, and it does not correspond to emulative envy as I define it.

At this point one may grant that emulative envy can be a virtuous emotion in all these senses, but object that its value is instrumental and not intrinsic. How does dispositional emulative envy qualify as a component of flourishing itself? In other words, in which way does emulative envy play an indispensable role in our moral lives, one that cannot be played by any other emotion?

I have two answers to this question. The short, and perhaps unsatisfying, answer is that emulative envy is the only morally and prudentially appropriate response to the comparative lack of important goods. It sustains the effort of overcoming a comparative disadvantage in an important self-domain. Remember that we can feel envy with regard to any good that is relevant to our identity, many of which qualify as components of human flourishing. Envy is the emotion that is best suited to playing this role, since admiration typically does not motivate short-term, focused improvement.

The long answer requires us to look at what emulative envy in action looks like. So far in this book I have employed a standard thought experiment technique: that of presenting the reader with a hypothetical scenario with the aim of eliciting certain intuitive responses. However, there are limits to what one can accomplish with it. Using vignettes and simplified cases allows one to carefully manipulate relevant variables and test changes in intuitions. But it also overtly simplifies complex realities.[34] I am not sure I can give an *argument* that shows conclusively how emulative envy is intrinsically valuable; arguing for intrinsic value in general is very difficult. It is not a coincidence that many philosophers who defend a virtue ethicist approach methodologically rely on extended narratives.[35] In Chapter 4 I show how emulative envy is a component in

---

[34] Note, then, that this is not akin to traditional criticisms of philosophy from the armchair. My vignettes are elaborated after careful consideration of empirical evidence. But psychological studies also greatly (and unavoidably) oversimplify the complexity of the envy experience.
[35] Martha Nussbaum's discussion of grief in *Upheavals of Thought* (2001a) exemplifies well this tendency. For an attempt similar to mine (namely to argue for the intrinsic value of a virtue by using examples) see Vigani 2017, 337–8.

the flourishing of two friends, fictional characters Lila and Lenù, whose complex relationship is narrated by Elena Ferrante through four novels (Ferrante 2012, 2013, 2014, 2015).

I shall end this section by considering a final objection, namely that there something inherently problematic with envy: its comparative nature. One could argue that no component of flourishing ought to rely on social comparison. Moral virtue, love and personal relationships, health, knowledge: aren't these all goods that require no comparison? What a virtuous agent cares about – the objection continues – is that they are knowledgeable, loved, healthy, and acting and feeling according to virtue. There is no need to compare oneself to others.

I do not have space in this book to fully address this objection, which would require us to delve deeper into theories of value. There are philosophical arguments in favor of the view that excellence of any kind is necessarily positional (D'Arms and Jacobson 2005; I come back to this idea in the Conclusion). Empirical evidence supports this view insofar as it shows how pervasive social comparison is, and how necessary to forming judgments of the self (Fiske 2011). Furthermore, an emotion such as admiration, which is generally considered the positive counterpart of emulative envy, nonetheless relies on comparison. For the purpose of this chapter I am happy to concede that, if social comparison is shown to be intrinsically bad, then no form of envy can ever be virtuous. But if one believes that social comparison is unavoidable, and that the very concept of excellence is necessarily comparative, then emulative envy is a virtuous emotion.

Note that arguing that emulative envy is virtuous does not imply that the wise person is disposed to feel it *often*. It is possible that emulative envy may be fitting and conducive to flourishing only in rare circumstances. Or it may be the case that a disposition to feel emulative envy is suitable to some agents more than others. People differ on how prone to social comparison they are, as measured by the scale of Social Comparison Orientation (SCO).[36] I am not sure how divergent from an Aristotelian orthodoxy this thought is, but it seems to me that not all *phronimoi* have to look alike (in fact, some will be *phronimai*). They will have different psychological traits and different relationships, cultural backgrounds, abilities, and experiences – they will lead different lives, and thus what constitutes flourishing for each of them will differ (see also D'Arms and

---

[36] See Gibbons and Buunk, 1999; Buunk and Gibbons, 2006. I discuss some characteristics of individuals who score high on this scale in Chapter 4.

Jacobson 2005 for an analogous position). In some lives, such as those I describe at the end of Chapter 4, emulative envy may constitute a central emotion, a necessary one to realize the agent's potential. In other lives emulative envy may occasionally arise, or arise frequently but with mild intensity or without playing a crucial role. Similar considerations may apply for emotions such as grief: imagine someone who has been spared great losses by fate. Grief has instrumental value because it leads people to celebrate and appreciate the loved ones in their lives and to strengthen relationships with them, and it brings them to reevaluate their priorities and values (Nolen-Hoeksema and Davis 2002; Ryff and Singer 2003); it has been argued to have also intrinsic value because it upholds just desert (Kristjánsson 2018). But someone who has never personally felt much grief may nonetheless be wise, insofar as they have witnessed other people mourn and have learned from that experience. I am unsure whether the same can be said for any emotion, since perhaps some emotions always play a central role in psychological development of healthy individuals (perhaps love is necessary for being a fully virtuous person). At any rate, that emulative envy can be virtuous does not imply that it should be felt all the time by everybody.[37]

3.9   Toward a Theory of Remedies of Envy

Chaucer wrote in *The Parson's Tale* that "envy is against all virtue and all goodness" and is therefore the worst sin (Chaucer 2011, 475). However, we have seen that he and the many other thinkers condemning envy have been too hasty in their judgment.

Even when envy is vicious, its viciousness manifests itself in quite different ways, and being able to identify them provides the means to find targeted remedies against them. While this is the domain of other disciplines, such as clinical psychology and psychotherapy, my taxonomy provides – I hope – some suggestions about how to approach these kinds of envy fruitfully.

Inert envy is mostly prudentially bad, and it stems from the perceived incapacity of the envier to actualize their emulative intentions. This is crucial in our moral evaluation of the enviers, and also has implications for how to help them cope with it: reinforcing their self-esteem, and encouraging them to believe that the good is obtainable, may push them toward emulative envy and self-improvement. Aggressive envy, on the other hand,

---

[37] I am thankful to Alida Liberman for encouraging me to think about this issue.

requires a very different treatment, since it is morally bad and stems from being focused on the rival and being motivated to level down. Different interventions may be recommended depending on the situation and the agent. First, from a cognitive perspective, enviers should be encouraged to redirect their concern from the target to the good, by reconceptualizing the good and thinking of the situation as non-zero sum. Perhaps this one specific good is not shareable, but there is another one in the vicinity that is. If this is not possible, very high costs should be associated with sabotaging the envied, so that the aggressive enviers are deterred from acting on it. Second, and in conjunction with cognitive interventions, one might try some kind of emotional reshaping in order to increase sympathetic attunement of the envier with the envied. Evidence shows that the more we bond with others, the more likely we are to envy them in a benign way (van de Ven 2016, 340).

Spiteful envy is radically vicious, being bad both morally and prudentially. It is possible that one has come to feel spiteful envy because the circumstances leave no space for hope, and have led the envier to develop an intense rivalry with the envied. If that is the case, perhaps the only remedy is to repress the envy altogether, or to acknowledge it while attempting to move on, or other forms of indirect coping. But one might feel spiteful envy because of a misguided understanding of the situation, or low self-esteem. For instance, one might see the good as exclusive, and interpret the situation as a zero-sum game, even when that is not the case. This impression may be corrected, and such correction might encourage the envier to focus on leveling up. Furthermore, the envier might be able to repair the wounds to her self-esteem, and become confident about the obtainability of their goal. On the other hand, one should implement the corrections recommended for aggressive envy, leading the envier to feel less hostility for the envied, and increasing sympathy and concern for them (in addition to making them aware of moral principles). It is not impossible, then, to move from spiteful envy all the way "up" to emulative envy.

Emulative envy is neither morally nor prudentially bad, and in some circumstances it may even be virtuous. Given that envy is an inescapable feature of human life, it is the only kind of envy that we should encourage ourselves and others to feel, express, and act on. If envy is the highest form of praise, as a Bulgarian saying goes, successful emulation may be its most desirable outcome.

CHAPTER 4

Love and Envy, Two Sides of the Same Coin

There be none of the affections, which have been noted to fascinate or bewitch, but love and envy. They both have vehement wishes; they frame themselves readily into imaginations and suggestions; and they come easily into the eye, especially upon the present of the objects; which are the points that conduce to fascination, if any such thing there be.

Francis Bacon[1]

4.1 Introduction: Love Does Not Envy, Or Does It?

Ellis and Richard, two surgery residents, are deeply in love. They have been drawn to each other by a shared passion for medicine, a focused ambition on their career, and a common perception of isolation in a world of people who do not look like them: she, a White woman in a traditionally male environment; he, an African American man in a predominantly White field. They decide to abandon their spouses, but, just when they are about to elope, Richard changes his mind, without telling her why, and their relationship ends. He cannot bring himself to admit to her that the reason he can't be with her is that he envies her: Ellis has just been nominated for a prestigious award, and he is incapable of rejoicing of her success and being in a loving relationship with a

For feedback on previous versions of this chapter I thank: Aaron Ben-ze'ev, Justin Clardy, Pamela Corcoran, Stephen Darwall, Jamie Dow, Tamar Szabó Gendler, June Gruber, Verity Harte, Jasper Heaton, Hud Hudson, Carrie Ichikawa Jenkins, Jonathan Jenkins Ichikawa, Michael Lacewing, Gerald Lang, Shen-yi Liao, Heather Logue, Dominic McIver Lopes, Nicholas Martin, Aaron Meskin, Donnchadh O'Conaill, Regina Rini, Aida Roige Mas, Matthew Smith, Zoltán Gendler Szabó, Neal Tognazzini, Pekka Väyrynen, Matthew Walker, Dennis Whitcomb, Justin Weinberg, several anonymous reviewers, and audience members at the University of Leeds and the EPSSE Annual Conference at the University of Edinburgh.
[1] Bacon 1999, 18.

woman who outperforms him professionally. Richard's intense envy has thus smothered his intense love.[2]

This story is exemplary of the widespread notion that love and envy are *incompatible* attitudes, both in the sense that they cannot be felt at the same time toward the same person, and that they are normatively antithetical – one a virtue, the other a vice.

This notion is foreshadowed in Plato's *Phaedrus*, where Socrates argues that true *eros* is free from *phthonos*, and it reaches maturity in Christian thought, where the capital sin of *invidia* is opposed to the cardinal virtue of *charitas*, as depicted in Giotto's Scrovegni Chapel.[3] Many a wedding ceremony include the famous quote from *Corinthians* 13:4 stating that "[l]ove is patient, love is kind. It does not envy, it does not boast, it is not proud." And it is not only erotic or Christian love that is expected to be free from envy. Siblings who envy each other – we are told – end up killing each other, as the stories of Romulus and Remus, and Cain and Abel, warn. As for friendship, Basil of Caesarea claims: "as the red blight is a common pest to corn, so envy is the plague of friendship."[4]

This opposition is a natural consequence of the prevalent understanding, in the history of philosophy, of envy being defined as a form of hatred, or necessarily involving malice and Schadenfreude, all of which are opposites of love and benevolence.[5] Still today, Rebecca Konyndyk DeYoung explicitly dubs envy "the enemy of love" (Konyndyk DeYoung 2009, 51) and claims that "the fundamental attitude of the envious is directly

---

[2] This vignette is inspired by *Grey's Anatomy*, season 11, episode 4. Here is a fan's synopsis: "[Richard] and Ellis made a pact to leave their spouses. [Ellis] had just received her first Harper Avery nomination. He was hatefully, hopelessly jealous, as if she was already too far ahead to catch up to. *Her success illuminated everything he hadn't yet accomplished.* The night before the carousel meeting, as he worked up the nerve to tell Adele [Richard's wife], he thought of Ellis and what she could do at such a young age. He thought of what she would do and he realized he didn't want to live his entire life feeling like that, so he ruined their pact" (http://greysanatomy.wikia.com/wiki/ Only_Mama_Knows, emphasis mine). Note that Richard says he was "jealous," but by now we know what that means.

[3] For more details on this fresco see the Appendix.   [4] Basil of Caesarea 1950, 469.

[5] Here is a quick review of what is discussed in greater detail in the Appendix: according to Descartes, envy qua passion is "a kind of sadness mingled with hatred, arising from our seeing good coming to those we think unworthy of it" (Descartes 1985, 394). For Spinoza, "[e]nvy is hatred in so far as it affects a man so that he is sad at the good fortune of another person and is glad when any evil happens to him" (emphasis in the original Spinoza 1949, 179). Hume says of malice that it imitates the effects of hatred and makes us rejoice in the suffering of innocent others. The only difference between malice and envy is that envy is a reaction to a "present enjoyment of another," while malice is "the unprovok'd desire of producing evil to another" (Hume 1978, 377). Kant calls envy, malice, and ingratitude "the vices of hatred" (Kant 1996, 206). While Aquinas defines envy as a form of sadness, he also sees a strong connection between envy and hatred, in that hatred stems from envy (*Summa Theologica* II-II, Q. 36).

opposed to love. To love is to seek others' good and rejoice when they have it. To envy is to seek to destroy others' good and sorrow over their having it." (ibid.).

While psychologists have not investigated the relation between love and envy in systematic ways,[6] there is plenty of evidence that (malicious) envy correlates negatively with feelings of sympathy and warmth, and positively with hostility and aversion. In light of all these considerations it is no surprise that clinical psychologists Julie Exline and Anne Zell, in a conceptual inquiry for envy's "antidotes," suggest that love may be a cure for, or a way of coping with, envy (Exline and Zell 2008, 325).[7] If one manages to feel love toward an envied person – they hypothesize – envy will be extinguished, since they cannot coexist. Thus, there is an overwhelming, cross-cultural and cross-disciplinary, consensus that love and envy are deeply incompatible.

In this chapter I challenge this consensus and argue that thinking of love and envy are incompatible is exceedingly simplistic, and that love and envy are compatible in at least two senses: first, they thrive in the same psychological conditions and thus are likely to occur together; second, love can benefit from emulative envy, and, when love is wise, it can tolerate some amount of inert, aggressive, and spiteful envy. In Section 4.2 I distinguish between two kinds of incompatibility: descriptive and normative. The descriptive version of the incompatibility thesis is shown to be too strong, so in the following sections I tackle the normative one. In Section 4.3 I propose an indirect argument, according to which we ought not to endorse an ideal of love free from envy, because that ideal is psychologically implausible. In Section 4.4 I rely on two case studies to show what envying the beloved looks like, and why it is not only a tolerable scenario but even a desirable one.

4.2   Preliminaries: Love, Envy, and Two Kinds of Incompatibility

Love is said in many ways, even more so than envy. There are (at least) two senses of love that we might be referring to when we ask whether envy is

---

[6] There are mentions of the relation between the two emotions in the psychological literature but are often brief and speculative. See for instance Fiske 2011, 59: "Envy is also likely to undermine friendship. ... A disposition toward envy makes for schadenfreude (glee at the envied other's misfortune), which hardly encourages friendship; responding to a friend's good news with resentment can destroy the relationship."

[7] The authors maintain that the idea that love is an opposite to envy is cross-cultural and cross-religious.

compatible with love: love as a mental state of the lover, and love as a relationship between two people who love each other.

There are many different theories of love in the first sense: philosophers have thought of love as an emotion, a desire, an appraisal – to mention just a few popular views.[8] I wish to remain uncommitted with regard to this issue since it does not appear to bear on our question: no matter how we conceive of it ontologically, love is always thought, on the one hand, to standardly involve caring for the beloved's well-being and rejoicing in their good fortune, and, on the other, to be void of hostility and Schadenfreude.

Furthermore, recall our initial scenario of love and envy. Richard is intensely envious of Ellis, but *does not fall out of love* because of that; his envy, that is, does not cause him to stop loving Ellis, at least not right away. What is destroyed by Richard's envy for Ellis is their loving relationship. No matter how Richard's mental states are characterized, the problem seems to be that he cannot *be with* Ellis: he cannot fulfill the role of a supportive partner who rejoices in her professional success. Indeed, it is clear that he still loves Ellis when he decides to break up with her, because he expresses that love later on. So, while his decision to end the relationship will indirectly and in due course smother his love qua mental state, envy directly and immediately affects his love qua relationship. Of course, the distinction between the two senses of the term is not always easy to draw, and the mental state and the relationship stand in complex relation to one another (and different theories of love have different takes on this relation). Throughout the chapter, for simplicity, I mostly talk of "love" without differentiating between these two senses, unless necessary.

When talking about envy I am initially going to *not* distinguish between varieties, and rely on the general definition of envy as an aversive reaction to a perceived inferiority vis-à-vis a similar other, with regard to a good that is relevant to the sense of identity of the envier, and which motivates to overcome such an inferiority either by bringing oneself up to the level of the envied or by pulling them down to one's level.

This definition fits Richard's emotion. He is pained by the perception that Ellis is a more skilled and accomplished surgeon (*aversive reaction to perceived inferiority*); such a perception stings because Ellis is similar to him in age, status, and capability (*similar other*) and because Richard identifies with being a surgeon (*domain of self-relevance*). Such a painful feeling motivates Richard to overcome his perceived disadvantage: he could either try to become as good as Ellis or he could try to make her worse off.

---

[8] For a review, see Helm 2017.

In fact, he does not quite do either, probably because he is inclined to "level down," but does not want to do something detrimental to Ellis, and so he breaks up with her.

So far, I defined love, and I defined envy. The only term that still requires an explanation is incompatibility. There are two possible interpretations of the idea that love and envy are incompatible: a *descriptive* and a *normative* one. I'll start with the descriptive interpretation, which in turn includes several variations.

First, one could think that love is incompatible with envy in the sense that the phenomenon of loving the beloved is simply *impossible*: while one can feel something that superficially looks like envy, in fact genuine envy can never arise in the context of an authentic loving relationship. Love and envy are thus contradictory states, as if we were saying: "love and not-love."

This interpretation, however, is too strong: we have no reason to look at Richard's behavior and declare either his love or his envy as inauthentic. He acts as passionate lovers do, and he is ready to leave his wife for Ellis; but he also confesses his envy to her even though people do not generally confess their envy, so when they do we have reason to believe them (*a fortiori*, given that he is in a loving relationship with the envied). Even though Richard's story is fictional it relies on realistic psychological assumptions, and it succeeds in depicting a *possible* scenario, which is all we need to refute the impossibility thesis.

Furthermore, notwithstanding a disappointing scarcity of rigorous empirical and philosophical investigations of this phenomenon,[9] anecdotal evidence concerning envying the beloved abounds with regard to all forms of love. The psychoanalytic literature, for instance, features many case studies of envy felt toward (or feared from) parents, children, friends, spouses, or siblings.[10] There is a wealth of self-help books on the topic

---

[9] I am not aware of any empirical research on envy in loving relationships. A related topic that has been investigated is that of *ambivalent* relationships (see Uchino et al. 2001; Bushman and Holt-Lunstad 2009). I am also not aware of any in-depth philosophical discussion of this issue. Aaron Ben-Ze'ev has a post on *Psychology Today* (www.psychologytoday.com/us/articles/200907/jealousy-loves-destroyer). Krista Thomason briefly argues for the possibility of envy toward loved ones (esp. "friends, siblings, parents, and colleagues" Thomason 2015, 45).

[10] See Stein 1990; Ellman 2000; Harris 2002; Polledri 2003; LaVerde-Rubio 2004; Anastasopoulos 2007; Gerhardt 2009; Zeavin 2012. The epistemological limits of psychoanalysis are notorious, even though some authors have recently suggested that psychoanalysis could become, and is on its way to becoming, a science (see Lacewing 2013). However, I am not using psychoanalytic research as a source of scientific evidence, but rather as a source of narratives that are akin to fictional examples or thought experiments in presenting nuanced and compelling pictures of human experience. For a defense of the thesis (which I do not endorse here) that psychoanalytic theory

(see, e.g., Cohen 1986; Barash 2006), and the internet is replete with articles on how to deal with either being envied by or feeling envy toward friends and other loved ones. The existence and popularity of such advice is indirect evidence that it is possible to envy the beloved.

A more plausible version of the descriptive interpretation of the incompatibility assumption is the one that I have implicitly adopted so far: envy kills love *after* it has already bloomed. If one finds oneself in the grip of intense envy toward the beloved, as in Richard's case, their love will unavoidably wilt, for instance because envy wounds the lover's self-esteem, provoking resentment instead of support or joy for the beloved's success. Vice versa, if one comes to love an envied person one's envy is supposed to fade away. On the surface this second case seems highly implausible, but that is after all what the idea of love as an "antidote" to envy is supposed to mean. According to this view, love and envy are like light and darkness: the more envy there is, the less love there can be, and vice versa. They are opposite, rather than contradictory, states.

This view seems more promising. However, this interpretation might be too weak. Opposite emotional states, such as sadness and joy, are compatible in the sense that one can feel a mixture of both, and the resulting state may be stable and even desirable (think of melancholia). But the alleged incompatibility between love and envy seems to imply its mixture would not be stable or desirable.

In other words, those who think of love and envy as incompatible in the way that I am trying to capture consider envy to be a pollutant: even a tiny bit in a clear puddle of water will make the water undrinkable. Conversely love is like a balsam that heals all wounds: if you manage to love the envied, you will stop envying them, as in the aforementioned speculation by Exline and Zell. (Note that one might be skeptical that there is a perfect symmetry here: it is much easier to spoil something good than to fix something bad.)

However, if interpreted descriptively this view is once again too strong. Most people would agree that a loving relationship can tolerate occasional and short-lived bouts of envy, in the same way as it can tolerate other negative emotions, including hatred.

The only plausible interpretation of the incompatibility between love and envy is thus *normative*: they cannot coexist in their ideal forms. In

pursues the same inquiry as philosophical moral psychology, see Harcourt 2013. For a non-psychoanalytic, *epidemiological* perspective on sibling relationships, which includes a discussion of envy, see Dunn and Kendrick 1982.

particular, *true love* should be void of *envy proper*. This is a thesis that is already found in Plato (see Appendix), and it is probably the thesis that is implicit in the opposition between envy as a capital sin and charity as a cardinal virtue. At any rate, this is the thesis that I am going to argue against in the remainder of the chapter.

I do so in two stages. I first propose an indirect argument. Because love and envy both thrive in the same psychological conditions it is not unlikely to feel envy toward the beloved. If we want ideals that do not go against our psychological propensities then we should not aim for a love that is wholly void of envy. I articulate this argument in Section 4.3.

I then propose a direct argument which aims to show that love can even benefit from envy, and which relies on my taxonomy of envy and, in particular, on the role emulative envy can play in a wise love.

4.3 Comparison, Similarity, and Desire for Esteem: Where Love and Envy Thrive

Imagine a beautiful ornamental plant that grows well in soil with a certain composition. Now imagine a weed that grows in the same kind of soil. Whenever the gardener tries to get rid of the weed by changing the composition of the soil, the weed grows stunted or stops growing altogether, but so does the plant they are trying to cultivate. If the gardener aims for a garden completely void of weeds, they are destined to be constantly frustrated. But if they accept the presence of weeds, they will get to enjoy the beautiful plant as well.

I submit that love – you guessed it – is like the plant and envy is like the weed. The soil is human nature. It is not possible to get rid of envy without getting rid of psychological and social mechanisms that favor the arousal of love as well, at least at the level of the species. The reason lies in the crucial role of social comparison in human psychology.

As I mentioned in Chapter 1, empirical evidence shows that while there are individual differences in how frequently and intensely people compare themselves to others, we all do it to a larger extent than we might realize. Social comparison is a process that fulfills three functions. First, it informs us about where we stand and how we stack up in comparison to others with regard to pretty much anything, from our abilities and opinions to facts such as how healthy we are; when the comparison is upward, that is, to our disadvantage, it may motivate us to self-improve. Second, when the comparison is downward, that is, to your advantage, it protects our self-esteem and makes us feel good. Third, it helps us fit into our social groups.

Some individuals are more prone to social comparison than others. Relevantly for our investigation, those who score higher on the SCO "tend to think about themselves a lot, but they also tend to think about others a lot" (Fiske 2011, 57); they are very self-focused and self-concerned, but they are also more empathetic and sensitive to the needs and perspectives of others. From an inclination to social comparison, then, stem both prosocial attitudes such as empathy, sensitivity, and feeling connected with others, and antisocial attitudes such as competition, envy, scorn, and shame.

These are deep psychological mechanisms that we are unlikely to eliminate from our nature anytime soon. We are prone to comparisons. But the most salient comparisons are those to similar others: those are the ones that are most likely to occur, and also the ones that are most diagnostic and significant for our self-assessment. It is this kind of comparison that is necessary to feel envy.

4.3.1   *The Role of Similarity in Envy and Love*

The review of both the history of philosophy and the contemporary empirical research highlights the central role of similarity in envy. Aristotle is among the philosophers who have paid attention to this aspect the most. Here is a relevant passage in the *Rhetoric*:

> It is evident, too, whom people envy; [. . .] for they envy those near to them in time and place and age and reputation, whence it has been said, "Kinship, too, knows how to envy." And [they envy] those they rival; for they rival those mentioned, [feeling] the same way toward them and on the same grounds, but no one rivals people ten thousands here in the future or dead nor those who live in the Pillars of Heracles nor those they or others regard as inferior or much superior. But since people seek honor in comparison with antagonists and rivals in love and in general those wanting the same things, necessarily they are most envious of these. This is the source of the saying "Potter [against] potter." And people are envious of those who have acquired something or been successful. These, too, are near and like; for clearly, they do not attain this good because of themselves, so distress at this causes envy. (*Rhet.* II.10, 1388a4–21, tr. Kennedy 2007, 145)[11]

---

[11]   The following translation makes the ending of the passage a bit clearer: "We also envy those whose possession of or success in a thing is a reproach to us: these are our neighbours and equals; for it is clear that it is our own fault we have missed the good thing in question; this annoys us, and excites envy in us" (tr. by W. Rhys Roberts, available at http://classics.mit.edu/Aristotle/rhetoric.2.ii.html).

Aristotle lists here many kinds of similarity: equality of reputation and social status, spatiotemporal proximity, commonality of background, equivalence of competences and skills, and affinity of goals and values.

Importantly for my purposes these are almost exactly the same kinds of equality, closeness, and likeness that he discusses in *Nicomachean Ethics* when talking about *philia*, that is, the loving relationship that can arise between husband and wife, between father and son, between brothers, between comrades, and between erotic lovers.[12] "Now equality and likeness are *philia*," he claims (EN, VIII.8),[13] and devotes a large part of book VIII to explaining the several ways in which *philoi* can be equal or similar. Affinity of goals and values[14] and equality of reputation and social status[15] are the basis of stable *philia*. In contexts in which social parity is necessarily precluded, as in the relationship between fathers and children, similarity is guaranteed by commonality of background.[16] Indeed, commonality is a characteristic of *philia* important enough to determine whether a relationship is "truly" or not a *philia*.[17] Not only does having things in common make people equal, but equality might in turn produce commonality,[18] and in general common upbringing and similarity of character go hand in hand.[19]

---

[12] *Philia* also describes the relationship between business partners and fellow citizens, which shows how much broader the Greek notion of *philia* is, compared to our modern notion of love.

[13] All citations in this paragraph are by W. D. Ross, available at: http://classics.mit.edu/Aristotle/nicomachaen.8.viii.htm.

[14] "For all friendship is for the sake of good or of pleasure-good or pleasure either in the abstract or such as will be enjoyed by him who has the friendly feeling-and is *based on a certain resemblance*" (EN, VIII.3, my emphasis). "However that may be, the aforesaid friendships [those based on virtue] involve equality; for the friends get the same things from one another and *wish the same things for one another*, or exchange one thing for another, e.g., pleasure for utility" (EN, VIII.6).

[15] "Now we have said that the good man is at the same time pleasant and useful; but such a man does not become the friend of one who surpasses him in station, unless he is surpassed also in virtue" (EN, VIII.6).

[16] "The friendship of children to parents, and of men to gods, is a relation to them as to something good and superior; for they have conferred the greatest benefits, since they are the causes of their being and of their nourishment, and of their education from their birth; and this kind of friendship possesses pleasantness and utility also, more than that of strangers, inasmuch as their life is lived more in common" (EN, VIII.12).

[17] "Now, but the others to whom we have referred have definite things in common-some more things, others fewer; for of friendships, too, some are more and others less truly friendships" (EN, VIII.9).

[18] "For where the citizens are equal they have much in common" (EN, VIII.11).

[19] "Two things that contribute greatly to friendship are a common upbringing and similarity of age; for 'two of an age take to each other', and people brought up together tend to be comrades; whence the friendship of brothers is akin to that of comrades. And cousins and other kinsmen are bound up together by derivation from brothers, viz. by being derived from the same parents. They come to be closer together or farther apart by virtue of the nearness or distance of the original ancestor ... The friendship of brothers has the characteristics found in that of comrades (and especially when these are good), and in general between people who are like each other, inasmuch as they belong more to

While he does not explicitly say that *philia* requires spatiotemporal proximity, that requirement is implicit in much else he says about intimacy (Cf. EN, VIII.3, 1156b26) and shared activities between *philoi*. Another kind of similarity Aristotle does not mention in the discussion of *philia* is equivalence of competences and skills, but it is not unlikely that *philoi* have similar skills at least in some domains: coming from the same background, engaging in common activities, and being guided by similar goals and interests are all likely to foster such equivalence.

Vice versa, there is one kind of similarity that is at play in *philia* – *similarity of characters*[20] – that is missing from the discussion of envy. That absence seems appropriate at least at a first pass: being similarly extroverted, or well-mannered, or courageous does not constitute a basis for being in the same comparison class or ranking order, and so does not trigger competitive reactions. However, character traits might indirectly contribute to developing a skill or talent, or to being socially esteemed. For instance, being extroverted might contribute to popularity, and being courageous might help to be a better soldier. Were that to be the case, there would be another kind of similarity in common between envy and *philia*, even if Aristotle did not remark on it.

In sum, similarity plays a fundamental role in love as well, in Aristotle's account. Here, too, his view is supported by contemporary psychology. There is extensive evidence that "when people have a choice, they choose relationships with people who are similar to them" (Bahns et al. 2012, 120). Contrary to the popular dictum, it is similars – not opposites – that attract.[21]

Thus, similarity in its various manifestations is a necessary condition for both love and envy. Both attitudes are ultimately dependent on the tendency and ability that human beings have to compare themselves to others, which is a fundamental, multifunctional component of human

each other and start with a love for each other from their very birth, and inasmuch as those born of the same parents and brought up together and similarly educated are more akin in character; and the test of time has been applied most fully and convincingly in their case" (EN, VIII.12).

[20] "Among men of these inferior sorts too, friendships are most permanent when the friends get the same thing from each other (e.g., pleasure), and not only that but *also from the same source*, as happens between ready witted people" (EN, VIII.4, my emphasis).

[21] At least most of the time. The empirical literature on similarity in personal relations is too vast for me to delve into it here, but one complication worth mentioning is that people may perceive each other as similar, *even when they are not*. Another one is that there are many dimensions along which an interpersonal interaction develops and is considered satisfactory. See Dryer and Horwitz 1997 for evidence that in some instances actual complementarity along the control dimension (i.e. submissive vs. dominant attitudes) predicts satisfactory interactions, provided that similarity along other dimensions (such as affiliation) is preserved.

psychology. But there is one more tile to be added to the increasingly complex mosaic of love and envy.

4.3.2   The Role of Esteem in Love and Envy

Social comparison favors the arousal of love and envy in at least one other way, which is highlighted in Jean-Jacques Rousseau's *Second Discourse*, in a passage that describes the genealogy of human society:

> [*Men*] *became accustomed to* looking more closely at the different objects of their desires *and to making comparisons*; imperceptibly they acquired ideas of beauty and merit which led to feelings of preference. *In consequence of seeing each other often, they could not do without seeing each other constantly. A tender and pleasant feeling insinuated itself into their souls*, and the least opposition turned it into an impetuous fury: *with love arose jealousy*;[22]
>
> discord triumphed, and human blood was sacrificed to the gentlest of all passions . . . *Each one began to consider the rest, and to wish to be considered in turn; and thus a value came to be attached to public esteem.* Whoever sang or danced best, whoever was the handsomest, the strongest, the most dexterous, or the most eloquent, came to be of most consideration; and *this was the first step towards inequality, and at the same time towards vice. From these first distinctions arose on the one side vanity and contempt and on the other shame and envy:* and the fermentation caused by these new leavens ended by producing combinations fatal to innocence and happiness.[23]

Rousseau's initial remarks are on physical proximity, but he then goes on to discuss the psychological mechanisms by which such a proximity produces both prosocial and antisocial feelings.[24] When human beings compare themselves to others they start to value *public esteem*, which is inherently comparative. Our estimable qualities make us appropriate potential recipients of either love or envy. Whether we are loved or envied, we come to perceive ourselves as having valuable traits that make us better than at least some similar others (who are our competitors, in love or other domains). Whether we love or envy, we look at the person who has those valuable traits and we are drawn to them, either to enjoy those qualities in and with our lovers, or to get them for ourselves.

---

[22] Since in French *jalousie* can be used to refer to *envie* as well, it is not clear if Rousseau means romantic jealousy, envy, or a combination of both (which seems to me the most plausible interpretation). In any case, he explicitly mentions envy at the end of the quoted passage.

[23] *A Discourse on the Origin of Inequality*, II, Rousseau 1973, 89–90, emphases mine.

[24] Remember how the evidence concerning high-SCO people shows that there is a connection between being prone to social comparison, being disposed to envy and being empathetic.

Love and envy, then, not only both require some sort of similarity, but also both involve seeing another person as uniquely valuable. Such a perception can conflict with the agent's own desire for public esteem, for standing out in a crowd as the *coolest* individual, she who is most lovable, but also most enviable.

4.3.3   Examples

Let us go back to our lovers, Richard and Ellis, and apply these ideas to their case.

Richard and Ellis share a social position: they are both at the margin of the profession and different from the majority of their peers, who are White men. They are obviously close in space and time. They are equally talented (well, Ellis might be just a little more talented) and they share the same goal and ambition: to become an excellent surgeon. These are the features that allow Richard to realize that he compares unfavorably to Ellis, and to feel the pangs of envy.

But these are also the features that ground his love for her! Richard and Ellis have fallen in love with each other, despite the fact that they are both already married, because they perceive themselves as soul mates: they strive for the same objectives, enjoy the same activities, thrive on the same challenges. Their spouses, on the other hand, do not understand their passion, and do not know what it means to save lives in the emergency room and discover exciting surgical techniques.

Furthermore, remember what triggers Richard's envy: that Ellis might win a prestigious prize, a tangible token of public esteem, that he was also in the running for. We can imagine that Ellis' estimable qualities made her stand out in the crowd of residents, rendering her attractive and desirable to Richard, who was also proud to have won her love. But once they become competitors those lovable qualities also become enviable qualities. Ellis is the most prominent resident – Richard is not.

So far I have only discussed a case of romantic love. But what about other kinds of love? Different kinds of similarity, proximity, equality, and affinity will be responsible for the arousal of envy and love, and estimable qualities will play different roles in different kinds of love.

Consider friendship first. Friendships often develop on the basis of similarity of a sort or other: our childhood friends are often those we happened to share a neighborhood or school with; later we choose friends on the basis of affinity of interests or character; even later friendships arise from sharing a workplace, or because our children go to the same schools.

In all these cases, perceived and salient similarities between us and our friends will make the arousal of envy likely: their toys or houses are bigger; their grades or salaries higher; their spouses more attractive or their children more obedient; they are more successful in their job or appear to be happier.

Sibling love is notoriously prone to rivalrous emotions such as envy and jealousy. Constant comparisons, made by siblings themselves, parents, or anybody else, explain the envy component of sibling rivalry, which is likely to be exacerbated by closeness in age, gender, and other salient identity characteristics.

Sibling love is very similar to friendly love, except that we do not choose our siblings as we choose our friends. However, both loves are character-ized by a peer relationship, and by sharing a background, or activities, or values and goals (where the disjunction is inclusive). In fact, Aristotle devotes particular attention to both loves and their different dimensions of similarity and equality.

Finally, even love between parents and children is characterized by certain kinds of similarities: whether genetically inherited or acquired through time, parents and children share many character features, values, and interests as well. Anecdotal evidence suggests that the more similar parents and children are, the more likely they will be to develop feelings of competition and envy. A typical case is the one, often represented in fiction, of parents who compare their children to their younger selves and resent the children's greater fortune or success.

Those familiar with the philosophical literature on love might won-der whether I am implicitly relying on the idea that love is grounded – that is, rendered appropriate or justified – in the beloved's personal qualities. While I am myself a defender of that view (Protasi 2014), I do not think such a commitment is required for the view I am presenting here because I am not discussing normative reasons at all. What reasons Richard has to love Ellis, I do not know. I am looking at Richard's love, and at the role estimable qualities have, from a purely psychological perspective.

Suppose that there are *no* justificatory reasons for love. It is still the case that he comes to appreciate her estimable qualities by loving her. Or consider familial love, which for most authors is grounded in the fact that there is a relationship between the parties: the justificatory reason I love my daughter is that *she is my daughter*. That does not bear on the fact that I appreciate her many qualities, I am proud of her for them, and I might come to envy her because of them.

4.3.4   *Qualifications*

Just as in Chapter 3 I defended the view that emulative envy may be virtuous without being felt frequently, my thesis here does not imply that envy is bound to occur in *every* loving relationship. There are many ways of loving and many ways of perceiving the beloved. Some loving relationships are less based on equality and similarity than others. A romantic relationship where partners see themselves as occupying unequal roles, for instance, as was common in the past, will not likely see the arousal of envy. Similarly, when partners value different things, or excel in different domains, they will also be less prone to envying each other. However, remember that evidence shows that stable and satisfying relationships occur between people who share values and interests. Furthermore, romantic relationships are increasingly based on equality, so one would expect an increase in occasions for feeling envy as well.[25]

Another way in which romantic partners might avoid envy is by identifying with each other very strongly. Recall the distinction, introduced in Chapter 1, between "comparison" and "reflection," different outcomes that can arise from upward social comparison (Tesser and Collins 1988). When lovers identify with each other they experience reflection and bask in reflected glory (Cialdini et al. 1976), rather than experiencing a process of comparison. I discussed earlier the many roles of social comparison: reflection, differently from comparison, is not diagnostic and informative of our position, but protective of our self-esteem. Basking in the beloved's success is a common experience, but for the aforementioned reasons it is not always possible. Furthermore, there are downsides to completely identifying with another person.

One could object that in love a full-fledged identification with the beloved is always supposed to happen, and therefore the very arousal of envy is evidence that love is not genuine or authentic. After all, some theorists define love precisely as the creation of, and desire for, complete union with another person (Helm 2013). Such a view, both in its descriptive and normative versions, has many advocates but also many opponents; I am in the latter group, but I cannot defend my position here. So, I will just offer the following qualification: if people experience their love as complete union then they will be unlikely to experience envy toward one another.

As to other forms of love, while friendship and sibling love might be the most prone to competition and rivalry and thus envy, there are exceptions

---

[25] I am thankful to Pamela Corcoran for a discussion on this issue.

there too, which may be the result of conscious choices: one might purposefully avoid engaging in activities that one's older siblings excel at, or one might choose friends that excel at things that one does not care about. (More generally, this might be a self-care strategy for people who score high on the SCO scale.)

Finally, consider parents–children love. In parental love envy is less likely when parents see their children as either an extension of themselves, or as very different from themselves; in filial love young children tend to see their parents as role models to emulate and, if the dissimilarity with them is salient, they will feel admiration and pride. And yet, again, we have much anecdotal evidence that both parents and children do feel envy toward one another, and that is especially likely when children grow older and the similarities between them increase.

In sum, many factors are responsible for the intensity and amount of envy individuals feel. The purpose of this section was to articulate a general principle: that the co-occurrence of love and envy is rendered more likely, at the level of the species, by the fact that they thrive in the same psychological conditions.

4.3.5   Against Psychologically Insensitive Love Ideals

Here, finally, is my indirect argument in favor of the normative compatibility of love and envy:

1. Envy for the beloved is an ingrained psychological propensity.
2. We should not endorse normative ideals that go against ingrained psychological propensities.
3. The ideal of love without any envy goes against an ingrained psychological propensity.
    Therefore, we should not endorse the ideal of love without any envy.

I have argued in favor of premise one throughout this section, and I take premise three to be a mere corollary of premise one. I will not give any argument for the second premise, since it is a version of the widespread notion that "ought implies can," a principle whose defense goes well beyond the scope of this chapter.[26] I should say that this premise should

---

[26] A reviewer suggests that, rather, the relevant principle is "difficult-implies-not-ought." It might be true that this is the principle at work here, but nevertheless this latter principle seems to me to *also* be a version of "ought implies can." I thank the reviewer for prompting me to expand on this point in the body of the text as well.

be interpreted as ranging over the species, not the individual. For instance, we do endorse, and enforce, normative ideals of non-violence, even though there might be individuals or groups of individuals for which exerting violence is a strong psychological propensity. But, overall, we think that most human beings at most times in their life can resist their aggressive tendencies.

Furthermore, I do want to provide a defense of a *particular version* of premise two, that is, the ideal of an envy-free love. I think the ideal is both self-defeating and too demanding.

In order to see the first aspect, recall what Richard did when he realized he was very envious of Ellis: he broke up with her. The strategy of interrupting the relationship when it becomes "toxic," as it is often represented in self-help columns, is not only costly but fundamentally misguided because it does not take into account how the co-occurrence of love and envy is likely to repeat itself. Richard, in particular, is bound to find himself in the same situation, given the kind of person he is (a driven competitive surgeon) and the kind of persons he is attracted to (similarly driven and competitive surgeons), and given his interests and values. In fact, he does later in life fall in love with another brilliant and ambitious surgeon, Catherine Avery, toward whom at times he feels inferior, and again envious (but they remain together, since he has seemingly learned to either cope with envy or feel the right kind).

As for the demandingness aspect, a natural objection to premise two is that ethics is *supposed* to be demanding and difficult, and that moral agents are *expected* to struggle and fail. Even if we never hit the target, we should keep aiming at it, as Aristotle recommends (EN, 1094a18–22). Remember the metaphor of the flower and the weed: those who are comfortable with ethics' demandingness would say that even if flowers and seed thrive in the same soil, that in itself is no reason to let the weed grow undisturbed: the scrupulous gardener will keep pulling it up indefatigably. Correspondingly we should keep uprooting envy from our loves, no matter how many times we have to do it, and even at the cost of terminating every relationship that involves envy. Perhaps Richard should learn to love different women; perhaps we should always look for friends whom we can admire but cannot envy; perhaps we should pursue loving relationships based on unequal roles or different interests and values.

It is in response to this approach that I present my final direct argument.

4.4 In Praise of Envying the Beloved

In this final section I argue that a certain kind of envy – emulative envy – can be beneficial to the loving relationship; in turn, a certain kind of love – wise love – can be beneficial to our lives. Thus, that love and envy are so linked in our psychology is not something that we should merely tolerate, but rather wholeheartedly embrace.

In the previous chapters I have detailed what emulative envy is, argued why it is a genuine form of envy, and showed how it does not involve ill will toward the envied. Here I only add that emulative envy is compatible with the duties of benevolence that love, in its best manifestations, prescribes.

We do not know what kind of envy Richard felt. Perhaps he wished that Ellis never gain her prize, or that she somehow lose it, in which case he felt some form of spiteful envy. Perhaps he imagined he won it instead in which case he felt some form of aggressive envy. It is possible that he felt the more innocuous inert envy, but that was enough to make him feel ashamed and incapable of truly loving her. Sometimes we are our harshest judge: perhaps the reason why he left her was not that his envy was malicious, but that the mere thought of envying her was unbearable.

Once again, one might suggest that Richard felt admiration, not envy. But, again, it is important to keep in mind that, while admiration is a good emotion to feel toward a beloved, it cannot fully substitute emulative envy, for two reasons. First, because it may be less conducive to an agent's self-improvement in certain cases, as we saw in previous chapters. Second, and more decisively, because whether or not we feel admiration or envy is not fully up to us. Admiration and emulative envy are different emotions that are characterized by different situational antecedents. Richard falls in love with Ellis, rather than someone whom he admires, because Ellis is *like him*; what makes him attracted to Ellis in the first place is precisely the fact that they are similar and equal on many levels. In the case of loves that are more unequal it might be easier to bring oneself to develop admiration, but there are limits there too: if envy arises in the first place it is because of perceived similarity – we can make that similarity less salient but we cannot eliminate it altogether. In general manipulating our emotional experience is possible, but some shifts are easier than others: for instance, it is probably easier to move from one variety of envy to another than to move from envy to admiration (even harder would be to move to scorn or pity).

In fact, another objection is that one might not be able to feel emulative envy either: after all, that is where Richard found himself. That is, the agent might not be in a condition that allows them to feel emulative envy as opposed to other, more pernicious kinds of envy. For instance, the envied good may be exclusive such that only one person can have it. There is only one Harper Avery Award a year, in this fictional context. However, Richard could have reminded himself that there was another competition in a year, and that if Ellis could get it so could he: it was possible for him to feel emulative envy even though he did not realize it. As I said in previous chapters, part of what is involved in emulative envy is the capacity to discriminate between actual and illusory goods, and between exclusive and non-exclusive goods.

However, there are some unfortunate cases, especially those that involve positional or zero-sum goods: for instance, two friends or romantic partners might compete for exactly the same dream job; a parent and a child might both want to be the person who is most successful in the family; two twins might strive for being valedictorian at the same high school. In all these cases, bringing oneself to feel emulative envy *with regard to this specific good* would in fact not be possible. Here we face a real limitation. Sadly emulative envy is but one form of envy. Other forms can arise – as we have seen in Richard's case – and that is truly problematic for the loving relationship. This is where the second ideal I advocate comes in.

4.4.1 Wise Love

Wise love is a loving relationship whose virtues are such that the lovers flourish in the relationship. If lovers love wisely, being together is a component of their individual *eudaimonia*. Wise love therefore involves striving for ethical virtues such as compassion, respectfulness, and thoughtfulness, and intellectual virtues such as truthful self-awareness and *phronesis*. The wise lover is committed to protecting the loving relationship and making it succeed notwithstanding and sometimes in virtue of negative, aggressive emotions that may arise. That commitment implies that the lover may encourage the beloved to feel emulative envy toward her. Envy can be an opportunity for growth, both for the relationship and the lovers.

When it is not emulative, loving wisely implies becoming capable of forgiving and forgetting, of understanding that the beloved is human and thus prone to human psychological propensities such as envy.

That wise love as an ideal implies acceptance of the human propensity to envy does not mean that wise lovers need to know all the research on envy described in this book! An intuitive understanding that envy is a common human emotion, and a sense that it is not all vicious, will suffice.

Furthermore, that wise lovers forgive and forget envy does not mean that they should forgive and forget each and every occurrence of envy: some envious actions or expressions are deleterious and immoral, and should not be tolerated. Likewise a wise lover might decide to part sides with a beloved who is disposed to intense malicious envy: no love relationship benefits from that, and no lover should tolerate that. But to a large extent what counts as intense or intolerable is an idiosyncratic matter, and part of the practical wisdom required by wise love involves precisely being able to assess this matter correctly.

When envy is emulative, loving wisely takes rivalry and competition as a chance for shared, genuine improvement, and reciprocal, altruistic support. While Richard has not experienced emulative envy with Ellis, he does in his subsequent relationship with his other brilliant surgeon wife Catherine.[27] He has learned that envy is part of the cost of loving women like Catherine and Ellis – his love has grown wiser.

Different forms of love will be wise in different ways. In particular, they may require different ways of managing envy. For instance, parents are expected to be role models for their children, provided they do so without excessive paternalism, and so it is appropriate for them to adopt an explicitly pedagogic attitude in dealing with their children's envy. For children it is less appropriate or feasible to do so, and so they might find it more fitting and helpful to adopt a nurturing and compassionate attitude toward their parents' envy. Sibling relationships can tolerate more open competitiveness than others, and so envy might be dealt with in the spirit of fair and affectionate competition. Similarly, some friendships will tolerate a higher degree of rivalry and competitiveness than others. I now turn to these kinds of *philia*.

4.4.2   Models: Two Women Friendships

Wise love cannot be fully defined since different loving relationships will suit different lovers, and their different talents and needs. Thus, my final argument consists in describing wise love by pointing at two case studies of *philia* among women.[28]

---

[27] Cf. *Grey's Anatomy*, season 8, episode 5 and ff.
[28] Many philosophers use extended discussion of fictional examples, literary ones in particular, to make philosophical arguments. Martha Nussbaum is one of the most prominent ones, and she defends such a practice in Nussbaum 1990.

There is not a lot of empirical evidence concerning potential gender differences in the way people feel, express, and cope with envy. There is some evidence that men feel envy more than women (Fiske 2011). It is plausible, however, that women may have a harder time dealing with envy given that they traditionally have fewer outlets to express their competitiveness openly. For instance, brothers may be given permission to engage in overt semi-serious fights, while sisters tend to be instructed to not fight. Similarly, men may be more explicitly rivalrous and competitive with their friends, while women are expected to be more sisterly.

Orbach and Eichenbaum (1988) present an analysis of envy in women's friendships from a feminist psychoanalytical perspective. One of their central claims is that envy among women is particularly destructive, and guilt- and shame-conducive, insofar as it clashes with the ideals of care that femininity is associated with. In a similar vein, but from a literature studies perspective, Wyatt (1998) suggests that Margaret Atwood's novel *The Robber Bride* is an accusation against feminism and its ethics of sisterhood, which risks reinforcing the traditional ideal of a nonaggressive, loving-at-all-costs woman. Wyatt claims: "The Robber Bride is on one level a story about restoring to a feminist community the right to envy" (1998, 52).

Similar attempts to restore the "right to envy" of women can be found in the two works of art I have already mentioned – TV drama series *Grey's Anatomy*, created by Shonda Rhimes, and the literary tetralogy *My Brilliant Friend*, authored by Elena Ferrante – from which I derive my case studies.

4.4.2.1   Cristina and Meredith

In *Grey's Anatomy* the characters, all driven surgeons, are often shown to envy each other. But the effects are not always as detrimental as in Ellis and Richard's case. Cases of envy within romantic relationships that is well-tolerated in the context of romantic relationships are shown frequently, even though they are generally not given particular emphasis in the plot – envy is often presented as an unavoidable by-product of a highly competitive environment, as par for the course.[29]

But there is one loving relationship where envy is sometimes explicitly featured: Meredith and Cristina's intense *philia*. Talking about *philia* is particularly appropriate in their case because this is not just your average friendship. As any fan of the show knows, Meredith and Cristina are each

---

[29] In addition to the envy and competitiveness present in Richard and Catherine's relation, we see similar dynamics between the "star couple" of the show's first eleven seasons, Meredith and Derek.

other's "person," which in the show denotes a role that is between "best friend forever" and quasi-romantic partner, a relationship that weathers all life changes the two women face, a relationship that in many ways precedes and supersedes sexual-romantic ones, no matter how passionate those may be. The depiction of Meredith and Cristina's *philia* was unprecedented in mainstream TV, insofar as it never shies away from the dark aspects of women relations, but it also glorifies the most luminous aspects.

In the episode "I'm Winning" (season ten), Cristina is nominated for the Harper Avery Award, the same that Ellis Grey (Meredith's mother) had won years earlier, and which had triggered Richard's envy. Meredith is, like Cristina and Ellis, an extremely talented and ambitious surgeon, and confesses to her husband Derek that she is envious of her friend.[30]

We know that Meredith is trying hard to be a supportive friend. At the beginning of the episode she tries to calm down Cristina, who anxiously waits for the phone call announcing the nomination. And yet Meredith is so envious that she has to fight tears throughout the day, and organizes a toast in Cristina's honor for the sole reason of masking her envy.

Or at least this is what she tells Derek, but things might be a little more complicated than that. Cristina clearly hates the idea of the toast because she fears it might bring bad luck, and Meredith, her best friend, must know that she would feel that way. Thus, one cannot help but wonder if Meredith's unconscious motivation is a little darker than the one she confesses, namely whether she is motivated by a bit of spiteful envy

Derek does not react to Meredith's confession with outrage or surprise. In fact, he is the one who started the conversation by guessing that Meredith is envious. That Meredith loves Cristina and is both happy for her and envious is presented as a normal feature of their relationship. I bet that no fan of the show was puzzled by what philosophers and theologians have for centuries decreed to be an impossible contradiction!

That is because Meredith and Cristina are shown to constantly compete with each other; it is only natural that they come to feel envy, whether spiteful, inert, or often emulative.

Meredith and Cristina's love is wise, since they are both aware of the beloved's shortcomings, including occasional bouts of malice, but they are always ready to forgive the other. It is also a relationship where emulative envy may be said to be *virtuous*. For both of them competitiveness is a

---

[30] Throughout the episode, which shows also another case of envy toward Cristina, the terms used are "jealous" and "jealousy," but the context makes clear that they function as synonyms for envy, as is often the case.

driving psychological force central to who they are, and witnessing each other's skills and achievements is a constant spur to self-improve and a source of respect for the other. They are attracted to each other from the start because of their similar characters and ambitions, and their relationship would be impoverished if it didn't contain emulative envy.

A similar dynamic can be found in a very different fictional context.

4.4.2.2   *Lenù and Lila*

Elena Ferrante has been acclaimed internationally as the most important Italian writer of her generation. She is best known abroad for a series of four novels, whose first volume is titled *My Brilliant Friend*, recounting the lifetime friendship between two Neapolitan women.

The complex story of Lenù and Lila, and of the multitude of side characters, unfolds over almost 2,000 pages, so I will not attempt to summarize it here. But envy is all over their, and other characters', relationship.[31] Lenù is the narrative voice and she often talks of the envy she feels for Lila, and the envy that in turn she perceives coming from her best friend. The very title of the first novel is ambiguous: until the end it is not clear who "the brilliant friend" is supposed to be. Often, given that it is Lenù who is writing and talking about how much she admires Lila, we tend to think that the brilliant friend is Lila, the amazingly gifted and charming woman capable of overcoming poverty, loss, and physical and emotional abuse of every kind. But at times we see that in fact it is Lila who thinks of Lenù as the brilliant one, the one who, thanks to hard work, determination, and strenuous self-discipline, made it out of the degraded working-class community the two friends grew up in. The crowd of secondary and tertiary characters also give discordant verdicts, praising and admiring now one, now the other.

By the end of the tetralogy the reader realizes that *both* are the brilliant friend – that that is precisely the point, and that that is why the story is so compelling and their friendship so durable, notwithstanding the many adversities, tensions, and fractures it goes through. They are both extraordinary people who manage to live lives that are far more meaningful and far richer than those of their neighborhood counterparts.

Neither woman could have achieved such a result without the other. From the very start, when they are little girls in primary school, Lila and Lenù prod and stimulate each other to do better, and they never stop.

---

[31] Envy also characterizes the relation Lenù has with her mother, among other negative emotions, but their relationship is far from ideal, and the envy present in it is mostly spiteful.

They will compete throughout their lives not just on the professional terrain, but also on the romantic one, unwittingly and resentfully sharing lovers and suitors. Their competition is often implicit and unconfessed, but fierce and obvious, and sometimes ugly and petty. Their rivalry leads Lenù, whose thoughts we are more privy to than Lila's, to wish that her friend die, and in turn to believe that the envy she perceives from Lila has cursed her own happiness, as in the superstitious notion of the evil eye. As a review of the book in *Intelligent Life* reads: "This is a story about friendship as a mass of roiling currents – love, envy, pity, spite, dependency and Schadenfreude coiling around one another, tricky to untangle."

Thus, their relationship seems to experience all varieties of envy, even the most spiteful kind. And yet they also experience the most noble kind, the one that constantly moves them to self-improve. It is a recurring theme of the books that neither friend would be who she is without the other as a model and as a rival. Their deep, intense, passionate *philia*, which is for both the most constant and enduring love in their lives, is, in the end, wise:[32] it knows that envy is the dark side of love, and that love can illuminate, but not annihilate, envy.

---

[32] However, they themselves are far from being *phronimai*, since all too often we see them acting quite viciously. The same may be said of Meredith and Cristina. Thus, I think a loving relationship can be wise even though the lovers could not be characterized as fully virtuous agents in an Aristotelian framework (full virtue does not make for very entertaining narratives, I suspect).

CHAPTER 5

Political Envy

Recall, firstly, how extreme racism expresses itself in emotion, the way it generates not only hatred and contempt, but fear, anger, reserve, suspicion, grief that one's offspring is going to marry a member of the rejected race, joy when evil befalls them, pity for members of one's own race who are bettered by them, pride when one succeeds in doing them down, amusement at their humiliation, surprise that one of them has shown signs of advancing humanity, horror or self-contempt at the discovery that one has felt fellow feeling for one – it is hard to think of a single emotion that is not corrupted.

Rosalind Hursthouse[1]

5.1 Introduction: Envy as a Political Emotion?

In a deservedly famous scene of Spike Lee's masterpiece *Do the Right Thing*, Mookie, played by Lee himself, is having a heated exchange with Pino, the son of the Italian American owner of the pizzeria at which Mookie works as a delivery boy. Mookie forces unabashedly racist Pino to admit that his favorite basketball player is Magic Johnson, his favorite movie star is Eddie Murphy, and his favorite rock star is Prince – all of Pino's favorite people, in other words, are Black.[2] Pino tries to explain how his idols are "different," how they are not "really Black." Mookie ignores

This chapter was extremely difficult to write and I am very grateful for the generous, patient, and often very detailed feedback of many colleagues, such as Aarón Álvarez, Emily Austin, Adrian Bardon, Bianca Cepollaro, Emanuela Ceva, Myisha Cherry, Samuele Chilovi, Francisco Gallegos, Manuel García-Carpintero, Barrett Emerick, Jonathan Gingerich, Marta Giunta, Stavroula Glezakos, Daniel Howard-Snyder, Frances Howard-Snyder, Martha Jorba, Adam Kadlac, Win-chiat Lee, Shen-yi Liao, Dan López de Sa, Alida Liberman, David Livingstone Smith, Pablo Magaña, Martha Nussbaum, Giulio Pietroiusti, Enrico Terrone, Neal Tognazzini, Patrick Tomlin, Giuliano Torrengo, Iñigo Valero, Ryan Wasserman, Dennis Whitcomb, and audience members of the Wake Forest University Philosophy Department Colloquia. I am also thankful to Agneta Fischer, Ruth Groff, and Vanessa Wills for bibliographic references and discussion (some of which ended up in the Appendix).
[1] Hursthouse 1999, 114.   [2] Both Pino and Mookie, however, often use the N-word here.

Pino's inconsistent blabbering and calmly and almost affectionately delivers the fatal blow: "You know, I think deep down inside you wish you were Black."

Race relations are a central aspect of the increasing political turmoil in Western countries. The United States' origin myth is that it is a country of immigrants, but it is also a country grounded in the genocide of the native American populations and the enslavement and exploitation of people of African descent. It is thus not surprising that race relations in the USA are as difficult as they are. But Europe is quickly becoming the theater of race-based tensions as well, and other countries are following suit. In general the world is likely to become a more racially mixed place, and thus a potentially more divided one, assuming racism is not extinguished soon, which seems unlikely.[3]

However, the role of envy in racial tensions and divides has thus far been completely ignored. Even those who realize that all emotions are essentially corrupted and involved in racism tend to ignore envy, as the quote in the epigraph exemplifies. This chapter aims to start remedying this lacuna.

In general, envy has not been studied much in its political dimension, which is surprising given the flourishing literature on political emotions.[4] Emotions that have been deemed to be political include love, anger, resentment, indignation, disgust, fear, guilt, pride, shame, and contempt.[5]

---

[3] Historians and sociologists might argue that migrations have always happened and that the world has always been racially divided: even in the absence of a modern notion of race, foreigners have always been looked at with suspicion and, even in relatively cosmopolitan societies such as the Roman Empire, there were large groups of people who were otherized and object of various forms of oppression, including, of course, slavery. But what interests me here is perceptions of racial diversity as we define it now. According to a 2018 poll run by the Pew center in twenty-seven countries in all continents, perceptions of diversity in one's own country has increased. See: www.pewresearch.org/global/2019/04/22/how-people-around-the-world-view-diversity-in-their-countries/.

[4] A notable exception is Martha Nussbaum, who talks about envy in *Political Emotions* (2013) and *The Monarchy of Fear* (2018). In both works Nussbaum has a very negative conception of envy as a narcissistic emotion, which, together with fear and shame, is the enemy of compassion. She talks about emulation and resentment as envy's positive counterparts, and overall endorses Rawls' framework with regard to the problem of envy: "[s]ociety's institutional structure supports emulation by leaving room for competition, without creating the sense of hopelessness and helplessness that can paralyze effort (and, we might add, the economy). Robust political and legal institutions also support constructive indignation and resentment, as citizens are encouraged to bring forward real grievances" (Nussbaum 2015, 345).

[5] While Nussbaum is probably the most prominent and prolific representative of this approach (see Nussbaum 2001a, 2013, 2016, 2018), feminist philosophers more generally have been at the forefront of it, and unsurprisingly so, given their understanding of the political as personal and their attention to the subjective, arational, and embodied aspects of human experience and knowledge. I don't have the space here to trace a genealogy of feminist philosophy of emotion, but it is worth mentioning Naomi Scheman's work on the politics of naming and recognizing emotions such as women's anger (Scheman 1980); Audre Lorde's discussion of anger as a powerful

Political emotions can be defined as "collective emotion[s] within a political context, such that a political event or issue is the target, but not necessarily the focus, of the emotion" (Protevi 2014, 327). Political emotions are thus a species of *collective emotions*, which are emotions that arise collectively and are shared by large groups of people. The study of collective emotions is an interdisciplinary field with many interlocking theoretical debates involving philosophers, psychologists, sociologists, and neuroscientists.[6] In social psychology there is a booming literature on *group emotions*, defined as emotions that individuals feel in virtue of identifying qua members of certain groups[7] and which may be argued to be distinct from emotions that people feel qua individuals (Mackie et al. 2008; Smith et al. 2008). I draw on some of this literature, but unfortunately there is very little empirical research devoted to group envy.

I believe there are two interconnected reasons for envy's neglect in both theoretical and empirical discussions of collective emotions. First, envy has been discussed in political philosophy in the context of what I shall call the Envious Egalitarianism argument. I argue that this debate is fundamentally misguided, and has skewed the discussion of envy's political role in a sterile direction, insofar as envy is narrowly defined as a malicious emotion that motivates to spoil the good even at the envier's personal cost. This kind of

and legitimate gendered political emotion (Lorde 1981), a thesis echoed by Marylin Frye a couple of years later (Frye 1983); the contemporary discussions of anger and oppression that include McRae 2017 and Cherry 2017; Alison Jaggar's discussion of outlaw emotions – emotions felt by members of subordinate groups which are incompatible with dominant perceptions and values (Jaggar 1989); Macalester Bell's feminist defense of contempt (Bell 2005); Alice MacLachlan and Katryn Norlock's work on resentment and forgiveness (e.g., MacLachlan 2009, 2010; Norlock 2009). Outside of a specifically feminist lens, see Samantha Vice (2017) on White pride. Black, gay, and disability pride are object of much interdisciplinary study, but the emotional components underlying these social movements are, in my view, not getting enough philosophical attention. Similarly, the vast and rich debate on political forgiveness and blame sometimes include emotional components (e.g., Emerick 2017), but is usually not primarily focused on them. Most recent moral psychological approaches to emotions focus on the personal as opposed to the political domain. For recent analysis of disgust, see, e.g., Kelly and Morar 2014; Kumar 2017; May 2014; Strohminger 2014.

6 Von Scheve and Salmela 2014 comprises many valuable essays on the topic from a wealth of disciplinary perspective. One debate worth mentioning here is that between emergentists and individualists: the former posit a distinct collective subject (so even corporations can have proper emotions, see Schmid 2014), while the latter believe that collective emotions are just the coordination or alignment of individual ones. Intermediate or alternative positions are possible (see Von Scheve and Salmela 2014, especially chs. 1–4). In this chapter I think of emotions that individuals feel in virtue of their group identity, even though I do not exclude the possibility that there might be group emotions in the stronger ontological sense. Here, too, I try to remain as neutral as possible with regard to these larger theoretical issues.

7 E.g., Doosje et al. 1998 is a seminal study on collective guilt, and van Zomeren et al. 2004 provides evidence for group-based anger. There are many more studies on anger and guilt, and also shame and Schadenfreude: see Leach et al. 2008 and van Kleef and Fischer 2016 for reviews.

envy is clearly immoral and prudentially bad, and its specter has forced progressives into a defensive position that required them to reject envy at all costs. Thus, the possibility that envy may play a positive role in the public sphere never emerged.

Furthermore, and this may be a second reason why envy is not more prominent in the political emotions literature, the parties involved in political and potentially envious relations have almost always been characterized as "haves" and "haves not," where the disadvantage that could potentially give rise to envy is implicitly seen as fundamentally a matter of material resources, of socioeconomic status, or of class differences in a "thin" sense. That is, the differences caused by, and entrenched in, cultural and ethnic identities have been ignored. But this, as I hope to show, is a mistake. Once we pay attention to the many facets of group identity we see that things are more complex and nuanced than that. For instance, a person can be lower in socioeconomic status (and consequently, in many societies, in access to political goods) and yet be an object of envy, much like Mookie is vis-à-vis Pino. Thus, we come to see that different varieties of envy can play different roles, including detrimental ones, in hitherto underinvestigated ways.

Here is an overview of the chapter, which is, unavoidably, more tentative and explorative than the ones that preceded it and which has two connected but distinct parts. The somewhat jarring argumentative shift from one to the other reflects the need to move away from the traditional approach to political envy and embark on a new sort of analysis. The first part (Section 5.2) is about the debate on envy in distributive justice. There are two main questions that are asked in this debate. One, from an ideal theory perspective, is whether envy can contribute to establish what justice requires. The answer to this question has traditionally been a resounding no: envy has been taken to be a vice that should not motivate political ideals, and thus by implication should not motivate justice ideals. A pivotal moment in this debate is John Rawls' discussion of "the problem of envy" in *A Theory of Justice*. Rawls inherits this concern from previous discussions, but he also passes it down to future generations of thinkers. Of particular note are some contemporary responses to Rawls which tackle the question of whether envy can contribute to moving us toward a more just society, thus shifting to a non-ideal theory approach.[8] What emerges from this review is that the discussion of envy in distributive justice, both in ideal and non-ideal theory, is influenced by too narrow a conception of

[8] Thanks to Patrick Tomlin for suggesting I clarify this methodological shift. For the difference between ideal and non-ideal theory approaches, see Mills 2005.

envy and, more generally, by too abstract an approach to the political sphere. Thus, the second part of the chapter considers the role of political envy in all its varieties with regard to a central political issue of our times: racism and racial tensions.[9] In Section 5.3 I introduce the idea of envious prejudice, specifically in relation to Asians and Asian Americans in the United States: I argue that those who are racialized as "Asian" have been subjected to a special kind of racism, namely one that is colored by envy more than any other negative emotion. I also note some limitations of political envy and the way in which it differs from envy in the private sphere. In Section 5.4 I apply my taxonomy to the political domain and detail some possible varieties of political envy. In the brief conclusion (Section 5.5) I note how tightly connected the personal is to the political, and how political envy might be harder to distinguish from political jealousy, thus ending this book like I started it and coming full circle.

Before delving into the discussion, a terminological note: I shall talk of "racialized groups" or "being racialized as" to signal my assumption that race is socially constructed. I will talk of "racial relations" as a shorthand for "relations between racialized groups."

5.2   The Rhetoric of Class Envy and Envious Egalitarianism

A frequent insult hurled at progressive politicians is that they feel "class envy." The rhetoric of class envy is at least as ancient as classical Greece (see Cairns 2003 and Appendix) and is based on the idea that those who ask for an egalitarian or at least progressive redistribution of resources are simply envious of those who are wealthy (for evidence of this rhetoric in US, UK, and Australian politics, see Bankovsky 2018).

In twentieth-century political philosophy the charge of class envy is brought up against egalitarianism by prominent conservative thinkers (e.g., Hayek 1960 and Schoeck 1969) and is distilled in what I shall call the *Envious Egalitarianism* argument (hereon EE):

1.   Egalitarianism is motivated by envy
2.   Envy is always a vice
3.   Political ideals motivated by vices ought to be rejected
        Thus, egalitarianism ought to be rejected.

---

[9] There are other contexts in which one could talk about envy in the public sphere. To mention but two: envy can be studied with regard to environmental policies, since envy toward other people's lifestyles is one factor in pernicious habits such as driving gas-guzzling cars and flying to exotic locations (Frank 1999; Morgan-Knapp 2014); one could also consider the role played by envy in contexts of corrective/transitional/restorative justice. I hope others will pursue those inquiries.

EE can be found in slightly different versions. Premise one is empirical, and Justin D'Arms (2017) distinguishes occurrent and genetic versions of it: *genetic* versions concern the origin of egalitarianism, and tell a story that is either historical (as in Nietzsche's *Genealogy of Morals*), or developmental (as in Freud's *Group Psychology and the Analysis of the Ego*); *occurrent* versions claim that those who defend egalitarian views of justice are personally motivated by occurrent bouts of envy (Hayek 1960; Schoeck 1969; Nozick 1974; Cooper 1982). Because it is the occurrent charge that tends to appear in the debate on distributive justice, I will focus on that here.

Most egalitarians accept premise two and focus on rejecting premise one, that is, they argue that egalitarianism is not in fact motivated by envy. There is no published view, to my knowledge, attacking premise three,[10] even though some have turned the argument on its head and suggested as a theoretical possibility that, if one and two hold, then, from a utilitarian perspective, we have reason to decrease inequality (e.g., Ben-Ze'ev 1992 and Norman 2002). There are also those who argue against the argument's appropriateness altogether, claiming that it suggests that psychological motivation is relevant, whereas what matters is whether egalitarianism is rationally justified.[11]

I, of course, hope to have shown in the previous chapters of this book that premise two is in fact false. Thus, from my perspective, this argument is a non-starter. However, in the distributive justice literature nobody argues against premise two. I believe that is because of how the debate has been shaped by John Rawls' influential discussion of envy in *A Theory of Justice*, to which I turn next.

5.2.1   The Problem of Envy in A Theory of Justice

With regard to envy Rawls faces two distinct issues: first, he has to preempt the charge brought about by EE and show that his principles of justice are

---

[10] Patrick Tomlin considers this possibility in his unpublished dissertation. A reviewer, whom I thank, suggests that "Machiavelli (*The Prince*) and Mandeville (*Fable of the Bees*) could be understood as thinking that political ideals motivated by vices can be a good thing and so ought not to be rejected." I find this suggestion plausible. I talk about Mandeville in the Appendix.

[11] As shown in Norman 2002, Parfit's Leveling Down objection (Parfit 2000) avoids the conflation between motivation and justification. The objection is that egalitarianism implies that it would be good that those who are better off would be worse off than they are now, even if nobody benefited from such a change. This is a counterintuitive view that, in turn, can be explained only as a rationalization of envy. In this version of EE the accusation of envy comes later. Parfit's solution is to endorse Prioritarianism, the view that we should give priority to the less well-off. But this is what most egalitarians, including Rawls, already claim to be after!

not motivated by envy; second, because his principles may give rise to a society that tolerates a decent amount of inequality, he has to show that it would not be destabilized by excessive envy. In a sense, he has to defend himself from critiques coming both the right and from the left. Consequently he adopts a two-pronged approach. (I am going to provide a sketch of the argument here, but interested readers can find a more detailed review in the Appendix.)

He starts, in chapter 3, by stipulating that there is no envy in the original position, at two levels: the highly rational individuals behind the veil of ignorance do not *feel* envy, and thus are not motivated by it in their deliberations, but also they do not *know* anything about envy and the role it plays in our social lives. Envy is thus excluded both psychologically and epistemically.

The exclusion might seem ad hoc, but Rawls justifies it by appealing to the fact that he sets aside "accidental contingencies" (Rawls 1999, 464) in order to simplify the bargaining process. He also adds that envy is a vice, and we do not want the parties to be motivated by any vice. Thus, Rawls feels comfortable "for reasons both of simplicity and moral theory" (465) to eliminate envy in the first stage of his argument. However, once the principles of justice have been chosen, he admits that he has to reckon with the possibility of envy, and ascertain whether "the well-ordered society corresponding to the conception adopted will actually generate feelings of envy and patterns of psychological attitudes that will undermine the arrangements it counts to be just" (465).

Rawls, then, concedes from the start premise two of EE (that envy is always a vice). Even more importantly, the definition of envy that he ends up using, borrowed from Kant's *Metaphysics of Morals*, is the following: "the propensity to view with hostility the greater good of others even though their being more fortunate than we are does not detract from our advantages" (466).[12] To which definition, he adds: "We envy persons whose situation is superior to ours ... and we are willing to deprive them of their greater benefits *even if it is necessary to give up something ourselves*" (466, my emphasis). Not only are the envious willing to spoil the good, but even renounce some other good on top of that! I shall call this envy *uberspiteful envy*.

Uberspiteful envy is obviously vicious: it is immoral and it also seems to detracts from personal well-being in a way that spiteful envy does not.

---

[12] There is a somewhat muddled discussion of various kinds of envy, which I review in the Appendix, which ends by declaring that the envy described above is *envy proper*.

However, Rawls claims that it may be *excusable* (468) in certain circumstances, namely when a person's social position, and thus access to objective primary goods, is so much lower than others that it would wound their self-respect. In such a situation it would be unreasonable to expect the envious to overcome their rancorous feelings, and it would be rational for them to try to satisfy those feelings – that is, to level down and strip the envied of their advantages even at a personal cost.

As we see in Section 5.2.2.3 the notion of excusable envy is taken up with a vengeance in the non-ideal theory approach. But Rawls does not really develop this notion. His mention of it a seems a sympathetic nod to those who see class envy as having powerful signaling value: if too many people feel lots of envy then something is wrong. The discussion is meant to acknowledge the relevance of the specter of envy before eventually shunning it: what Rawls ultimately wants to do is to show that his well-ordered society does not risk this plague, because his society is well-ordered and will be well-functioning.

He goes on to explain that in the well-ordered society citizens' self-respect is supported by the sense that everyone is treated as equal and, furthermore, that in practice the principles of justice will not give rise to excessive material inequalities (see Appendix for a more detailed explanation).

Rawls' final verdict is thus that the well-ordered society is not likely to be destabilized by excessive (excusable) envy. It is at this point that he finally tackles the charge against egalitarian conceptions of justice, under whose heading his two principles fall. Much like other egalitarians, he highlights how the problem is not inequality per se, but fairness, and that his focus is on improving the situation of the less advantaged. He reiterates the classical distinction between envy and resentment: the parties might be motivated by the latter, and thus by a concern for injustice, but not by the former. To the extent that his theory of justice is egalitarian, Rawls believes that he has shown it to not be envious.

5.2.2 *Responses to Rawls*

Rawls' influence on anglophone political philosophy can hardly be overestimated, and that holds true for the discussion of envy as a political emotion as well. I have to postpone to another time a detailed discussion of the responses to Rawls' treatment of envy. Here I shall only provide a brief review. The responses can be divided into three groups: there are those who are sympathetic to the general Rawlsian framework and only point out some limitations of his views; those who critique Rawls from the right and are not sympathetic to egalitarian/progressive views; and those who critique Rawls from the left and are skeptical of an ideal theory approach. The responses are all quite different but, spoiler alert, they all share a fundamental feature: *none of them rejects the assumption that envy is a vice.*

5.2.2.1 Sympathetic Objections: Ben-Ze'ev and Tomlin

Starting with the most sympathetic responses, Ben-Ze'ev (1992) agrees with Rawls that egalitarians are motivated by resentment and thus that there are good moral reasons to increase equality, but correctly individuates a significant flaw in his entire approach to the problem of envy: as we saw in Chapter 1, envy does not primarily concern itself with great inequalities but with small ones![13] Envy thrives in similarity of status and conditions, not in the large gaps. (Ben-Ze'ev presents an interesting case study: envy in Israeli kibbutz, a strictly egalitarian society by design.[14]) It may be that Rawls does not realize this, because he is so influenced by the weight of EE in the literature, or perhaps it is because he takes his cues from Kant and the Aristotle from the *Ethics* rather than Hume and the Aristotle from the *Rhetoric*, with the former accounts being less psychologically refined than the latter (see Appendix). Either way, it is empirically problematic that Rawls focuses so much on showing that his principles are not going to cause envy because they keep at bay great inequalities, when what really stimulates envy are the small differences. The stability test, then, loses significance.

However, Rawls could respond to this objection that at least he has excluded envy from the start, by precluding the parties under the veil of ignorance to be motivated by, or even aware of the existence of, envy. Here is where Patrick Tomlin's critique comes in.

Tomlin (2008) argues that Rawls cannot exclude envy from consideration in the first stage of the argument. Rawls can postulate that the parties be not personally motivated by envy, but he cannot exclude envy from the knowledge the parties can use in their determinations. That human beings feel envy is an important fact about human nature that parties should be informed of. The same reasons that bring Rawls to consider the problem of envy in the stability test should have brought him to include knowledge of

---

[13] See also in the Appendix the many discussions of this feature of envy in Aristotle, Bacon, and Hume.

[14] The observation that envy thrives in societies designed to be egalitarian is not new. The 1927 novel *Envy* is a biting satire of communist Russia (Olesha 2012).

envy in the first stage of his argument. Tomlin, however, believes that this is not a damning criticism, since he thinks the parties might get to the same conclusions anyway.[15]

Whether or not the well-ordered Rawlsian society is immune to envy thus remains open, even though, again, both Ben-Ze'ev and Tomlin are overall sympathetic and optimistic about the success of Rawls' project. Robert Nozick, on the other hand, is notoriously not so sympathetic.

5.2.2.2   Conservative Critiques: Nozick and Cooper

Nozick discusses the relation between envy and egalitarianism in *Anarchy, State, and Utopia* (1974). Nozick, like Rawls, adopts a fairly narrow conception of envy, albeit not quite as narrow as Rawls. He defines envy thus: "The envious man prefers neither one having it, to the other's having it and his not having it" (239). Thus, also for Nozick envy is always spiteful. However, Nozick does not mention the possibility of an additional cost to oneself, as Rawls does, and therefore his envy is not *über*spiteful. Nozick muses that envy is a "strange" emotion: why are people so pained by unfavorable comparisons, to the point of holding the irrational preference that a good be spoiled, rather than possessed by another person? His answer is, insightfully, that self-esteem is inherently comparative: "There is no standard of doing something well, independent of how it is or can be done by others" (241). Therefore he realizes what Rawls seems to have missed: that equalizing people on some dimension will not reduce envy, given that people will find other dimensions of comparisons, including "quality of orgasm" (243)![16]

Nozick seems fairly attuned to some real-world features of envy and thus he concedes that the occurrent version of EE is implausible, given that egalitarians are personally willing to lose some of their advantage for the sake of egalitarianism. However, Nozick does not think that egalitarians have conclusively proved that they are not motivated by envy. He suggests that perhaps what they gain in exchange for their seeming righteousness is a boost in their self-esteem, a sense of superiority.

---

[15] To repeat: I am presenting very simplified reviews of these articles. Tomlin in particular presents an objection to Rawls concerning different kinds of envy that is worth looking at. I hope to discuss this dialectic in greater detail in future work.

[16] Nozick might have meant this remark to be tongue in cheek, but it is true that people's sexual lives, and in particular men's alleged sexual prowess, can be a powerful source of envy. Tomlin 2008 provides a response to Nozick on behalf of Rawls that I ultimately find unconvincing, but unfortunately I do not have the space to discuss it here.

Similarly, David Cooper (1982) suggests that egalitarians, even when they appear to be among the "haves" and thus presumably unaffected by envy, unconsciously (in the technical Freudian sense) identify with the "have-nots" and are thus similarly motivated by a lack of self-esteem and powerlessness.

Robert Young (1987) points out that Cooper's is far from being the simplest explanation for a behavior that seems to be motivated, simply, by a sense of justice, a retort I find convincing. As for Nozick, Young has a more complex reply. First, he rejects that self-esteem is comparative by saying that "[it] can rest on normal capacities and achievements; to be outstanding is not required" (271). But I think that Young here equivocates on two meanings of "outstanding": while it is true one can have self-esteem even if they are not outstanding, in the sense of being superior to everybody, it is not true that one can have self-esteem without standing out in some way with regard to a few others. Empirical evidence seems to suggest that self-esteem is unavoidably comparative in this second way. Second, Young distinguishes between self-respect and self-esteem, and claims that since self-respect grounds self-esteem and an egalitarian society is the best means to fostering individual self-respect, then an egalitarian society will also best favor self-esteem. I find this argument interesting, but underdeveloped and also unsupported by evidence.

In general I worry that all of the authors cited so far (with the partial exception of Ben-Ze'ev) rely too much on speculation, introspection, and anecdotal evidence when it comes to making empirical claims, and thus the debate surrounding the first premise of EE – that egalitarians are motivated by envy – ends up devolving in a clash of intuitions, even though the premise is purportedly descriptive.[17] While they surely contribute to the understanding of various issues in political philosophy, they do not shed much light on the role of envy as a political emotion.

---

[17] To be fair, I do appreciate that Young painstakingly combs through many egalitarian views in order to provide textual evidence that equality is said to be valued only insofar as it brings more just outcomes or establishes more fraternal societies; that egalitarians claim to be willing to tolerate inequalities provided they serve the interests of the most disadvantaged; and that hostility to less than perfect equality, when present, is often motivated by a pragmatic skepticism: in the actual world tolerating significant inequalities rarely ends up improving the situation of the worse-off. Still, this is not quite evidence concerning the psychological motivation of egalitarian thinkers. Some indirect empirical evidence can be found in Starmans et al. 2017, where the authors convincingly argue that the wealth of cross-cultural evidence on people's preferences for equality is actually better interpreted as evidence that people care about fairness, and that equality only functions as a proxy for fairness. Thus, equality is not preferred for its own sake.

The third group of responses to Rawls is, at a first pass, more promising. Since they reject an ideal theory perspective and are thus more attuned to features in the real world, they may be more empirically grounded (although not with regard to envy, as we shall see). Furthermore, while they still think of envy as a vice, they at least consider the possibility that it may be excusable, or useful in some other way.

5.2.2.3   Non-ideal Perspectives: Frye, Green, Bankovsky

To reiterate, we witness here a methodological shift: from an ideal theory perspective, the question is whether envy can contribute to establish what justice requires; from a non-ideal theory perspective, the question becomes whether envy can contribute to moving us toward a more just society. Correspondingly, rather than attempting to envision a (relatively) envy-free society, these thinkers consider how we can deal with envy given an unjust society.

Harrison Frye (2016) emphasizes nonideal circumstances and explores the concept of excusable envy as a powerful tool in an unjust world. While he agrees with Rawls that envy is an immoral emotion and that resentment is the most apt response to injustice, he defends envy as a second-best tool when "civility and dialogue break down" (519) and when citizens are blinded by their self-interest and are seemingly unaware of the large inequalities plaguing many contemporary liberal societies. (Frye, like Rawls, is seemingly unaware that envy is triggered by small inequalities.) Rational appeals to justice in public deliberation will thus be ineffective, and more unconventional measures will be needed: "[p]erhaps broader social movements that include public protest among other disruptive activities are called for in order to shift public perceptions of inequality" (520). Furthermore, and relatedly, envy can be a trigger for reflection. Envious feelings might move the individual to interrogate the conditions that have provoked those feelings. That is how Frye interprets Rawls' claim that an individual in the face of great inequalities may "resent being made envious" (Rawls 1999, 468).

Frye is explicitly critical of more revisionary approaches to political envy, such as that of Jeffrey Green (2013). Green, in an article provocatively titled "Rawls and the Forgotten Figure of the Most Advantaged: In Defense of Reasonable Envy toward the Superrich," argues that Rawls' notion of excusable envy is better understood as *reasonable* envy, and, further, that "*implementation* of liberal justice requires identifying and potentially regulating the economic expectations of the most advantaged, *sometimes without any (or even negative) economic benefit to the rest of society*"

(Green 2013, 124, my emphases). The gist of Green's argument is that, in implementing the principles of justice, legislators have heuristic, protective, and redressive justifications for imposing burdens on the most advantaged class.

While Green focuses on the implementation of Rawls' principles of justice, Miriam Bankovsky (2018) thinks more generally in terms of actual, existing liberal societies and the forms that condemnation of envy takes in them. She shows that "arguments [against envy] are overwhelmingly marshalled in opposition to redistributive or inequality-mitigating policies in advanced capitalist societies" (260). Like Frye and Green she adopts the Rawlsian conception of envy, which necessarily involves a desire to level down even at one's own cost.[18] Like Green she is more sanguine than Rawls about the value of this malicious kind of envy, and argues that in conditions of systematic injustice it may be not just excusable, but rational and prudent. She notes that resentment cannot arise when one feels powerless to correct the injustice one is witnessing or suffering. Thus, she interprets protests involving property destruction and occupation of public spaces, such as those by the Occupy movement, as acts of *civil disobedience*, even though by classical liberal standards they count as criminal acts of vandalism (recall that Frye also deemed them necessary sometimes). She sees those acts as expression of uberspiteful envy that the 99 percent feels toward the 1 percent, and she thinks that they are not only excusable, but warranted and rational from a prudential perspective, because protesters feel they have no other means to reduce a huge and unjust economic gap between the very rich and everyone else, a gap that affects all primary social goods: basic liberties, access to education, sporting facilities, jobs, government offices, etc. "The moral implication of excusable envy is an assignation of accountability to the social structures that reproduce envy-excusing inequalities" (270). Punishment for these acts should thus be mitigated in a juridical setting. Furthermore, from a political perspective, legislators should rectify the conditions that have made envious individuals incapable of bringing about change in other, more normal and legitimate, ways.

Bankovsky's article constitutes an important contribution to the topic of envy as a political emotion, among other reasons, because she introduces a

---

[18] To be precise, Bankovsky adopts an ever narrower conception of envy, which she borrows from Morgan-Knapp 2014, according to which envy necessarily involves a wound to self-esteem and a subjective perception of undeservingess. I evidently disagree with this definition. However, I don't think the narrowness of the definition bears on what I have to say about Bankovsky's view, so I set it aside.

factor that was until that point absent in the debate on envy as a political emotion: race. As far as I know Bankovsky is the first author in this literature to utilize extended narratives, in which agents are not described in abstract terms as "haves" or "haves-nots," or as "citizens" without any other demographic characteristics, but as real people with names such as "William" and "Rajeev," and specific interests such as cricket.

But even here, racialized identity intervenes only as a mediating factor, as affecting economic privilege and access to primary social goods. Rajeev is meant to represent – it seems to me – second-generation citizens of South Asian descent, who live in poorer neighborhoods. But Rajeev's race is not per se made salient (in fact, race is never mentioned in the article). Relatedly, Bankovsky talks about the Occupy protests, but not of non-peaceful protests in response to racism and racial injustice. And yet, the unlawful activities she describes ("contravening municipal and other laws regarding the habitation of public spaces, and engaging in property destruction," 272) are the same as those seen in the so-called "riots" that took place, among others, in the Parisian *banlieues* in 2005, and in US cities several times in their history but most notably in Los Angeles in 1992 and more recently in 2020.[19]

Even Bankovsky's (excellent) piece is unsatisfying in my view, because, even though it refers to some empirical evidence on envy and alludes to a more multilayered reality, it still accepts the Rawlsian premise that envy is uberspiteful, and it still focuses on socioeconomic status.

In the remainder of the chapter I expand the range of envy while shifting the focus from distributive to racial justice. I attempt to apply my taxonomy to the context of relations between racialized groups. As we shall see, the application is not straightforward, which is to be expected given that group relations are not simply "bigger" than individual relations, but come with their own history, structure, and complications. I argue that emulative envy is less likely and more unstable in this context, and that aggressive envy is particularly scary.

Before proceeding I ought to acknowledge two limitations of the following analysis. First, for reasons of space I focus only on race as opposed to other kinds of identity. This is not because these are not interesting or worthwhile pursuing. Martha Nussbaum has recently argued

---

[19] The 2020 protests took place in several US cities in response to the murder of George Floyd, an African American man killed in Minneapolis by a White American officer, who knelt on his neck for almost nine minutes. Similar protests include those triggered by the murder of Freddie Grey in Baltimore in 2015, and by the murder of Michael Brown in Ferguson in 2014.

that misogyny, defined as a set of behaviors aimed at enforcing men's privilege, is partially driven by what she calls "fear-envy": women are now perceived by men as successful competitors, and, in the eyes of misogynists, they need to be put back where they belong (Nussbaum 2018). I think Nussbaum is primarily thinking here of misogynistic *men*. But of course women can be misogynistic and sexist too, and I suspect that some of their misogyny and sexism stem from envy: for instance, envy for the perceived superior freedom that liberated women enjoy (I admit, this is not based on any kind of scientific evidence and it is most definitely a biased perspective). Another instance of group envy with regard to gendered relations can be witnessed in a particularly vile species of misogyny, the one exemplified by so-called incels (a portmanteau for "involuntary celibates"): it seems to me that incels feel a strong aggressive and spiteful envy for the "Chads" who "steal" all the women, which results in violence not only against women but also those men.[20] In addition to gender there are surely many other interactions between identity and envy that are worth exploring, but I chose race because it is both a timely and urgent topic, and one in which envy has been almost entirely ignored. I shall limit my analysis to the US context, which I know best. Not everything I say will generalize to other contexts, but I hope that some of it will.

A second limitation is that I am speaking as if gender, race, and other identities are separate and discrete. That is, I am ignoring the *intersectional* aspects of social identity (Crenshaw 1989; Carbado et al. 2013). This is a very significant issue, but I hope I can be allowed such oversimplification in virtue of the fact that I am merely dipping my toe in a new and unexplored treacherous body of stormy waters: this is extremely preliminary work. I hope I, and others, can pursue more sophisticated analyses in the future.

5.3 Envy and Prejudice

Racial relations in the USA have always been tense, especially along the White–Black divide, but have been further exacerbated by an ever-accelerating convergence along political lines.[21] Furthermore, there is a demonstrated economic gap between races,[22] and related gaps in

[20] www.lawfareblog.com/incels-americas-newest-domestic-terrorism-threat.
[21] www.pewresearch.org/fact-tank/2019/04/09/key-findings-on-americans-views-of-race-in-2019/.
[22] www.bls.gov/spotlight/2018/race-economics-and-social-status/pdf/race-economics-and-social-status.pdf.

education,[23] health,[24] and other socially primary areas, thus racial inequality often corresponds with the kind of socioeconomic inequality that is of interest in the distributive justice debate (although, as I said, the overlap is not perfect).

Emotional arousal has always been a political tool, and that is truer than ever in the era of identity politics:[25] anger, resentment, indignation, fear, contempt, suspiciousness, even disgust and hatred are being recruited and stirred in ads, debates, and rallies from both sides of the aisle. I said at the beginning of the chapter that accusations of class envy are still being flung from the conservative side. But, in such a racially divided context, envy cannot be exclusively class-based. It will be unavoidably mixed with racial and racist prejudice. Even when people seem to talk of socioeconomic status only, there is often an implicit racialization. (For instance, "welfare recipients" are often expected to be Black or Latino; "working class" often refers to *White* working class; if I ask you to visualize a member of the 1 percent you will likely think of a White man.)

In order to better see the relation between envy and prejudice, let us go back to *Do the Right Thing*. After Mookie accuses Pino of secretly wishing he were Black, thus implicitly accusing him of being envious,[26] Pino laughs dismissively. The dialogue continues and ends "in a tacit stalemate and a mutual, and almost cordial, exchange of 'fuck you(s)' insulting each group's cultural icons" (Guerrero 2020, 54). This scene is followed by another famous one, the "racial slur montage," in which a member of a different racial and ethnic group stares at the camera and angrily vomits racially charged insults at another group (the groups involved are Italian Americans, Blacks, Jews, Koreans, and Puerto Ricans).[27]

One way to think about the connection between the two scenes is that the racial slur montage is the collective version of the first one. The first scene is a dialogue between two people who are not exactly friends but who have known each other for a long time. They are the same age and gender, and work together for Pino's father, Sal, who later claims that Mookie is like a son to him, much to Pino's outrage (and notwithstanding Sal's own only slightly more benevolent racism). Even though Mookie and Pino may appear very different and they clearly identify with different groups (groups

---

[23] https://nces.ed.gov/pubs2016/2016007.pdf.   [24] www.ncbi.nlm.nih.gov/books/NBK425844/.

[25] I do not mean this expression in its pejorative meaning. See Heyes 2020 for a review of the concept.

[26] One could object to my interpretation. I cannot defend the hermeneutical claim in detail here, but I am not the only one who sees envy here (e.g., Burgin 1994, 239).

[27] See the two scenes here: www.youtube.com/watch?v=cOxOR3x8FBQ. Content warning (perhaps obvious): repeated use of racial slurs.

which end up engaging in violent confrontations by the end of the movie), they are very similar in some respects. This is the perfect breeding ground for envy to arise, as I showed in Chapter 4.

Pino is in a position of privilege with regard to his socioeconomic status: he is the heir of the joint, after all, and he lives in a different, probably slightly wealthier neighborhood; he is White, and that comes with a hefty amount of political and social privileges. Nevertheless, he lacks Mookie's self-assuredness, and he is resentful he has to work in a situation that he sees as beneath him. He is jealous of his declining privilege and tries to protect it against people like Mookie, whom he sees as undeserving but whom he is secretly envious of. He constantly tries to put Mookie down, in a way that Hume would have well understood.

The second scene amplifies the meaning of the first one, insofar as it shows the negative collective emotions that are felt by the ethnic and racialized groups that live in the same Brooklyn neighborhood. One of the central themes of the movie is the dialectic of similarity and differences between the groups: all of the people who live in the neighborhood, with the exception of the lone White gentrifier, share the fact of being of low socioeconomic status and being racialized as non-White. The few White people who are somewhat integrated and tolerated in the neighborhood are Italian Americans, who have a (quickly forgotten) history of being otherized and racialized as non-White. The coexistence between the different racial groups is possible, but difficult and fragile. It is premised on the similarities, but disrupted by the differences and the many negative emotions that these differences trigger: distrust, fear, contempt, anger, resentment, and, often neglected in the debate on racial tensions, jealousy and envy.

Envy *has* been cited as a contributing factor to the *Shoah* (the Jewish genocide) but also in the extermination of the Tutsis in Rwanda, the Chinese in Indonesia, and the Indians in East Africa (Glick 2002; Staub 1989).[28] However, in most discussions of racism, genocide, and dehumanization the word envy rarely appears. Both in scholarly and everyday conversations the emotions that are usually discussed are anger and resentment, fear, contempt, and, of course, hatred/hate (which are sometimes used as synonyms, sometimes as different technical notions, as in Green

---

[28] There is also the idea, popular in the early Christian tradition, that Jews killed Jesus out of envy (Aquaro 2004; Schimmel 2008). The connection with anti-Semitism is obvious, and it would be interesting to discuss how reciprocal accusations of envy play out in prejudiced and hostile interactions between groups, but I won't be able to do so here.

2007). White racists, for instance, are said to fear immigrants, resent the loss of supremacy, despise those who are different, and hate people racialized as non-White. All these emotions are surely crucial in understanding racism and, more generally, tensions between not just racial groups but all social groups: these emotions play crucial political roles and deserve to be studied. But envy (together with jealousy) has been underestimated in these discussions and it is time to start reflecting on how it shapes political relations between groups.

Now, this is somewhat surprising, given envy's infamous reputation in the history of ideas. One might argue that this neglect is warranted and due to the fact that envy necessarily involves upward comparison. But most relations between groups, especially the adversarial ones that characterize racism, involve *looking down* on the target and being *proud* of oneself. The racist typically sees the racialized other as inferior, worthy of contempt, to be rejected. When the object of contempt attempts to fight back, the resulting emotional responses are hostile aggressive emotions that focus on putting the inferior other back where they belong. When fear is involved the other might be seen as a threat, but in a way that is rarely understood as being compatible with envy (even though, as we shall see, it should). When jealousy is evidently in place, where groups covetously protect what they believe they are entitled to, then it may be the other who is seen as envious, but never the racist. White supremacists, for instance, are proud of their alleged superiority and see themselves as rightly protecting their role in society. How could they ever perceive themselves to be lacking in any way?

And yet racial prejudice is well compatible with envy. The most straightforward case is that of prejudice against Asians/Asian Americans, and it is to this particular case that I devote Section 5.3.1.[29]

5.3.1   Yellow Peril: Historical and Contemporary Forms of Envious Prejudice Toward Asians

Racism takes many different forms, and I submit that anti-Asian racism is particularly imbibed with envy. It seems to me that one of the reasons anti-Asian racism is overlooked is that it is either masked as admiration (which

---

[29] Distinguishing appropriately between "Asians" and "Asian Americans" is tricky, since in many contexts, including empirical investigation, the distinction is not drawn. I will discriminate between the two when appropriate, but in most discussion of stereotypes, for obvious reasons, the two expressions are conflated.

in fact is more often malicious envy, as I will argue) or "positive prejudice," such as sexual objectification toward Asian women, which is not actually beneficial.

Group envy is admittedly a complex subject to study empirically. As I mentioned earlier, the blooming literature on group and collective emotions is overall silent on envy. The role of envy in anti-Asian racism, in particular, has not been discussed, with one important exception, namely the work of Susan Fiske and her collaborators (Mina Cikara, Amy Cuddy, and Peter Glick).

Fiske et al. have argued that prejudice is often ambiguous. Rather than a univalent antipathy toward outgroups it is better conceived as *ambivalent* across two dimensions: *competence* and *warmth*. Groups that are high in the social hierarchy, that is, perceived as socially powerful, are deemed to be competent, while groups perceived to be cooperative or nonthreatening are judged warm. According to this 2-by-2 Stereotype Content Model (SCM), bias toward outgroups assumes very different emotional shapes: pride is felt toward, for instance, Christian middle-class Americans; pity is directed at the elderly, the disabled, and the mentally ill; disgust is reserved for the homeless, poor Blacks, Arabs, and Feminists, among others;[30] and finally envy is targeted at the rich, Asians, and Jews.[31]

There are several concerns with regard to this work. First, there is a question about the subject of the prejudice. Fiske's book, *Envy Up, Scorn Down* (2011), which summarizes and popularizes the many studies Fiske and her collaborators have run, often talks in terms of "we" and "Americans," used interchangeably. But, given that the majority of the participants in these studies are White,[32] this use of the first person, and the assumption that that is representative of "Americans," is problematic. Is Fiske talking about the "average" American? Who is that? Someone who is *not* Asian, or Black, poor or rich, disabled, Jewish, old, mentally ill, etc.? We get uncomfortably close to the "mythical norm" decried by Audre

---

[30] Pity and disgust are conceptualized in this model as forms of scorn, of looking down to the other. When the target scores higher on warmth, the agent feels pity; when lower, disgust.

[31] Cuddy et al. 2008; Fiske et al. 2007; Fiske 2011; Cikara and Fiske 2012. See Glick 2002 for an explanation of envious prejudice against Jews according to the same model (SCM). I should say I don't think the *Shoah* can be attributed solely to envy. An immoral abomination such as genocide is too complex for its motivations and causes to be reduced to one emotion, albeit one as powerful and destructive as spiteful envy. Surely other emotions, desires, and beliefs are at play and some of them might be more weighty factors.

[32] The race of subjects in many of the cited studies is actually not reported. When it is, the large majority is Whites (as in the first study in Cuddy et al. 2008). But in many cases, as when the subjects are Princeton undergraduates, we can still infer a White majority.

Lorde (1984) as both impermissibly exclusionary and epistemically unfounded: most of "us," either in the USA or in the world, are not middle-class White able-bodied young Christians. But in these studies there seems to be no conscious engagement with the question of whose perspective is being assumed as normative, and why.

Furthermore, if the race of the subjects is not analyzed separately and considered as a variable, it is hard to tell whether Whiteness is a mediating factor (although that is almost surely the case!), and in general what is the relation between one's racialized identity and one's prejudice.

Second, there are more worries about how envy is measured. In some of the studies envy is measured only via the combination of low warmth and high competence, which is, however, compatible with a variety of emotions and attitudes. In others, envy is measured via single-item feelings, which are not valid measures of envy (Lange Weidman, and Crusius 2018; Crusius et al. 2020).[33] Finally, envy is only considered in its malicious variety. In Fiske (2011), for instance, Iago is presented as the "paragon of envy" (14), but, as I have shown, Iago's envy is only one kind of envy.

So I think we need to supplement these ambiguous data with anecdotal evidence. As *Do the Right Thing* illustrates, relations between racialized groups are colored by many aversive emotions, which include anger, hatred, contempt, jealousy, and also envy. One of the reasons for envy's neglect in the discussion of racial relations is that racism is often thought to necessarily involve a perception of inferiority and/or a perception of injustice. Envy necessarily involves the perception the envied is in a superior position, and for most scholars it is void of a perception of injustice. But we know that envy masquerades as resentment, and this is particularly plausible where claims of injustice are bogus, as in the case of White supremacists talking of "reverse racism." And it is possible to scorn or despise a group for some reasons, but envy it for others. Blacks may be scorned for their supposedly inferior intelligence, but envied for their alleged hypersexuality, athleticism, and exoticism.[34] Jews are envied for their supposed cleverness, but despised for their alleged greed.

Both Asians and Jews are mentioned by Fiske and collaborators as targets of group envy. I shall set envy toward Jews aside, even though I find it plausible that group envy has been and still is at least one factor in anti-Semitism. I set it aside both because I cannot tackle a topic with

---

[33] I am thankful to Jens Lange for references and an explanation of this issue.
[34] I thank David Livingstone Smith for a discussion on this topic. See also discussion of Hume in the Appendix.

such a huge literature even superficially, and because it is not an original suggestion.

The case of Asians and Asian Americans is also complex, but I think it is worthwhile to think about it because to my knowledge the connection between envy and anti-Asian racism has not yet been made. Even Fiske (2011), notwithstanding her discussion of group envy toward both Jews and Asians, does not draw that connection, and mentions racism briefly and only in relation to scorn.

Hostility toward successful Asian Americans can be found throughout US history: while manifestations of anti-Asian sentiment can be found in America as early as in the 1600s, more systematic discrimination and persecution starts against Chinese immigrants in mid-nineteenth century, with the "Yellow Peril" movement booming around the late 1870s and culminating in the Chinese Expulsion Act of 1882 (which barred diligent and previously praised Chinese laborers from entering the USA) and in bloody massacres in 1885 and 1887. Hostility toward the Japanese has its obvious apex in the internment of Japanese Americans (1942–6), which scholars argue was also motivated, perhaps primarily, by economic reasons.[35] The history of anti-Indian sentiment is particularly interesting, given that Indians initially enjoyed the more privileged status of Caucasians – until they too started to appear as a threat to White laborers and were relegated to an inferior position as "nonWhite" Caucasians (1923). Helen Zia's review of the history of immigration and persecution of these three ethnicities (among others) clearly shows how White laborers felt envy and resentment toward these competing outgroups (Zia 2000, ch. 2). Jean Pfaelzer explicitly calls the ethnic purges against Chinese immigrants in the Pacific Northwest "pogroms" (Pfaelzer 2007, xviii), and defines the Chinese expulsion and persecution process as one of "ethnic cleansing" (Pfaelzer 2007, xxix), comparing it to Jewish genocide of World War II, but also to the massacres that occurred in Rwanda, Indonesia, Bosnia, Nigeria, Eritrea, Iraq, and Darfur.

In more recent years Asian Americans have often been dubbed the "model minority," while "Asian" as a general category has been neglected in discussions of racism, at least in part in virtue of the perception that they are not as badly off as other racialized groups. However, the seemingly positive prejudice makes them an ideal target for public envy and does not detract, and rather actually contributes to, acts of racism

---

[35] https://fee.org/articles/special-interests-and-the-internment-of-japanese-americans-during-world-war-ii/.

against them.[36] Remember that aggressive and spiteful envy are defined as aversive responses to perceived disadvantage or inferiority toward a similar other[37] with regard to a domain of self-importance and which motivates to "level down," to steal or spoil the envied good: such an emotion is perfectly compatible with the acts racism motivates. Furthermore, Asian Americans' status as a model minority can be easily revoked, as the sudden increase of hate crime and derogatory commentary following the COVID-19 pandemic has shown: many Asian Americans (including Canadians) have reported suddenly finding themselves the object of street harassment for the first time in their lives.[38]

Dehumanization is a common component of racism, and Asians are dehumanized in ways that are consistent with that of other racialized groups: they are seen as vermin and as subhuman, their phenotypical traits are caricatured in grotesque way, and so forth.[39] However, there is a kind of dehumanization that is usually not shared with Blacks, Native Americans, or Latinos, and that is the idea that Asians are like robots: efficient artificial beings devoid of feelings. This comment can often be heard with regard to both Asian Americans and citizens of countries like China or Japan, where people are compared to cogs in a machine. Or think about the idea of a "Tiger Mom," which is only superficially positive, and in contrast to the traditional expectation of maternal nurture.[40] (Recall also the discussion of dehumanizing praise and backhanded compliment in Chapter 2 with regard to inert envy.)

---

[36] It is also worth remembering that racism is always contextual and intersectional: Asian women are objectified by those who claim to have "yellow fever" and thus may be envied by other women, while Asian men are perceived as emasculated and asexual, and will thus be non-Asian men's object of contempt and ridicule.

[37] Remember that the envied can be perceived as similar in some respects but not others, so it is compatible with a perception of inferiority and otherness.

[38] For the USA see here: www.pbs.org/newshour/nation/we-have-been-through-this-before-why-anti-asian-hate-crimes-are-rising-amid-coronavirus; and www.bbc.com/news/world-us-canada-52714804. The same phenomenon has been witnessed worldwide and denounced by many organizations: www.hrw.org/news/2020/05/12/covid-19-fueling-anti-asian-racism-and-xenophobia-worldwide.

[39] In addition to Zia 2000 and Pfaelzer 2007, see also David Livingstone Smith's work on dehumanization (2011, 2020).

[40] It should be noted, however, that the expression was coined by Asian American law professor Amy Chua, and has been embraced by many Asians with pride (https://en.wikipedia.org/wiki/Tiger_parenting). Also, many Asian Americans do seem to find pride in their model minority status and use it sometimes to distinguish themselves from other non-White people, toward whom they might harbor racial prejudice of their own. These are well-known phenomena I won't comment on, but I want to flag that this kind of pride is well suited to provoking envy in others, envy that combined with racist prejudice can turn easily into the White supremacist desire to "put them back where they belong," much as with "uppity," a derogatory expression US southerners used for Blacks who didn't know their place.

Envious prejudice against Asians and Asian Americans has implications for a variety of policies. Starting with domestic policymaking, for instance, whether or not Asians and Asian Americans are considered an underrepresented group in education will affect whether they are included in public initiatives aimed to increase diversity. Envious prejudice also affects implementation of anti-discrimination efforts. Such prejudice also affects decisions about allocation of federal aid across social groups: while it's true that, as a whole, Asians are the highest-earning non-White group in the USA, they are also affected by the greatest internal inequality, even compared to Whites[41] (that is, among Asians the inequality gap is the widest) and poverty is steadily increasing among the Asian elderly.[42]

With regard to international policies, envious prejudice conditions how citizens feel about a variety of trade and defense issues. A strong anti-China sentiment has been stoked by politicians from both conservative and progressive parties since China has become a superpower. The COVID-19 outbreak in 2020 exacerbated this sentiment; fanned even by the president of the United States, it has assumed explicitly racist aggressive forms, targeting not only the government and the citizens of the People's Republic of China, but "Asians" in general, and just about anyone who *looked* Asian to the racist eye.[43]

While anti-Asian prejudice is, together perhaps with anti-Semitism, the most plausible example of racialized envy, I suggest that there are other ways in which envy seems to intervene in racial relations. But before finally delving in the varieties of political envy, I have to acknowledge the ways in which my taxonomy may fall short in the political sphere.

5.3.2   Limits of Political Envy

While I do not have a theory about the differences between the moral and political domain, I think it is safe to assume that the political sphere is not simply larger than the moral one: a society is not just the sum of its

---

[41] www.pewsocialtrends.org/2018/07/12/income-inequality-in-the-u-s-is-rising-most-rapidly-among-asians/.

[42] See www.aarp.org/content/dam/aarp/home-and-family/asian-community/2016/09/capacd-report-aarp-2016.pdf?intcmp=AE-ASIAN-COMMUNITY.

[43] www.politico.com/news/2020/05/20/anti-china-sentiment-coronavirus-poll-269373; www.aljazeera.com/opinions/2020/4/16/anti-asian-racism-must-be-stopped-before-it-is-normalised/; www.nationalgeographic.com/history/2020/09/asian-american-racism-covid/.

individuals, and adapting my taxonomy to the political and social domain is not just a matter of scalability.[44]

With regard to envy there seem to be at least two factors that differentiate the public/political domain from the private/moral one (I use the labels somewhat loosely so as to cast as wide a net as possible, rather than assuming that the terms are interchangeable).

First, my sense is that the baseline for hostility and antipathy is higher at the political level. In the United States the political climate is increasingly more polarized.[45] Rawls' notion of "overlapping consensus" (Rawls 1993) strikes me as a mirage: the overlap of values and ideals and, perhaps more importantly, the willingness to work through differences seem to be shrinking, even if we reject comprehensive views that do not qualify as reasonable (such as White supremacy). While citizens might still be similar in respects relevant to an ideal legislator – they all want happiness, safety, love, freedom to develop their talents according to their preferences, etc. – they nevertheless perceive others as fundamentally different, alien at times, and often untrustworthy and in bad faith, even evil. Crouched in their epistemic niches, shielded by their cultural self-conceptions, American citizens look at outsiders with suspicion, fear, and hatred. Most of them have good reasons to feel resentment (even if they do not always direct their resentment correctly): they live in a deeply unjust society, riddled with huge economic inequalities, plagued by gun violence, and seemingly doomed by climate change.[46]

In personal interactions it is much easier to find common grounds, develop a liking for a person, bring oneself to overcome a rivalry, and focus on achieving the lacked good. Or sometimes we simply distance ourselves from the envied, cut ties, and focus on some other goal, thus coping with envy indirectly. But in public interactions the other party is often abstract, an image on a newspaper, often a caricature or stereotype in a political ad or satirical piece. People who have different comprehensive views are demonized and otherized, and that makes communication difficult or impossible. Furthermore, communication with members of an outgroup

---

[44] One way to see this is to think about the related distinction between public and private morality. Bernard de Mandeville famously claimed that private vices can be public virtues (see Appendix for his take on envy) and, independently from whether one agrees with the normative thesis, one ought to concede that such a thesis could not even be articulated if the only difference between the public and the private sphere were one of size. The point is that they are structurally different.

[45] See: www.pewresearch.org/topics/political-polarization/.

[46] This is not meant to be a neutral diagnosis: many Americans would say that the real problems are uncontrolled immigration, political correctness, destruction of traditional values, or the demise of American manufacturing.

often takes place on the internet, which notoriously makes interactions among strangers trickier, less authentic, and often nastier.[47]

In such a context I fear that envy devolves easily and quickly into its worst varieties and cannot play a robust role in creating societal flourishing; as I have argued, it can play at the personal level. Envy inherently focuses on perceived individual disadvantage from a nonmoral perspective; that is why even in its malicious form it has a powerful signaling and motivating value. It tells the agent what they care about at a self-interested level and it prompts them to do something – anything – about it. But its strength is also its weakness: it is first-personal, self-reflective, inward-looking, and amoral. While emulative envy can in certain conditions be a virtuous emotion it is not really "made" to address systemic injustice or wrongdoing, as anger and resentment are.[48]

The second and related feature that limits the positive role of envy in the political/public sphere is perception of control. It seems to me that perception of control is likely to be lower on average in political and public contexts. There are many politically relevant factors we cannot control. We cannot easily move away from our city or country, we do not have as much control over what our government decides to do, and yet we all care about our place in society and about what (we perceive) our government does or does not do for us. Social mobility may be perceived as impossible (and that perception is sadly often correct) and, by most accounts, we cannot change our race. Other group identity factors may be changeable but not easily, such as gender, while others we may not want to change, such as religion. When perception of control is low, and hostility is high, emulative envy has a hard time arising and may be more ephemeral than in the personal sphere. Nevertheless, I believe that there are some instances of political emulative envy, as we shall see in Section 5.4.

---

[47] Barnidge 2018 shows that people perceive interactions on social media to introduce more negative affect, and to be characterized by higher perceived political disagreement compared to face-to-face interactions. He suggests this might be one factor in increased political polarization. On negative affect and polarization, see Iyengar et al. 2012. For a critical review of studies of the internet's effects on politics, see Farrell 2012. See also Wojcieszak and Mutz 2009 for the claim that fruitful online political exchange takes place in non-dedicated platforms.

[48] This is a version of the long-standing concern that envy is not a moral emotion, unlike resentment, and is thus not suited to address injustice (among others, see Ben-Ze'ev 2002 and Miceli and Castelfranchi 2007).

5.4 Varieties of Political Envy

5.4.1 Aggressive and Spiteful Political Envy

As I said in Chapter 3, aggressive envy is particularly worrisome in virtue of its prudential benefits. If the envier is not caught they can benefit from their immoral actions. However, the kinds of behaviors that *individual* aggressive envy elicits is disincentivized through moral disapproval and legal sanctions: stealing, sabotaging, cheating, and murdering are actions that people can occasionally get away with (some people more so than others), but there is at least prima facie consensus on their being impermissible.

The same cannot be said at the group level. As I already mentioned, Adam Smith talks about *wars* as being motivated by envy (1976, VI. II. 28). Given that many if not all wars are sanctioned by the governments who wage them, and granting that at least some wars are motivated by (aggressive) envy, then envy's aggressive tendencies are not clearly condemned at a group and political level.[49] Two potential examples of successful aggressive envy at a group level have obvious connections to racial prejudice: the Jewish genocide in Nazi Germany and the internment of Japanese Americans. More generally, if I am right in my diagnosis of racism against Asians as having envy at its core, then the kind of envy that is being felt here is clearly aggressive or spiteful. It aims to deprive the target of its perceived superior status and in many cases it does succeed not only in bringing the envied down, but also in stealing the envied good.

Much like Jews were deprived of all they had in Nazi Germany, Japanese Americans who were interned saw their properties vandalized or confiscated and their wealth all but stolen, either by the government or by their "fellow" White Americans. In these cases aggressive envy is possible: economic advantage can be taken away, and so can social status.

I am not sure whether we can attribute the killing and other physical harm of a targeted racial group to aggressive or spiteful envy. It seems that in many cases the distinction is not sharp and the envy that is felt oscillates between spiteful and aggressive, or is hybrid: pogroms or riots against Asian Americans and Asian immigrants saw rioters destroying property,

---

[49] The US invasion of Iraq in 2003, which critics believed was motivated more by the desire for economic gain than by the desire to quash a "rogue state," may be an example of what Smith had in mind. Colonialism may also be seen in part as motivated by both greed and envy, with post hoc rationalizations fueled by racist prejudice. There is a question of whether we can think of *nations* as subjects of emotion proper, but I cannot address it here.

looting and vandalizing homes, and beating their targets, but also pocket-
ing valuables. Putting people in concentration camps allows property
confiscation but also humiliation, pain infliction, and, of course, in
the case of Jews, physical elimination – the ultimate form of leveling
down. (Note that some of the peculiar behavioral tendencies of envy
require seeing the target as human, albeit a lesser kind of human, or else
there would not be the pain of inferiority, nor the desire to put the
target down.)

Here, too, we can see the difference between the personal and political
sphere and the way in which thinking about racial relations matters. In
personal interactions, defined as interactions in which group identity is not
salient, factors such as dehumanization or otherization do not intervene.
But in envious prejudice the high degree of hostility and the intense desire
to harm the target make the distinction between aggressive and spiteful
envy blurry and less significant.

An interesting case is that of the White poor who are against social
welfare policies, even though they themselves may benefit from them. This
irrational behavior can be more easily explained by the combination of
envy and racism: taking away resources from "welfare queens" and "thugs"
is more important to them than having access to those resources themselves.[50] This seems to be a case of uberspiteful racial envy, and one that,
differently from the cases discussed by Bankovsky, is never reasonable or
justified, even though perhaps it may be excusable in some circumstances,
at least from the perspective of assessing individual blame. (I am thinking
of people who grow up in extremely poor rural areas and who are raised in
very homogenous communities, where racist thinking may be very widespread. Perhaps these agents may be excused for their envy. Another
possibility is to think they are morally unlucky but still accountable.)

Against my characterization of racial envy two possible objections arise.
First, one may say that what motivates people in many of the cases
I described is resentment, not envy. This is certainly the feeling expressed
by many Whites: they lament the injustice being perpetrated against them,
the fact that, for instance, Asian workers stole their jobs by accepting lower
wages. This is a complaint that is often repeated today both toward
immigrants and oversea workers in less developed countries. I also frequently hear the same complaint voiced with regard to Asian students,

---

[50] I do not mean, once again, to reduce a complex phenomenon to a single explanation. Envy is not
the only causal factor, but it seems to me to be an important one.

whose allegedly high academic standards and achievements levels are perceived as threatening.[51]

There are two ways to respond to this objection. One is to say that this is envy's well-known strategy to mask as resentment. Enviers talk about injustice but, whether they are aware of it or not, that is often is a lie. In the discussion of EE the defenders of egalitarianism often point to the evidence that what they feel is resentment or indignation, for instance by gladly renouncing some of their own advantage in favor of more equality (see discussion in Young 1987, among others). Counterfactual scenarios (and veils of ignorance) are useful here: if the situation were reversed, and the agent complaining about injustice were actually profiting from it, would they complain? As far as I know many of the White workers rioting against Asian immigrants were not previously advocating for everyone's right to work, even though some of them might have in fact been in favor of unions and solidarity among all workers. (An analogous sort of partial solidarity can be seen in the women suffrage movements, which often excluded non-White women, although in that case it does not seem envy-related.)

The second way is to acknowledge that things may be complicated, once again, due to the racial prejudice component. The White workers attacking Chinese laborers, the White Americans supporting the internment of Japanese Americans – they probably *also* truly believed that they were the victim of injustice, or that the Japanese were the enemy. Granted, some self-interest was lurking right nearby. But, again, these are complex large-scale social phenomena that are bound to be overdetermined and racial prejudice by itself has many causes and components. So surely there was some resentment and jealousy involved (more on jealousy later).

Note that the two responses are connected: one of the reasons why the White laborers, in a counterfactual scenario, would not be supporting the Asian immigrants' right to work is precisely because of racism and the perception that an asymmetry in wages and job opportunities is justified by race differences.

Whites are used to their privilege; in many cases this privilege is invisible to them and thus they feel entitled to it, and so when it disappears or is threatened their jealousy is very intense and righteous, and it transforms

---

[51] Again, "Asian students" here is stereotypical, since not all people who have Asian ancestry can achieve high academic performances, and given the variety of cultural norms and even just ethnicities that the category "Asian" actually encompasses. I have encountered this sort of barely veiled hostility in my classroom. More anecdotal evidence is provided in Senior 2014, ch. 4.

into resentment and indignation. Allow me a quick detour to religion. Think about the idea of "the war on Christmas." Conservative pundits in the USA popularized the concept in response to the idea that Christian holidays should not be imposed as the default holiday in December, since there are many people who celebrate other religious festivities, or none at all.[52]

The idea that printing "Happy Holidays" on coffee cups constitutes an attack to Christianity may seem ludicrous, but it becomes more plausible when one thinks that most American Christians were used to Christianity being the default religion for a long time. The idea that that is not so was scary and upsetting to many. Some of them have become entrenched in their belief that Christianity is under attack in their country, even though 70 percent of Americans identify as Christian.[53] This belief is not intelligible in the absence of a whole system of beliefs, desires, and emotions, according to which Christianity is the only true religion and which rejects the possibility of religious pluralism. In a sense this is the kind of attitude portrayed in the Old Testament of a "jealous" God, who demands that the Israelites be faithful to Him only. Similarly the resentment that may be genuinely felt by White workers toward non-White workers, in the past or present, is not fully intelligible outside of a White supremacy and/or nationalist perspective, broadly construed, and the resentment and distrust toward Japanese Americans could not have been genuinely felt outside of some implicit endorsement of racist ideas such as racial essences.

Thus, even if one were to insist that what is at stake in the situations I described is unjustified resentment, a genuine emotion different from envy, my reply would be that this resentment is so drenched in racist prejudice and dehumanization that it becomes its own, very scary, green-eyed but white-skinned monster, a hybrid emotion of jealousy-envy-resentment, coveting an undeserved privilege that is slipping away, intertwined with contempt, fear, and hatred of the "other."

Remember the hybrids of jealousy and envy that I described in Chapter 1. What we see here is the political, and uglier, version, the emotional counterpart of White privilege and entitlement, which motivates one to guard land, resources, jobs, women, and natural God-given talents, and to steal or spoil any "undeserved" advantage and perceived

[52] https://en.wikipedia.org/wiki/Christmas_controversies#Present-day_controversy.
[53] www.pewforum.org/religious-landscape-study/. About 7 percent practice non-Christian or "liberal" (e.g., Unitarian Universalist) faiths, 7 percent profess to be atheist or agnostic, and the rest don't care.

superiority, even when that superiority is gained at the cost of enormous hardship and adversity, as in the case of exploited immigrant laborers.

5.4.2 Emulative and Inert Political Envy

Can there be any positive role for envy in the public sphere, then? I think the answer is a *cautious* yes, because I am not as sanguine about political envy as I am about personal envy. There are situations in which a group can look at another and realize that they are not doing as well as they could, without there being any wrongdoing involved in their disadvantage, in which case envy, rather than resentment, is the fitting response. If the group cares about the good for its own sake and believes it can emulate the envied, then emulative envy is possible and appropriate in these conditions. However, emulative envy may be very fragile in a context of great inequalities and injustice.

Another scene from *Do the Right Thing* may help illustrate what I mean. The scene involves three secondary characters: ML, Coconut Sid and Sweet Dick Willie, three Black men who are often shown sitting together on the street and commenting on passersby. At some point Coconut Sid comments on how a Korean family has opened a successful business in the neighborhood, in a building that was previously boarded off, just a year after "getting off the boat." He wonders whether Koreans are "geniuses" or whether Black people are just "plain dumb." ML replies that "it's got to be because we are Black" but Sweet Dick Willie interjects that he's tired about that "old excuse." Coconut envisions a future in which a Black person will open their own business, but he seemingly can't even see himself as being the owner because he talks only about being the first customer. A small hope such as that is still mocked by Sweet Dick Willie, who forecasts that Coconut is not going to do "one damn thing" because he never does. And he adds, before heading toward the Korean store to get himself a beer, that Coconut has some nerve to speak like that since *he* got off the boat too.[54]

The scene is about two and a half minute long but there is a lot to unpack. Each character in it identifies as Black. However, there is also an implicit divide between the two African American men and the immigrant Coconut. It is not obvious what exactly Sweet Dick Willie may be implying in alluding to Coconut's immigrant status, but nothing he says presents a reason to believe that the Korean immigrants' success is *undeserved*. This is not a scene showing righteous resentment: this is about

---

[54] www.youtube.com/watch?v=ZUbvT6YKPzk. I am grateful to Myisha Cherry for this reference.

envy, and this envy could become emulative if the men felt they could emulate the target. But it's implied in the movie that none of these three men will ever open their own business. Their inert envy can easily become aggressive: Sweet Dick Willie addresses the Korean man as "Kung fu" and a brief altercation follows.

The movie foresees a dark outcome of these tensions: in 1992, during the Los Angeles riots following the beating of Rodney King, more than 2,000 stores owned by Korean Americans were ransacked and looted by African Americans. Tensions between these two groups had been mounting in the previous year, with the murder of a young Black woman, Latasha Harlins, at the hands of Korean-born store owner Soon Ja Du. Such intense hostility was likely driven by a host of aversive emotions – not just envy, but fear, resentment, contempt, and hatred. Spike Lee masterfully illustrates the complex interaction of envy with these other emotions, including some positive ones such as admiration, hope, and pride, which can prevent emulative envy's devolution into its worse counterparts. These positive emotions can be self-directed, that is, within a group, or directed to another group.

The flourishing of "Black excellence" hashtags (and related others such as #blackgirlmagic) on social media is illustrative of the hopefulness felt by younger generations and of the role that emulative envy, together with admiration, can play *within* the Black community.[55] Bolstering one's collective self-esteem, however, is going to increase the possibility of emulative envy not just within but *between* racialized groups.

A case in point is that of the historical emulation of Asian Americans of African Americans' struggle for civil rights.[56] This emulation has sometimes given rise to alliances and direct solidarity (e.g., Asian American students joining African American ones in protests and initiatives), but sometimes it has proceeded in a parallel fashion (e.g., the "Yellow power" movement). Furthermore, Asian Americans are justified in feeling emulative envy toward African Americans with regard to contexts where African Americans are in a comparatively privileged position. To mention just three cases where this might be the case: Asian athletes who play in sports dominated by Whites and Blacks, such as basketball, tend to be underrated;[57] Asian men are assessed as less masculine than men of other races

---

[55] I am grateful to Quinelle Bethelmie for having suggested this perspective to me.
[56] The same holds for disabled college students, who were inspired by Black activism in the 1960s to fight for disability rights (Shapiro 1993).
[57] www.scmp.com/sport/other-sport/article/2187416/jeremy-lin-says-it-kind-sucks-being-only-asian-american-nba; www.scmp.com/sport/other-sport/article/2170300/deceptive-jeremy-lin-freakish-john-wall-and-why-we-need-mind-our.

(Galinsky et al. 2013); Asian Americans struggle to be perceived as truly American, while African Americans are more rarely perceived as foreign.[58]

While these are injustices that are most appropriately responded to with resentment, emulative envy can work well as a *transitional* emotion: one that helps subjects of injustice overcome a state of inertia, hopelessness, and depression. Furthermore, emulative envy is not an affiliative emotion and is thus compatible with not liking the envied; therefore it is an appropriate emotion between groups whose relations are neither hostile nor friendly. Emulative envy constitutes an appropriate stepping stone to subsequent feelings of admiration and solidarity.

A virtuous cycle might be triggered such that, once relations reach a certain threshold of non-hostility, groups become able to feel emulative envy, or perhaps initially inert envy, as shown in the Spike Lee movie. Hostility might then decrease and groups might become more amenable to collaboration and alliances.

One could object that emulative envy, qua envy, cannot be a fitting political emotion given its amoral nature. But most political emotions are not about addressing systematic injustice, and yet are still often advocated as tools for political change. Hope and courage are paradigmatic examples: they are not *about* injustice, but they can help to bring about justice nonetheless.

5.5   Taming the Green-Eyed Monsters

I started this book by distinguishing between envy and jealousy through a simplified version of *Othello*, which portrayed Iago as the prototype of envy and neatly differentiated him from the jealous Othello. But here I want to end by going back to the complications and nuances of the relation between envy and jealous, a complication that is already present in the Shakespearean work.

The subtitle of *Othello* is *The Moor of Venice*. While commentators disagree on the extent to which we can apply contemporary notions of race

---

[58] Although they, too, face this bias, especially in politics. See for instance the phenomenon of "birtherism" that affected US president Barack Obama, who was accused of not being born on US soil, and similar instances of racist bias against US congresswomen Kamala Harris, Alexandria Ocasio-Cortez, Ilhan Omar, Ayanna Pressley, and Rashida Tlaib, who are similarly accused of not being American and asked to "go back to their country" (see, e.g., www.cnn.com/2019/07/17/politics/donald-trump-greenville-rally/index.html). It is notable that some of these accusations have come from African Americans (e.g., www.thedailybeast.com/kamala-harris-is-surging-and-birtherism-is-back), thus again showing a tension within the Black community.

to the text, the consensus is that Othello was indeed not White, and that Desdemona's father's opposition to the marriage is due to Othello's race (Singh 2003, 493; for the scene, see Neill 2006, 45–7). Many of the insults directed at Othello are most easily explained as racist epithets that foreshadow subsequent anti-Black tropes ("Barbarian," "Barbary horse," "lascivious Moor," "thicklips," "sooty bosom").[59]

While in my simplified version the paradigm of jealousy is Othello and Iago is all envy, in the actual play Iago's spiteful envy is tinged with jealous entitlement, and it also often masks itself as resentment, in line with envy's psychological script.[60] His personal envy is thus political, insofar as it involves vindicating certain privileges due to his class and race (in addition to perceived personal merit).

Furthermore, Othello's jealousy also has a political component. He is more vulnerable to suspicion, insecurity, and being manipulated given his isolation in Venetian society, and he is trying to defend his hard-won fortune and happiness within the context of social pressures and norms such as anti-miscegenation: his union with Desdemona is called "unnatural" by Brabantio, and Iago suggests that his and Desdemona's offspring are "coursers" and "gennets," thus anticipating analogies between miscegenation and breeding with animals. His military valor is what propelled him to where he is, but that is going to prove insufficient to keep him there, his success as fragile as that of many contemporary African American men and much more prone to reversals of fortune than their White counterparts.[61]

The personal is then political also with regard to envy, and in the public sphere the distinction between envy and jealousy is more tenuous because public goods are more subject to being perceived as a matter of desert and justice, whether that is in fact the case or not. The role of emulative envy is also more transitional and subject to devolutions than in the private sphere, for individual control is more limited and fragile.

Where does that leave us?

I think it leaves us to acknowledge that negative emotions have to be handled with particular caution at a group level, as Gustav Le Bon (1947)

---

[59] Othello's full text can be found at http://shakespeare.mit.edu/othello/full.html.

[60] Again, I do not aim to defend a hermeneutical thesis about the Shakespearean text, since I am no literature scholar. Those who read the play differently can think of this as a discussion of an *Othello* from a close possible world.

[61] There is a wealth of data on this topic, but this is the most striking visualization of the fate awaiting even wealthy Black boys in America: www.nytimes.com/interactive/2018/03/19/upshot/race-class-white-and-black-men.html.

warned us (van Kleef and Fischer 2015, 2). Unlike in Kallipolis, the flourishing of our city may depend on different emotional dynamics than the ones governing the flourishing of our soul.[62] Even though I have argued that emulative envy can be a private virtue, I am hesitant about its potential as a public one. But I hope I have suggested some of its possibilities as well as its risks, and that others will take these ideas and develop them further.

---

[62] I am, of course, alluding here to Plato's *Republic*.

Conclusion
Envy and Human Goodness

Whenever I praise my younger daughter's achievements, her older sister *immediately* jumps in: "What about *me*? Am *I* good?" And my usual response is: "This is not a competition."

Notwithstanding all of my theoretical beliefs, my immediate response to my children's sibling rivalry, their jealousy and envy, is to fall back on conventional expectations. I refuse to make comparisons. I say the things parents are supposed to say: "don't compare yourself to others; what matters is what you do, who you are." But the truth is more complex and perhaps less reassuring.

The truth is that our lives are often competitive; that our standards of goodness are almost always comparative; and that envy, jealousy, and other rivalrous emotions are often *appropriate*. Thus, I should let my children feel, and learn from, those emotions. I should teach them how to cope with those unpleasant feelings productively, rather than rushing to make them feel better, to eschew the difficult interactions caused by them.

Toward the beginning of the book I made a crucial assumption: that envy can be fitting. That, in other words, there are certain circumstances in which anybody has a *pro tanto reason* to feel envy, no matter their other predispositions or values. All my controversial claims about envy – that it can be prudentially or morally good and even virtuous – rely on this initial assumption.[1] But that is also a controversial assumption.

I have mentioned envy's *signaling role* before.[2] From a psychological and sociological perspective envy reveals to the individual what they care about,

---

[1] There might be cases where unfitting envy is prudentially or morally good from a consequentialist standpoint. A presumptuous emulative envier, for instance, might end up improving themselves even though their assessment of the situation was mistaken.

[2] The signals might be mixed, and confused, and might take some reflection and introspection to decipher. We can draw a distinction between goods that make us aware that we envy another person (call them *triggering goods*) and goods that we truly envy people for, the ones that we care about (call them *primary goods*). For instance, I might envy's someone fancy clothes, but then realize that I don't

whether they are aware of it or not, and the same holds for society at large: looking at what people envy in different countries or groups is very indicative of the values of those collectives. But the psychological and sociological approach ignores deeper issues of value. Many philosophers resist the idea of fitting envy on the grounds that comparative assessments of value are never appropriate. They think that what matters to flourishing is what one has, not what one lacks, and that consequently envy is necessarily unfitting and genuine goodness is never worth of being envied (see for instance the discussion of Plato and Kant in the Appendix).

D'Arms and Jacobson offer a persuasive defense of envy's fittingness conditions, which I draw from here. But my argumentative strategy is different from theirs. Their aim is to demonstrate that all *human sentiments* (defined as syndromes of thought, feeling, and motivation, and which constitute a core subset of the emotions) can be fitting, insofar as they detect authentic and distinctive human values. They use envy as one particularly hard case. Once it can be shown that even envy can be fitting, then *a fortiori* their general claim follows. Thus, they show that envy is an emotional response to comparative ranking. "The propensity to envy is a price of caring about relative standing," they say (D'Arms and Jacobson 2005, 123), and they go on to argue that this psychological concern is both deep – that is, hard to get rid of at the species level – and wide, which means that it is enmeshed with a variety of psychological responses (such as envy and pride) and values such as excellence. They show that excellence is an inherently comparative notion, starting with its very etymology, since "to excel" means "to surpass, to do better than." Given that excellence is a central human value, emotional responses to relative standing, such as pride and envy, can be fitting.

One obvious difference between my view and theirs is that I do not think envy always constitutes a "price" to pay just so that we can have pride and excellence on the positive side. They take envy to be necessarily malicious, and thus an emotion we should try to not feel and definitely ought not to act on. I obviously disagree; envy contains both its costs and its benefits within itself. But, also, what I aim to do here is to expand on their discussion of goodness. They use the notions of positional goods and

---

real care about fancy clothes, but I care about having such financial security that I can afford to buy fancy clothes. We can also draw a distinction between primary goods and goods that we come to envy people for as a consequence of the fact that the envied values them (call them *secondary* goods). For instance, I might envy someone because they are much more confident than me (that is the primary good), and as a consequence of this envy I come to envy their success at ballroom dancing, even though I don't really care ballroom dancing.

of comparative excellence in order to show that envy can be fitting. I go further and distinguish different ways in which social comparison intervenes in shaping human goodness at both a metaphysical and epistemic level.

Let us go back to my daughter's eagerness to hear that she is better than, or at least as good as, her sister (often it's the former she wants, but she will grudgingly settle for the latter).

In my children's case sometimes I refuse to draw a comparison because it would be an unfair and meaningless one: one is three years older than the other, and so usually I praise them for skills or outcomes that cannot be sensibly compared. When my daughter complains, I respond, "Do you want to be praised as if you were a little child?" and then I go on to explain their different but equal virtues, or I try to induce a mindful exploration of her own feelings ("Why do you feel that way?").

But, like many other parents, there are times when I cannot help but compare them, especially where the comparison is appropriate: one is kinder, while the other is tidier; one is more affectionate, while the other more generous. In general I am keenly aware of the many different ways in which one is more or less gifted or advantaged than the other. Comparing them is unavoidable, and it is normal (recall that frequent comparison to one's sibling contribute to the intertwining of love and envy discussed in Chapter 4).

One of the main reasons parents are told to never compare a child to another is that it may elicit envy. But this injunction is in tension with the practice of pointing out the positive behavior that we want our children to emulate (Kant coherently condemned this pedagogical practice, insofar as it was based on a comparative understanding of goodness that he wholeheartedly rejected; see Appendix).

But can children be assessed as good on their own merits? Can a person, more generally, be said to be excellent without there being an implicit comparison with other individuals in the same comparison class?

Moving from children to parents we see more comparisons taking place. In *All Joy and No Fun: The Paradox of Modern Parenthood*, Jennifer Senior writes endlessly about how parents of both genders compare themselves to others in order to figure out whether they are doing it right. She cites another author, Michael Lewis, who confirms this in the context of division of labor with regard to childcare: "They don't care if they are getting a raw deal so long as everyone is getting the same deal" (Lewis 2009, as cited in Senior 2014, 92). Lewis goes on to say that the problem with modern parenting is that "there are no standards and it's possible that there never again will be" (Senior 2014, 92). But that is false: there are standards, much as there always were, namely based on what other parents, taken as template or models, are doing. What modernity has changed in this regard is the amount of available models and the difficulty in knowing what to do with them. I started with the example of my daughters wondering whether they are good children, but the same applies to parents: am I a good mother? How can I tell? By comparing myself to other mothers: do they yell less than me? Do they spend more time with their children? Being a parent is exhausting these days for many reasons, but one is the immediate access to an apparently infinite number of mommy blogs providing innumerable chances to compare oneself – just one of the many ways in which the internet has multiplied our chances at social comparison.[3]

Instagram, Facebook, and all the other social media are replete with people boasting about their good fortune, talents, and achievements, and they become mirrors on the wall who constantly refuse to tell us that we are the fairest in the land. D'Arms and Jacobson, in making their case that many goods that are central to flourishing are necessarily dependent on social comparison, claim: "Part of the desire to achieve is surely an aspiration to excellence, and excellence in various endeavors – from scholarship to the arts, industry, even athletics – contributes to human flourishing. Yet which accomplishments count as excellent, or sufficiently good to be worthy of pride, is largely a function of the performance of others (especially those who are nearby)" (2005, 123). Note the list of domains: scholarship, arts, industry, and athletics. In all of these central areas of our lives our standards of excellences are determined in crucial ways by other people's achievements. I provide more examples below, but one that concerns me personally comes from a field that is at the intersection of art and athletics, namely ballet. Thirty years ago, being able to do thirty-two *fouettés* on pointe was considered the pinnacle of a ballerina's technique. Nowadays it would be unthinkable for any "principal dancer" to limit herself to that. Complications and embellishments of various sorts, such as extra pirouettes or changes in direction, need to be added. This is simply because too many people are now capable of what used to be an amazing achievement, and the standards have changed. Similar points apply to sports records: Simone Biles has obliterated record after record

---

[3] Many of these versions of parenthood are of course very curated and not necessarily authentic, which makes the comparison to oneself both more painful and less informative. Thanks to Vanessa Carbonell for pointing this out.

in gymnastics,[4] Eliud Kipchoge can run a marathon in under two hours (his official world record hovering barely over that), and so forth.[5]

Any threshold that is used to judge success is going to be determined by looking at what other individuals on average accomplish, or even just *are*. Seemingly intrinsic physical properties such as normal growth are measured with inherently comparative tools: growth charts that are used by pediatricians are based on measuring thousands of children, against which each child is now compared. Being a "small" child actually means being *smaller* than the average child in that original sample. Similar considerations hold for the majority of properties of bodies and minds that we deem good, whether it is IQ or endurance and speed.[6]

More precisely, many intrinsic physical or mental properties are uninteresting in themselves. Perfect symmetry is an inherent property of an object, but whether or not it is aesthetically valuable seems to depend on how many objects possess it; the physical attractiveness of people may also be said to be a function of symmetry, but if all humans beings were perfectly symmetrical we would likely not be attracted to it, or prize it as much as we do. Similarly, health standards are contextual and culturally relative for this reason. What counts as being healthy varies depending on time, place, and circumstances.[7]

You might think that there are components of flourishing that are obviously non-comparative. Pleasure seems like a good candidate because certainly it is a component of a good life, and most pleasures seem to have nothing to do with what others feel. But even with pleasure there is space for comparison. Recall Nozick's seemingly jocular reference to the quality of orgasm as something people may envy each other for. Everybody who

---

[4] It is worth noting that Biles defies conventions of gymnastics, in that she is Black in a traditionally White-dominated field, thus having faced some challenging, and unfair, comparisons (https://time .com/4450741/olympics-gymnastics-diversity/). She also been featured in a beauty campaign with the hashtag #nocompetition (promoted by a cosmetics brand – the ad asks: "When did beauty become a competition?" Since forever, is my answer). Biles and her peers train many more hours than their counterparts in the 1960s, which is the only way to achieve the technical feats that are expected of them (see: www.sutori.com/story/the-ideal-gymnast-body-type–gvHzFRrQZFZJhU3g383BrwpU).

[5] This is not to say such progression is unavoidable or linear. Some limits are set by what human bodies can or cannot achieve, and some record holders from past decades remain unbeaten.

[6] Here I am only alluding at a host of complex issues having to do not just with goodness, but with the very concepts of normalcy and normality. I cannot possibly do justice to those issues here, but want to at least acknowledge the important contributions of philosophers of disability on the topic of who counts as a normal, well-developed child or person. Readers who are unfamiliar with those contributions would do well to start with Kittay 2019, especially part I.

[7] For a discussion of healthiness as a relative/contextual, yet real, property, see Bloomfield 2001, esp. ch. 1.

can have an orgasm surely enjoys it. But notice how quickly comparison creeps in. People often wonder whether others experience more sexual pleasure than they do, whether they are more adventurous, or whether they live more exciting lives. Comparison may also take place within oneself, with one's younger self, for instance, or simply yesterday's ("today's wasn't as good as last week's").

In general the question is often: how can I tell whether *this thing*, this experience here, this event, this trait, is good? I compare. And often I compare to what others have. How else are we supposed to know what is normal, what is achievable, and what is superlative?

Note that there are two ways in which goodness or value may be said to be comparative: metaphysical and epistemic.

Some things cannot *be* good (and hence are not properly judged to be good) without some people doing better than others. The comparison here is metaphysically and logically necessary. This is the case of *positional goods*, which are defined as "goods the absolute value of which, to their possessors, depends on those possessors' place in the distribution of the good – on their relative standing with respect to the good in question" (Brighouse and Swift 2006, 474). A standard example of a positional good is honor: to be honorable in a certain society means to be anointed, to be given a social status that is higher than other people's. To be in any honor association is valuable precisely because not everybody gets in – only a small portion of individuals gets in and *that* is where its value stems from.[8]

Other typical examples of positional goods are connected to social status, and in a consumeristic society they are often luxury material goods, objects or experiences that cost a lot of money and cannot be afforded by many people and thus function as status symbols. These tend to often be dismissed as inauthentic goods, not only by moral philosophers but also by sociologists and psychologists, for good reasons: evidence shows that they do not actually bring happiness, and one of the reasons why they don't is that agents are caught up in an arms race, which is never-ending and collectively damaging (see, e.g., Frank 1999). But there are positional goods that are not so easily rejected as false idols: educational pedigrees are one such case. An Ivy League degree has value also (some might say primarily) in virtue of the social currency it carries, and not just because of

---

[8] In economics the discussion on positional goods is often framed in terms of "positional concerns" (Solnick and Hemenway 1998). Note that *bads* may be less positional than goods (Solnick and Hemenway 2005), but I won't be discussing this asymmetry here. There is some evidence that everyone has positional concerns in at least some domain (Solnick and Hemenway 2005).

the education that is expected to be associated with it, as is shown by the success of many an underachieving student who can nevertheless tout having graduated from a prestigious institution (the list of US presidents provides some examples). These degrees are prized because it is very difficult to be admitted to one of those schools. Similarly with publications: the higher the rejection rate of a journal the better the journal is taken to be. (We can quibble about the causal chain here: it is possible that initially a journal is taken to be very good because of its editors – editors who often come from prestigious institutions, but never mind that – but soon enough the rejection rate by itself becomes a measurement of goodness all by itself. A journal is deemed prestigious *insofar as* it is hard to publish in it.) Variations of this mechanisms can be found everywhere: it seems a robust feature of human psychology that we value being part of exclusive clubs. Groucho Marx's joke that he does not want to be a member of a club that admits him relies in part on this truth.

Furthermore, many goods, whether they are themselves positional or not, have *latent* positional aspects, as argued by Brighouse and Swift (2006, 478–9). Even if healthiness is not positional in itself, the healthier a person is the greater access they have to jobs, education, and other scarce goods.[9] Similarly with prestigious degrees and publications: even if you do not consider them positional in themselves they surely have positional aspects insofar as they are part of a causal chain such that it is in virtue of the fact that they are scarce goods that they play a crucial instrumental role in achieving goods such as well-paid rewarding jobs. Similar considerations apply for beauty, or wits, insofar as those properties allow people to get ahead in the world.

But many of the objects and properties described above rely on comparison in a second, *epistemic* sense: their standards are set through comparison, as I illustrated at the beginning. Whether I am perceived by others as healthy, beautiful, intelligent,and so forth depends on how I compare to others in my comparison class, on community standards, on ideas of "normality" and "function" that cannot but be comparative. Thus, I have made a metaphysical claim (that much human goodness

---

[9] I want to flag that Brighouse and Swift's discussion contains ableist passages, such as when they claim: "[t]he value to me of my health does depend on how healthy others are. In the land of the blind, the one-eyed man is king" (Brighouse and Swift 2006, 479). It is far from obvious that in the land of the blind the one-eyed man is king, since presumably in the land of the blind everything is set up to accommodate the blind, and the one eyed-man might actually be at a great disadvantage: there would be no use of artificial lights, everything would be written in Braille, etc. However, I think their general points are still valid.

depends on implicit or explicit rankings and positionality) and an epistemic one (that we use implicit or explicit comparison to know what position we occupy in this continuum of goodness).[10]

These are claims that go against, or at least are in tension with, multiple venerable traditions, such as Platonism, Stoicism, Christianity, and Kantianism. I cannot possibly defend them in full here, which is why I sneakily relegate them to the end. But they are not at all shocking from a layperson's perspective. As Brighouse and Swift put it: "[i]t is a commonplace that people's happiness depends, in part, on their perceived place in the distribution of other goods" (2006, 480; see alsi Frey and Stutzer 2002; Layard 2005). This is true even with regard to the most quantifiable, seemingly non-positional good of all: money. You would think it's always more valuable to have more money rather than less. But people prefer to make less money in absolute terms, provided that they make as much or more than their peers (Boyce et al. 2010), which is why employers have such strong incentives to keep salaries private: people are much more likely to ask for raises once they discover they make less than others, even when they are satisfied with their salary.[11]

The connection between happiness and positionality may be seen as an example of human irrationality and it often surprises those who are not familiar with the empirical literature. But it is neither irrational nor surprising once we consider how not just our psychology but our social reality is deeply shaped by comparison. It is not simply that our conception of the self, of our talents, of our character is inherently comparative. It is our conception of pretty much *anything that matters* that is based on interpersonal comparisons, and, in many cases, it is strictly dependent on one's position in those comparison scales. This is especially true with regard to scarce or finite resources, but we live in a world where socioeconomic inequalities are rising and natural resources are diminishing.

Martha Nussbaum (1986) has already argued that human goodness is necessarily fragile. Her argument was based on the role that *luck* plays in human events. Here I suggest that one element of luck, one other way in which humans lack control over their fate and happiness, is how they

---

[10] Thank you to Vanessa Carbonell for help with this formulation and for much helpful feedback on this Conclusion.
[11] One might reply that the concern here is fairness. But again, how is fairness assessed? By comparing oneself to others. A second reply might be that actually money is for a lot of people always positional, since what people care about is to be rich, not to have a certain amount of money, and so the example about money is not as powerful as I make it sound. But if that is true, it is still a confirmation of how widespread positional goods are.

compare themselves to others with regard to their physical and mental talents, their material resources, their health, their relationships, their achievements, and even their pleasures.

In this list of contributors to *eudaimonia* one is notably absent: moral virtue. The Stoics are not listening to me already, but perhaps a Kantian reader is still around and might at this point triumphantly point out that none of this truly matters: that what we ought to care about is the quality of our will. Emboldened by such a resistance a reader of Plato might add that surely *sophia* or intellectual wisdom is not wholly comparative; a religious reader might jump in to say that God's love is infinitely shareable and we do not need to compete for it.

Now, a first response is to happily concede that I do not think that goodness is *always* comparative or positional. A walk in the park on a sunny day when the birds are chirping and the children are laughing is a source of joy, pleasure, and goodness that has no need for comparison or competition. There are many such goods. And surely some of us may be more attracted to those goods. Much like D'Arms and Jacobson (2005) I am a pluralist in terms of value and think there are many ways to thrive, some of which do not involve a role for rivalrous emotions such as envy, or for comparative goods such as excellence. The life of religious contemplation can be a blessed one, and so is the life of a satisfied pig. Neither of them attracts me, however, and I suspect the same holds for many of us.

I do care about being a morally good person, but there are many ways in which comparison affects morality too. Virtue ethics is a clear example, especially in an Aristotelian framework where both the notion of the mean and the idea of the *phronimos* as a moral exemplar are relational and comparative, at both an ontological and epistemic level. Consequentialist approaches always rely on comparison, especially if they involve maximization.[12] Even an ethics of care, as shown by the discussion of good children and good parents, will end up having to rely on comparisons sometimes. Is my child well cared-for? The answer in part depends on how well cared-for other children are.

Whenever we ask the question of goodness ("Am I good enough?" "Is this object a good instance of its kind?" "Is this a good life?") we search for an answer by looking around, we cast a sidelong gaze, we compare

---

[12] Consequentialist comparisons, however, may be between states of affairs, and thus not be interpersonal. I am thankful to Francesco Orsi for pointing this out, and for insightful comments on this Conclusion.

ourselves to others. If we perceive ourselves – what we own or how we live – as falling short, then we envy.

Envy's signaling value, then, may be much more important than we previously thought.[13] If most of human goodness is relational, comparative, competitive, or positional, then it is not surprising that envy is a universal emotion. It safeguards our chance at happiness.

---

[13] For a different (compatible with mine) perspective on the intrinsic moral value of envy, see Thomason 2015. Thomason argues that envy is intrinsically morally valuable because it signals our investment in our values and is thus integral to moral agency.

In the Beginning Was Phthonos:
A Short History of Envy

What could be more fatal than this disease? It ruins our life, perverts our nature, arouses hatred of the goods bestowed on us by God, and places us in a hostile relation toward Him. What drove the Devil, that author of evils, to wage furious war upon mankind? Was it not envy? Because of envy, too, he was guilty even of open conflict with God. Filled with bitterness against God because of His liberality toward man, he wreaked vengeance upon man, since he was unable to avenge himself upon God. Cain also attempted this maneuver – Cain, that first disciple of the Devil, who learned from him envy and murder, crimes of brother against brother.

Basil of Caesarea, *Homily on Envy*

A.1 Introduction: Envy in Western History of Philosophy

Envy is considered the motivation for the first murder, a fratricide no less, as recounted in Genesis 4:3–8.[1] It is a vice that appears repeatedly in the Bible,[2] in the Rabbinic literature and the Jewish moralists' writings,[3] and, as we shall see, in the works of Christian and Islamic philosophers. But the condemnation of envy as a destructive anti-goodness force precedes, and

I am extremely grateful to Michael Della Rocca and Fatema Amijee for very helpful feedback on this Appendix. I am also thankful to Andrew Arlig, Matteo Di Giovanni, Elizabeth Goodnick, Hadi Jorati, Marcy Lascano, Stephen Ogden, Gary Ostertag, Kevin Timpe, and Christina Van Dyke for help with bibliographic references. Finally, I thank Stephen Darwall, Scott Edgar, E. Sonny Elizondo, Tamar Szabó Gendler, Lisa Gilson, June Gruber, Verity Harte, Austen Haynes, Amy Lara, Kelley Schiffman, Alex Silverman, Kenneth Winkler, and Alexander Worsnip and all the participants of SEMPY at Yale for their feedback on previous versions of this chapter.

[1] Both Augustine and Basil interpret Cain's actions as due to envy. See Section A.3.1.
[2] In addition to the killing of Abel, envy arguably motivates Joseph's brothers to sell Joseph as a slave, Saul to try to kill David, and the false mother in Solomon's story to accept that the baby whom she claims to be hers be cut in two – just to mention the most famous examples (the last one being the most ancient instance of what is now labeled as "baby envy," a popular topic on the internet). See Simmel 2008 for a discussion of these and other examples of envy in the Old Testament.
[3] See Schimmel 2008 for a review of envy in the Jewish tradition. Conversely, Christians have accused Jews of being motivated by envy when they failed to welcome Jesus as their savior. See Section A.3.1.

extends beyond, the Judeo-Christian tradition: Daoism (i.e., Taoism),[4] Confucianism,[5] Buddhism,[6] Hinduism,[7] and Islam[8] all condemn envy. However, even within this global and far-reaching antipathy we find the seeds of a different, more optimistic approach – one that foreshadows the thesis I have defended in this book: that envy is not all bad.

In this Appendix I provide a short, and somewhat opinionated, history of envy in Western philosophy, with a focus on ancient and modern philosophy. My hope is to provide a starting point for historians interested in emotions and for moral psychologists interested in the historical roots of envy, so that they can develop and pursue the connections highlighted here. It may also be interesting for any reader to see how the notions discussed in the book have developed through time and place. However, the Appendix can also be read independently from the book (hence some redundancies and repetition with regard to the central notions).

As I said, the scope of this survey is limited to what is traditionally, if imprecisely, called the "Western" tradition – with the (arguable) exception of Arabic philosophy, which is itself deeply interconnected with the Greek, Jewish, and Christian traditions. However, since all world philosophies and religions talk about envy, I think the philosophy of envy would benefit from cross-cultural investigations. I regret not being able to pursue this task myself at this time.

Here is an overview of what follows. I start by discussing envy in the ancient Greek tradition. In particular, I review various notions of *phthonos* (roughly translated as "malicious envy") in the Platonic corpus, Aristotle's discussion of both *phthonos* and *zēlos* (benign or emulative envy/emulation) in the *Rhetoric* and in the *Nicomachean* and *Eudemian Ethics*, and Plutarch's analysis of hatred and envy in *De Invidia et Odio*. I then move on to five thinkers in the Christian tradition (Basil of Caesarea, Augustine, Gregory the Great, Thomas Aquinas, and Catherine of

---

[4] The *Xiang'er Commentary* (*c.*200 CE) contains explicit injunctions against envy, but allusions to the problems caused by envy can be found already in the third verse of the *Daodejing* (i.e., *Tao-te ching*), whose date of composition is debated, but cannot be later than the third century BCE (cf. Chan 2012).

[5] We find an indirect criticism of envy in Confucius' *Analects* 14.1; one in Mengzi's (i.e., Mencius') eponymous collection of book VI, Part A, 17, and another one in Xunzi's work *Human Nature Is Bad* (23.1). Even though there are no passages that are consistently translated as explicit condemnations of envy, David Wong in an email correspondence assures me that "it is uncontroversial to say that all three of these would condemn envy if presented with a case of it." See also Wong 2013, par. 2.6, for some relevant context.

[6] "Irshya" ("envy" in Sanskrit) is condemned in every Buddhist tradition. Cf. Tuske 2011.

[7] Cf. the *Bhagavad-Gita* (12:15 and 16:3), and also the envious Duryodhana in the epic work *Mahabharata*.

[8] The Islamic condemnation of envy ("ḥasad" حسد) is unsurprising given that its theology and ethics derive from the Judaic tradition. See Section A.3.5 for more details.

Siena) and two Islamic ones (Al-Qushayrī and Al-Ghazálí). With these theologians, envy, already considered vicious by their predecessors, becomes demonic and sinful.

By the end of the Middle Ages the main characteristics of envy, the conditions in which it arises, the kind of behaviors it motivates, the dispositions it is associated with, and its difference with cognate emotions like emulation, resentment, and Schadenfreude have all been discussed, and arguably correctly identified by one author or other.

And yet, early modern reflections on envy are both rich and diverse, bringing to light novel concerns and perspectives. I analyze envy in Francis Bacon, Descartes, Hobbes, Butler, Spinoza, Leibniz, Locke, Mandeville, Smith, Hume, and Kant. I discuss these authors according to two themes. The first one concerns the underlying psychological mechanisms of envy, and, in particular, the role that cognitive and affective processes such as comparison, imitation, and sympathy play in our social emotional lives. These authors show, sometimes unwittingly, that the same psychological tendencies that motivate our darkest side are also responsible for our brightest one. Relatedly, the second theme is that of political implications and public manifestations, of our private passions and vices. How does envy affect social realities and political institutions? It is often assumed in contemporary discourse that envy cannot but be a destructive force, but many of these philosophers find in envy some silver lining, or even consider it a necessary feature for civilization.

I end this historical review with an author from the twentieth century: John Rawls. Even though he is much closer to us chronologically than a Rousseau or a Kant, it seems to me that his discussion of envy, as of many other things, has been so influential in the following tradition that deserves to be included here.

A.2 Envy as a *Pathos* in the Ancient Greek Tradition

How is envy said in ancient Greek? There is no simple answer to this question. Partly this is due to the fact that "ancient Greek" in its broadest construal spans from the ninth century BCE to the fourth century CE, and partly it is due to the fact that even within much narrower time frames (e.g., the classical period) the same words are used with different meanings by different authors, and are, furthermore, translated and interpreted differently in English versions. The usual issues concerning translation and interpretation, and the relationship between language, concepts, and emotions (Lutz 1988), are even more thorny when it comes to a culture such as the ancient Greek one.[9] David Konstan warns us that "we cannot take it for granted that the Greek words map neatly onto our own emotional vocabulary" (Konstan 2006, x), and Ed Sanders is similarly wary of an approach that looks for "one-to-one equivalents" (Sanders 2014, 4). However, being aware of cultural differences and specificities does not imply that we cannot find meaningful and even large overlaps between Greek notions and ours. As Sanders puts it:

> certainly an ancient Greek might express *orgê* in some different situations and some different ways to when or how modern Anglophones might express anger, and they might think of the emotion in subtly different ways (e.g., as expressed by different metaphors), but understanding those differences is the entire purpose of a scholarly study; if anger will perfectly well translate *orgê* 95 percent of the time, it seems otiose not to use that perfectly respectable word when discussing a given instance of *orgê* in (or translating one into) English – unless the instance falls within the other 5 percent. This problem is in fact not confined to the study of emotions but covers a wide range of ethical, social, political, and institutional vocabulary for which there is no absolute equivalence between ancient Greek and modern terminology (in any language). To translate only where there is complete equivalence would, if pursued rigorously, lead to "translations" in which most of the words of necessity remained in Greek. (Sanders 2014, 6)

What is "envy" then, in ancient classical Greek culture? The simplest answer is *phthonos*, which is usually translated as "envy," "ill will," "begrudging," or "malice," and which always denotes a malicious emotion or attitude.[10] Sanders, however, in his comprehensive 2014 study on envy in the archaic and classical period, has identified *twelve* different "scripts," that is, distinctive kinds of emotional scenarios, for *phthonos* and cognate forms: begrudging-refusal (only archaic); odious/hateful/hostility; spite/malice/Schadenfreude; censure; begrudging envy; covetous envy; rivalry; begrudging sharing; two slightly different variations of possessive jealousy; sexual jealousy; and finally the so-called envy of the gods (*phthonos theōn*).[11]

Sanders argues that his script approach is particularly suitable to investigating the Greek notions of envy and jealousy insofar as they not only differ from ours, but are also stigmatized and often unconscious emotions,

---

[9] For an overview of these issues, see Konstan 2006 (introduction) and Sanders 2014 (ch. 1).

[10] Some interpreters advocate for translating it as "jealousy," e.g., Brisson 2000, but that is uncommon (even though it might be appropriate in some linguistic contexts). See also discussion about "scripts" below.

[11] For details and explanation of these scripts, see Sanders 2014, 33–46 and table 3.1 for a summary.

and thus one might find descriptions of the emotional experience without a corresponding label.

Both Sanders and Konstan, however, end up focusing on narrower – and closer to ours – notions of *phthonos* as it is employed in classical Athenian contexts, with a particular interest in Aristotle's works. I follow a similar approach, and review the most notable accounts of envy: those found in Plato, Aristotle, and Plutarch.

For all of them, *pathē* (from which the word "passion" ultimately derives) are different from drives or appetites (such as sexual desire), and they are not conceived in terms of "internal states of excitation" (Konstan 2006, xii), which is how modern philosophers thought of emotions. Rather, "the emotions are elicited by our interpretation of the words, acts, and intentions of others" (ibid.) and thus they can be affected by rational deliberation and can be shaped by persuasion and by education. In general, Greek philosophers gave prominence to the role of cognition in emotional experience (with some significant differences regarding the role of affect, which is important in Aristotle). But here too, as I have done in the rest of the book, I shall remain uncommitted on general theories of emotions unless it directly affects the present discussion.

A.2.1   *Phthonos in Plato*

In the classical period *phthonos* appears mostly, albeit not exclusively, in negative terms. That is certainly the case within the Platonic corpus, where *phthonos* is consistently presented as a vice. There are six dialogues where *phthonos* makes a significant appearance.

In three of them – *Menexenus, Republic, Laws* – nicely distributed across the three groupings of Platonic dialogues,[12] *phthonos* refers to what we would call envy in a traditional sense, as a malicious and thus vicious emotion, but the mentions are not sufficiently extensive to provide further details about a Platonic[13] conception of envy.

In the *Menexenus*, Aspasia (through Socrates) talks about how peace following the defeat of the "barbarians" (that is, the Persians) brought on the city "what people generally inflict on the successful: jealousy

---

[12] See Cooper 1997, xxi–xxi for a review of the "thematic" versus "chronological" way of distinguishing among dialogues. Independently from one's preferred way, these three dialogues belong to different groupings.

[13] To keep things simple I assume that even in the Socratic dialogues we find a "Platonic" account, at least in the weak sense that Plato agreed with it, even though the position expressed might have been Socratic in origin.

and – through jealousy – ill-will" (*Mx.* 242a, tr. Paul Ryan, where "jealousy" translates *zēlos* and "ill will" translates *phthonos*). In the *Republic, phthonos* is one of the many vices that afflict the tyrant (e.g., IX 580a1, tyrant is *phthoneros,* consistently rendered as "envious" across different translations). Finally, in the *Laws* it is presented among the passions that are a source of injustice and disorder (IX 863e5–8, usually translated as "envy," again).

In the remaining three dialogues, however, we find longer, or at any rate more significant, analyses.

In the *Timaeus,* Plato is responsible for an innovative conception of deity: in contrast with the traditional image in Greek mythology of *phthoneroi theoi* (envious/jealous gods), he remarks that the Demiurge, being good, is free from *phthonos* (*Timaeus* 29d7–e2). According to F. G. Herrmann (2003), the Demiurge is in this respect similar to the real philosopher (and thus to a philosopher king), as conceived by Plato. Thanks to his envy-free nature the Demiurge is able to create a world that is, like himself, as good as possible.[14]

In the *Phaedrus,* too, envy is said to be absent in the gods' chorus (247a7), but there is also a much more detailed discussion of *phthonos* in human lives. According to Alessandra Fussi, "[j]ealousy in Phaedrus's speech and envy in Socrates's subsequent harangue are shown to be typical expressions of vulgar *eros,* while in the Palinode Socrates explains that noble *eros* is without *phthonos,* both in its divine and in its human incarnations" (Fussi 2017, 83).

Thus, in *Phaedrus phthonos* is used in both the "sexual jealousy" (232c–232e, and 240d–e) and in the "begrudging envy" and "spite/malice Schadenfreude" (239a–240d) scripts, to use Sanders' definitions, according to which the envier wants primarily to deprive the envied of the good, and to spoil the good, respectively (again, cf. Sanders 2014, 46).[15]

True, noble love is based not on physical beauty, which is not only ephemeral but out of our control, limited, nonshareable, and positional, but rather on a more transcendental and divine kind which we do not have to compete for: "[i]f we understood that we can all be equally nourished by

---

[14] Herrmann provides a detailed analysis of the role *phthonos* plays in *Timaeus,* and puts it in relation the discussion in other dialogues, primarily *Phaedrus* and *Republic.* Among other claims, Herrmann argues that Plato's treatment of *phthonos* breaks with tradition not only with regard to deity, but also with regard to the norms of an honor culture: Plato rejects a competitive picture of society, which Aristotle seemingly endorses, in which social esteem and external recognition assert individual worth. For a consonant view, see Gill 2003.

[15] Both Fussi 2017 and Herrmann 2003 have rewarding discussions of these passages.

beauty without consuming or destroying it, *phthonos* would not arise" (Fussi 2017, 85).

The common denominator among these very different discussions is that *phthonos* is vicious insofar as it hinders the pursuit of authentic goodness (of philosophical truths, and of true love, which of course for Plato are closely related) and consequently it damages individual and collective flourishing. Gods, true lovers, and philosophers should all be free from *phthonos*.[16]

However, *Philebus* 48b–50e offers a most intriguing, but also obscure, picture, which stands in partial tension with this otherwise coherent and consistent condemnation of *phthonos*. The interpretation of this short passage is debated,[17] and this is not the place for a fine-grained analysis or a hermeneutical attempt on my part. I shall only highlight some features relevant for our topic.

In *Philebus* Plato talks about *phthonos* in the context of a discussion of mixed pleasures of the soul, and, more specifically, he refers to a specific kind of *phthonos*, a "childish" (*paidikos*) one that we feel especially toward comic characters.[18] He again claims that *phthonos* is "unjust" (49d6–7) but he introduces two novel elements. First, he presents it as a pain mixed with pleasure. Therefore, *phthonos* here cannot refer only to what in English we call envy, not even malicious or begrudging envy, as in the dialogues mentioned before. This pleasurable component is a response to seeing others make a fool of themselves, in particular, but in general being subject to misfortune. Thus, it seems that Plato is thinking here of what Aristotle later will call *epichairekakia*, that is, pleasure felt at other people's misfortune – what we now call Schadenfreude. *Phthonos*' semantic range is thus wider in *Philebus* than in the other Platonic *loci*. It is better thought as malicious envy + Schadenfreude, and it is usually and aptly translated as "malice."[19] In subsequent philosophical accounts, and in contemporary empirical investigations, this form of malicious pleasure is generally

---

[16] As remarked in Herrmann 2003, 59, lack of *phthonos*, *aphthonia*, is recommended in both *Protagoras* 320c1, 327a–b and *Symposium* 210d6, 213d2, both in tune with the *Republic* and *Laws* passages mentioned above.

[17] See, e.g., Hackforth 1945, 92–3; Frede 1992, 1993, lii–liii; Migliori 1993, 249–54; Delcomminette 2006, 444–8; Halliwell 2008, 300–2; Austin 2012; Cain 2017; Fussi 2017.

[18] Whether he is talking *only* of an emotion directed at comedic characters or *also* at real-life people is controversial. I lean toward the latter, but I do not defend this view here.

[19] Sanders calls this script "spite/malice/Schadenfreude" (Sanders 2014, 46, table 3.1; see also discussion on pp. 101–3). Frede 1996, 275 seems to think of the Rhetoric's *phthonos* as a mixture of pleasure and pain as well. However, Aristotle seems to not go as far as Plato in thinking that envy *itself* includes pleasure at others' misfortune. Rather, he talks of a common state of mind for both (1388a24–7), which is compatible with conceiving of them as separate

considered to stem from the separate and distinct, albeit often co-occurring, emotion of Schadenfreude.[20]

Giving a fuller account of *phthonos'* ontology in the *Philebus* requires committing to a specific interpretation of Plato's theory of pleasure and pain. Dorothea Frede (1992) has argued that pleasure is perceived restoration and pain is perceived destruction. If that were correct we might think of *phthonos* as a mixed pleasure because it involves both a perceived destruction and a perceived restoration. One might venture to say that *phthonos* is thus the consequence of a perceived destruction because it is connected to a wounded self-esteem, which is then perceived to be restored, correctly or incorrectly, through bringing down the object of one's envy by rejoicing at their misfortune. If this turned out to be a plausible interpretation, we could see in Plato a precursor of contemporary philosophers such as Gabriele Taylor (see Section 2.4.1.1).

There is a second interesting novelty in *Philebus*: Plato seems to think that feeling *phthonos* toward enemies is not objectionable, perhaps because, as Fussi puts it, "we do not owe everybody a sympathetic response" (Fussi 2017, 79).[21] This is the only place, as far as I am aware, where Plato talks about *phthonos* as justified.

Setting aside these more speculative observations, it remains that Plato's account of *phthonos* well represents an important trend in the philosophical discussion of envy, which we see more prominently in the Christian tradition: the conviction that (malicious) envy is, as Chaucer puts it in *The Parson's Tale*, "against all virtues and against all manners of goodness" (Chaucer 2011, 475). Envy is an attack to goodness itself, when goodness is conceived of as inherently shareable. But a much different approach is taken by Plato's disciple.

A.2.2   Phthonos *and* zēlos *in Aristotle*

Aristotle's account of the envious emotions is routinely cited by contemporary psychologists, and for good reason. It is psychologically subtle and even visionary, since it foreshadows many contemporary findings. Philosophers also often start their inquiry with Aristotle's account, since

emotions, albeit ones that often co-occur in people disposed to feel *phthonos*. Also, it is important that Plato defines *phthonos* as a mixed *pleasure*, while Aristotle defines it first and foremost as a *pain*.
[20] Cf. Smith et al. 1996 and van Dijk et al. 2006. See also Chapter 3.
[21] Fussi also points out that in the *Republic*, however, Socrates' response to Polemarchus' definition of justice as owing good things to friends and bad things to enemies seems to show a change of heart. Given that *Philebus* is a Socratic dialogue, perhaps Plato is here adhering to a Socratic view.

it is normatively complex. Here I can only present an all too brief review. I refer the interested reader to more specialized discussions.[22]

A.2.2.1   Rhetoric

Aristotle's most detailed and perceptive account of envy is in the second book of the *Rhetoric*, which contains the richest account of emotions in his corpus. There, Aristotle analyzes a group of emotions concerning the fortunes of others, which includes *eleos* (pity), *to nemesan* (indignation), *zēlos* (usually translated as "emulation"), and *phthonos* (envy).

Phthonos appears to be opposed to pity, since it involves what we would now call upward social comparison ("looking up" to someone who is doing better than us), and pity involves downward social comparison (or "looking down"). Aristotle warns us against confusing *phthonos* with *to nemesan*, which, unlike *phthonos*, is a righteous emotion that necessarily involves a moral element: the assessment that the good fortune of others is *undeserved*. *Phthonos* contains no such moral judgment.[23] He defines *phthonos* as "a certain kind of distress at apparent success on the part of one's peers in attaining the good things that have been mentioned, not that a person may get anything for himself, but because of those who have it" (*Rhet.*, 1387b 22–5).[24] He then goes on to provide a prescient and influential analysis of this *pathos*'s situational antecedents, typical motivations, and behavioral outputs.

Phthonos always involves a triadic relation between an agent, a good that the agent perceives herself as lacking, and another person who possesses it. Aristotle carefully spells out each component of this relation.

First, the agents: those who feel *phthonos* are similar to the envied ones with regard to age, class, wealth, character, and ends (1387b25–6 and 1388a5–16), and who are just slightly inferior to them (1388a4). *Phthonos* simply cannot arise in the absence of similarity of some sort. As seen in Chapter 1, the importance of similarity has been corroborated by contemporary psychological research.

Second, there are the things that are envied, which are goods that are, in Aristotelian terms, "external" (that is, susceptible to luck), relatively scarce, and positional,[25] such as reputation and honor, wealth, beauty, and in

---

[22] Among others, Konstan 2006, ch. 5; Sanders 2014, ch. 4; Fussi 2017.

[23] Whether or not envy contains some sort of moral judgment of desert is still debated in both psychology and philosophy.

[24] All *Rhetoric* passages cited here are from George Kennedy's translation (Kennedy 2007).

[25] I adopt the following definition of positional good: "Positional goods [...] are goods the absolute value of which, to their possessors, depends on those possessors' place in the distribution of the

general the "gifts of fortune" (1388a1–4). (These are also objects of envy in Plato.)

Finally, Aristotle mentions that the *phthoneros* feels pleasure at seeing the envied incur misfortune, and that they do not feel pity for the envied, information which is relevant to the orator whom Aristotle is addressing here: the purpose of this discussion is to help a speaker persuade, even emotionally manipulate, an audience. *Phthonos* was often carefully aroused in political contexts (Cairns 2003), not unlike current political rhetorical discourse (Bankovsky 2018) (see Chapter 5).

Aristotle then juxtaposes *phthonos* to *zēlos*, which is

> a kind of distress at the apparent presence among others like him by nature of things honored and possible for a person to acquire, [with the distress arising] not from the fact that another has them but that the emulator does not (thus *zēlos* is a good thing and characteristic of good people, while *phthonos* is bad and characteristic of the bad; for the former, through *zēlos*, is making an effort to attain good things for himself, while the latter, though, *phthonos*, tries to prevent his neighbor from having them). (1388b 30–6; Kennedy 2007, 146. Kennedy uses "emulation" and "envy" for *zēlos* and *phthonos* respectively)

Thus, *zēlos* is quite similar to *phthonos* phenomenologically: they are both painful reactions to a similar other being better off than we are. However, *zēlos* arises when we are bothered by the fact that we don't have the good, more than the fact that it is the other person who has it: we are concerned with our lack, that is, not the other's possession. Because of this different concern the behavior that follows is radically different: instead of attempting to deprive the other person of the good we try to acquire it for ourselves, thus making one emotion good (*epieikes*) and the other bad (*phaulos*).[26]

Aristotle adds that those who feel *zēlos* "think themselves deserving the good they do not have (for no one thinks himself worthy of things that seem impossible)" (1388b2–3; Kennedy 2007, 146). Note that he does not say that *zēlos* itself is about desert, but only that people who feel it like to think of themselves as deserving. They might as well be wrong. The reason why they think this is psychological: in order to be motivated to acquire the good they have to think of it as a possible, achievable goal. Thus, Aristotle thinks they conceive of this possibility in terms of desert.

---

good – on their relative standing with respect to the good in question" (Brighouse and Swift 2006, 474). See also discussion in the Conclusion.

[26] For an interesting discussion on the semantic range of *epieikes* and *phaulos*, and the implications for Aristotle's normative theory, see Sanders 2014, 64–5.

However, Aristotle adds an unnecessary element here, notwithstanding his previous claim that *zēlos* and *phthonos* are pains felt at similar others, rather than deserving or undeserving others. One can perceive a goal to be possible on grounds other than desert; we shall see that Descartes defines emulation as a form of courage that stems from seeing someone similar to us attain something, without any reference to desert. If I see someone who is my age and gender who can run a marathon, for instance, I may feel I can emulate them, without thinking they deserve to run a marathon. The notion that emulation or benign envy cannot arise without this perception that leveling up to the similar other is possible has been confirmed by empirical evidence, as I detail in Chapter 2.

The other differences between *zēlos* and *phthonos* stem from the definitional distinction: *zēlos* is the emotion of the young and magnanimous, while *phthonos* is the emotion of the old and small-minded. But the objects of the two emotions are the same in kind: honor and offices, great deeds and wealth, and friendships. The only difference is that the goods object of *zēlos* tend to be those whose "enjoyment can be shared with neighbors, for example, wealth and beauty more than health" (Kennedy 2007, 147). Even the intellectual virtue of *sophia* is mentioned as potential object of both emotions (1387b31, 1388b17). Now, setting aside the specific examples (it is not clear that beauty, if it is meant to be personal beauty, can be shared any more than health) the point is clear: the good in question needs to be conceived of as achievable. The question of the envied good and its nature is a recurring theme of this book.

The contrary (*enantion*) of *zēlos* is contempt/disdain (*kataphronēsis*). Being contrary is the stronger kind of opposition for Aristotle (*Metaph.* 5.10, 1018a25). The contrary of *phthonos* is spite (*epichairekakia*), that is, pleasure at someone's misfortune, independently of whether it is deserved or not.[27]

A.2.2.2 *Is* Zēlos *Envy?*

Whether *zēlos* should be thought of as a form of envy, or as an emotion different in kind from envy, is controversial.[28] It is usually been translated as "emulation," and historically it has been thought of as a distinct

---

[27] "We therefore find that in the *Rhetoric* Aristotle posits three pleasurable emotions — pleasure at deserved misfortune, spite, and disdain — respectively contraries to indignation, envy, and emulation. Pity also has a contrary: 'happy for.' Each pair of emotions is aroused in the same individual in directly contrary circumstances." (Sanders 2014, 63).

[28] E.g., La Caze 2001, Sanders 2014, and Fussi 2017 are roughly in the former camp, while Kristjánsson 2002 (see esp. p. 139), 2006 is in the latter.

emotion. In the history of philosophy, as I discuss in Section A.4.2.2, both Hobbes and Butler seem to have in mind this Aristotelian distinction when they juxtapose envy with emulation. But while Hobbes and Butler distinguish the two emotions exclusively on the basis of their different motivational tendencies and behavioral outcomes, Aristotle identifies the element in the intentional structure of the emotion that those different motivations and behaviors stem from: the difference lies in what I have called *focus of concern*, that is, whether the envier is focused on the lack of the good itself or on the fact that the envied has it. (See Section 2.3.1 for a detailed discussion of this notion, and Section 3.8 for a discussion on emulative envy as virtuous according to Aristotelian criteria.)

In favor of the "distinct from envy" interpretation stands the intuition that envy is necessarily bad. But, as culturally widespread as it is, it is still a culturally specific notion, and we should not project it on other cultures or on a single author. Furthermore, as I show in Chapter 2, contemporary psychologists increasingly think of envy as being both malicious and benign, and if we read the text with that possibility in mind *zēlos* starts to appear a lot closer to *phthonos* than previously imagined.[29] For the sake of remaining relatively uncontroversial, however, I use the Greek terms untranslated throughout this book, leaving in the background the question of whether *zēlos* corresponds to a benign form of envy.

What matters for the present discussion is that *zēlos* is a painful emotional reaction to a perceived inferiority to a similar other, which, however, does not motivate the agent to deprive the envied of the good, but that rather motivates them to self-improvement, and which is a *virtuous emotion*. This is the first time in Western philosophy that something very similar to envy is presented as potentially virtuous. Christopher Gill (2003) proposes a persuasive and explanatorily powerful analysis of Aristotle's view: he argues that Aristotle's acceptance of what Gill calls rivalrous emotions is grounded in a theory of the good that is more in line with the conventions of his times, one that acknowledges the importance of honor and social esteem in human lives. Thus, according to Aristotle, human happiness includes external goods, "bodily goods such as health and beauty, material possessions, and, also, social relationships and

---

[29] Fussi 2017, 74 presents the correspondence between *zēlos* and benign envy as straightforward. I agree with her that the emotional phenomena to which the two terms refer greatly overlap. However, I think they are both social kinds, with specific cultural differences, and their conceptual analyses differ insofar as psychologists emphasize descriptive features such as perception of control over the situation (see Chapters 1 and 2), while Aristotle emphasizes normative aspects, such as the moral goodness of the agents, and whether or not the agents care about the good for its own sake.

position" (Gill 2003: 31–2). Such a theory is critiqued earlier by Plato, and later by Epicureans, Stoics, and Christians.[30] According to the latter thinkers rivalry cannot be a virtue because genuine goodness (God's love, virtue, intellectual wisdom) is infinitely shareable, not dependent on ranking and not susceptible to competition.

The extent to which Aristotle differs from Plato is, of course, debatable and depends on entrenched hermeneutical debates concerning the *Nicomachean Ethics*. In the ethical treaties, furthermore, the discussion of envy and related passions is a bit different from the *Rhetoric*'s.

A.2.2.3 Phthonos *in the Ethical Treaties*

The emotions relating to the fortune of others are analyzed in the ethical treaties with attention to their role in the Aristotelian doctrine of the mean, where virtue is a mean between two excesses. *Phthonos* is analyzed in relation to the virtue of *nemesis*, which roughly corresponds to the *Rhetoric*'s *to nemesan*. According to Konstan (2006) and Sanders (2014), *nemesis* in *Eudemian Ethics* is a complex emotion that involves both painful and pleasurable reactions to good or bad outcomes. *Nemesis* is thus the virtue concerning appropriate emotional responses to other people's fortune, even though in *Nicomachean Ethics*, it is defined more narrowly as the appropriate painful reaction to undeserved success.

In both the *Eudemian* and *Nicomachean Ethics*, *phthonos* is a vice of excess since it is a painful reaction to others' good fortune, independently of desert. In *Eudemian Ethics* Aristotle adds that the envious person feels pain, even if success is deserved. Aside from configuring *phthonos* as a vice, this is not a significant departure from the *Rhetoric* per se, which already characterized *phthonos* as insensitive to perceived merit. The opposite vice, which goes unnamed in *Eudemian Ethics*, is *epichairekakia*, that is, feeling so little pain to the point of feeling joy at people's misfortune.

Contemporary commentators have highlighted the artificiality of the ethical approach to *phthonos*, and the related tension with the *Rhetoric*'s approach.[31] In the latter work Aristotle is interested in providing tools to

---

[30] Gill, thus, follows Konstan (2003, 2006) and Sanders (2014) in approaching the study of this emotions from a culturally specific standpoint.

[31] E.g., "We see then that Aristotle is undertaking to measure on one scale data which require three scales. [. . .] The treatment in the Aristotelian ethical treaties of those three types of envious emotion [*nemesis*, *phthonos*, and *epichairekakia*] and of pity offers a curious example of the difficulties encountered in Aristotle's theory of mean and excess and deficiency, especially when this theory is made to embrace the emotions" (Stevens 1948, 182). Konstan talks of "Aristotle's rather confusing attempts to adapt the opposition between *nemesis* and *phthonos* to his tripartite model of mean and extremes" (2006, 115), in reference to both *Nicomachean Ethics* and with regard to the

manipulate these emotions to the speaker's advantage, and ends up emphasizing more clearly envy's insensitivity to perceived desert, the importance of the similarity condition, and its frequent conflation with the righteous *to nemesan.* In the ethical treaties Aristotle attempts to force these complex multidimensional emotions into the unidimensional notion of excess and defect, thus falling short. While he remains consistent with regard to the maliciousness of *phthonos,* however, he never presents it as necessarily self-defeating, as other philosophers before and after him, not even in the ethical context, thus leaving open the possibility that the envier, for instance, obtain some external good by sabotaging the envied. Furthermore, as highlighted by Gill, he allows for the possibility of a positive rivalrous emotion: *zēlos.*

A.2.3   Phthonos *and* Misos *in Plutarch*

Another ancient author who discusses envy with insight and subtlety is Plutarch, who in his short treatise *De Invidia et Odio* has the merit of distinguishing carefully between hatred and envy. According to him we do not envy those who have wronged us, or who are wicked, but rather those who are *fortunate.* Since "no one is unjust in being fortunate," envy itself is unjust, the wrong reaction to people's prosperity and nobility. Envy is a base emotion, which men deny, and "if you show that they do, they allege any number of excuses and say they are angry with the fellow or hate him, cloaking and concealing their envy with whatever other name occurs to them for their passion, implying that among the disorders of the soul it is alone unmentionable."

Plutarch here correctly identifies two connected phenomena that will later be confirmed by empirical investigations. First, envy often presents itself as *resentment* or *indignation,* which, differently from envy, are moral emotions, in the sense that they necessarily involve a moral claim: when

---

Eudemian Ethics in particular: *Eudemian Ethics,* "Aristotle's effort to contrast *nemesis* with *phthonos* in this treatise appears to be something of a dud" (ibid.). However, I think Konstan's rendition of the relevant passage (1220b39–40) is misleading. He says that *phthonos* is a reaction of pain at "those who are doing well *and* deserve to" (114, my emphasis), which makes it sound as if *phthonos* is sensitive to desert and reacts negatively to it. But the passage can be translated as follows: "Envy consists in being annoyed at prosperity *more often than one ought to be,* for the envious are annoyed by the prosperity *even of* those who deserve to prosper" (my emphases, tr. Rackham, Harvard 1952) or "A man is envious through being distressed at good fortune *in more cases than he should* (*Even those* who deserve to do well upset the envious man when they do do)" (my emphases, tr. Woods, Clarendon Press 1992). So perhaps Konstan overstates the difference with *Nicomachean Ethics* here. See also Sanders' discussion (2014, 66–7). See also my discussion in Chapter 3, Section 3.8.

Table A.1 *Summary of Aristotle's views of phthonos and related emotions across the three works*

Rhetoric	*Phthonos* (malicious envy): painful response to the perceived good fortune of another, not because it is undeserved, but because they are similar to us (1386b16–20), with a focus on the rival – felt by bad people, and motivating the agent to deprive the envied of the good (1388a34–8). Desire is *not* a concern in *phthonos*. The agent of bad character is both *phthoneros* and *epichairekakos* (spiteful, feeling pleasure at others' misfortune per se, independently of desert). Thus, *epichairekakia* is the contrary (*enantion*) of *phthonos* (1388a24–7).	*To nemesan* (indignation): painful response to someone's undeserved *good* fortune (1386b8–12) – felt by good people. Opposed (*antikeisthai*) to pity (*eleos*), which is pain at someone's undeserved *bad* fortune (1385b13–14). The agent of good character who feels *to nemesan* and *eleos* will also feel their unnamed contrary emotions: pleasure at deserved good fortune (1386b30–1) and pleasure at deserved bad fortune (1386b26–8 and 30).	*Zēlos* (emulation/emulative envy): painful response to the advantage of a similar other, with a focus on the lacked object – felt by good people and motivating the agent to acquire the good (1388a32–8). Its contrary (*enantion*) is *kataphronēsis* (disdain/contempt): pleasure we are not suffering the other's bad fortune (1388b22–3), or shallow, inauthentic good fortune (1388b26–8).
	The agent of good character feels both *zēlos* and *to nemesan*.		
Eudemian Ethics	*Phthonos* is a vice of excess: pain felt at good fortune, *even when merited* (1220b39–40, 1233b20–1).	*Nemesis*: the virtuous mean, which is righteous indignation (feeling appropriate pleasure and pain for the fortune of others according to desert) and thus includes *to nemesan*, *eleos*, and their unnamed contraries in the *Rhetoric* (1233b26–30).	Unnamed joy at *undeserved* misfortune (1233b21–4). (In practice, this is spite, or *epichairekakia*.) (Vice of deficiency, because the agent lacks pain.)
Nicomachean Ethics	*Phthonos* is a vice of excess: pain felt at anybody's good fortune (1108b4–5).	*Nemesis* as righteous indignation and virtuous mean, but only defined in terms of pain at unmerited success (1108b3–4).	*Epichairekakia*: pleasure at misfortune (1108b5–6). (Vice of deficiency, because the agent lacks pain.)

I resent someone, I must think that they have wronged me; when I am indignant about something, I must think that some wrong has been done to someone.[32] But envy requires no such claim: I can be envious of someone even if they deserve what they have (indeed, I may be even more envious because of that!). Even though Plutarch does not discuss these issues we should notice that the masking of envy as a moral emotion may be either in good or bad faith. When it is in good faith and thus unconscious (because enviers cannot admit of being envious even to themselves) we can call it a form of *confabulation.* But it can also happen in bad faith, because expressing either of these moral emotions has few of the drawbacks envy has, and can even bring some advantages to the envier if she succeeds in convincing others that the envied's advantage has been obtained unjustly. The masking thus takes the form of manipulation or a lie. Finally, sometimes envy actually *becomes* resentment or indignation, via a process of *transmutation.*[34]

Plutarch identifies a second phenomenon, connected to the first one: envy is rarely, if ever, openly *confessed* (qua envy). Sanders observes that in "[I]n the whole Classical corpus, there are only three surviving instances where someone explicitly says: 'I' feel *phthonos*" (Sanders 2014, 36), and in the seventeenth century, as we shall see, the difficulty to admit to envy is a recurring *topos.* The reluctance to admit to envy affects the way envy is currently investigated: psychologists sometimes use alternative terms or proxy concepts, but this solution of course makes the interpretation of the results difficult.[35] The reluctance to confess envy also affects linguistic usage: English speakers, for instance, often resort to the term "jealousy" when they want to admit to envy without risking the social and moral condemnation that often follows envy declarations.[36] This practice in turn further complicates empirical investigations because

---

[32] Thus, resentment is *personal,* while indignation is *impersonal* (that is, the wrong is seen from an impartial perspective, even when I am the person who has been wronged). Cf. Strawson 1962. Both share what Darwall 2006 characterizes as *second-personal* nature.
    Some authors (e.g., Smith 1991) believe that envy necessarily involve at least a claim of subjective injustice, but I agree with the criticism of this position argued by Miceli and Castelfranchi 2007, 466–7.

[34] Cf. Smith and Kim 2007, 56–7. This can be seen as a (sometimes successful) *coping* mechanism.

[35] See Smith and Kim 2007, 54–5.

[36] The substitution is not consciously motivated, but rather an ingrained linguistic practice. Jealousy's wider semantic scope is such that it functions as a synonym for envy so automatically that speakers often do not even realize the difference between the two emotions until prompted to do so. Thanks to Verity Harte for suggesting a clarification on this point. See also Chapter 1.

it may sometimes be hard to distinguish discoveries about envy from discoveries about jealousy proper.

A.3   Envy as a Sin in Christian and Islamic Thought

In late antiquity envy's reputation further worsens as the Christian Church Fathers include it among the worst human sins. In this section I highlight the most significant features of the sin of envy according to some prominent Christian theologians and philosophers, without attempting to situate their accounts of envy in their philosophical systems. It is noteworthy that only one of them, Catherine of Siena, considers any potentially positive aspect of envy, and even she talks of envy positively only in relation to an attitude, "holy envy," that seems different in kind from envy proper. This is not surprising given that envy in these religious contexts is by definition a sin and a vice, and thus nothing good can come out of it. A similar attitude can be found in Islamic philosophy. Section A.3.5 is thus devoted to medieval philosophers Al-Ghazálí and Al-Qushayrī, who also condemn envy on religious and ethical grounds.

A.3.1   Early Christian Thinkers: Basil of Caesarea and Augustine of Hippo

This Appendix's epigraph is from a homily[37] by St. Basil of Caesarea, a fourth-century Cappadocian theologian who is venerated by most Christian churches, known for extolling and practicing ascetical ideals, and contributing to shaping Western monasticism.[38] According to Monica Wagner, writing in the introduction, Basil regulated and systematized communal practices such as the common table and prayer in common, and insisted on moderation with regard to practices such as fasting. Such moderation, however, should be interpreted in light of the standards of the time, not ours: "[t]here is [...] a marked strain of Stoic rigorism in St. Basil's insistence upon the extreme gravity of sin to the extent that he

---

[37] Abridged versions of this homily (often not clearly marked as such) can be found online, but for the scholarly edition cited here, see Basil of Caesarea 1950. See Limberis 1991 for an analysis and the socio-historical context. Limberis argues that "[w]hat is significant about the homily is that it demonstrates how Basil continued to work within the indigenous code of Mediterranean social behavior that was dominated by honor, shame, revenge, and envy. Thus what Basil offered his congregation as a solution to the grave problem of envy is really a recasting of the pursuit of virtue, so common to Christian Neoplatonists, into the Mediterranean social code. Virtue is rewarded by the most valued possession: honor" (164).

[38] Among his many venerable relatives we can count his siblings Makrina the Younger and Gregory of Nyssa.

does not recognize degrees of heinousness – all sin is equally serious – and also in his stern demand for the renunciation of all fleshly pleasures" (Basil of Caesarea 1950, x). Not surprisingly, in light of this context, Basil's condemnation of envy is absolute and thunderous, and it is in the moral dimension that Basil's analysis of envy is most innovative.

With regard to the emotion's phenomenology, appraisal, situational antecedents, and behavioral consequents, he does not add much to the Greeks' understanding. He defines envy as a pain arising from other people's good fortune, and describes in vivid terms the immoral and imprudent behaviors that it motivates. Like the Greeks he points out that we feel envy toward those who are similar and close to us, including our neighbors, relatives, and friends; like Plutarch he also remarks on how difficult it is for the envious to confess their envy, which makes it harder for them to heal from it. Even the metaphors he uses to characterize envy's phenomenology as a self-consuming, rotting disease are borrowed from the Greeks: he talks of envy as "red blight" and "rust," both of which are images found in the aphorisms attributed to the Seven Sages (cf. Sanders 2014, 33–4). However, he does introduce, as far as I can tell, an original simile: he talks of envy as an arrow that, if thrown against a hard object, may come to strike the thrower (if only he had heard of boomerangs!). This idea of envy as a necessarily self-defeating attitude recurs in the history of ideas.[39]

I focus on this image of the arrow, in particular, because in Basil it depends on the belief that the good the envier is after is never genuine. This is an idea that we have already seen in relation to Platonic and Stoic theories of value (recall Gill's interpretation), according to which moral virtue is the only authentic good. In an Aristotelian framework, *phthonos* is malicious and unethical, but is not necessarily self-defeating: if the envier sabotages the envied, for instance by stealing the envied good, they might get something for themselves. But if one believes that no external, exclusive, or positional good can ever be genuine, then envy can never bring any real advantage.

In Basil and his Christian successors we find this notion developed according to a Christian ethos, and it seems to me that therein lies their novel contribution. Basil states that the many things we envy people for (wealth, health, beauty, wisdom, ethical and intellectual qualities) are only instrumentally, never intrinsically good: they have to be used well by those who believe in God.

---

[39] I critique a modern version of this idea (from Gabriele Taylor) in Chapter 2.

The remedy to envy is thus, according to Basil, to reframe our value system according to the word of God and to be ambitious only with regard to virtue. Furthermore, we ought to be kind and forgiving toward our neighbor, just like God has been toward man. The opposition between *charitas* and *invidia* (in some way foreshadowed in the envy-free nature of deity in the *Timaeus*, and perhaps even in the opposition between *phthonos* and *eros* in *Phaedrus*) is another recurring theme in the Christian condemnation of envy. Its seeds can be found in St. Paul's second letter to the Corinthians ("Love is patient, love is kind. It does not envy, it does not boast, it is not proud," Cor. 13:4) and we see its development in Aquinas in the next subsection.

Unfortunately, in Basil we also find another Christian *topos*, that of the Jews' envy for Jesus. Basil claims that Jews were envious and enraged by his miracles and this is why they persecuted him.[40]

Many of Basil's ideas can be found in his contemporary Augustine of Hippo.[41] While Augustine does not speak about envy as extensively as other Christian thinkers, we can infer his beliefs from sparse remarks in his works. Like Basil, Augustine interprets Cain's slaying of Abel as motivated by envy and inspired by the devil. In *De Civitate Dei* (XV. 5) he compares this fratricide to the one committed by Romulus, who killed his brother Remus according to the myth. What is relevant for our purposes is that Augustine claims the reason for the murder is that the brothers did not want to share the glory of ruling Rome. Cain and Abel's situation is not exactly analogous, in that they were not after the rule of an earthly city, but in both of these rivalries envy is premised on a mistaken assessment of the good: authentic goodness is not diminished, but rather increased, by shared possession.

Like Basil, therefore, Augustine explicitly opposes envy to *charitas*. In *De Civitate Dei* he says that "the possession of goodness is increased in proportion to the concord and charity of each of those who share it" (*De Civitate Dei* XV. 5), and in *De Catechizandis Rudibus* (4, 8) he claims that nothing is more opposed to charity than envy. This opposition will prove influential: not only is charity the traditional opposite of envy in Christian theology and iconography, but also love more generally is proposed as an

[40] Basil presents this as a particular case of the general rule that the envious will be angry, rather than grateful, at their benefactor. This is a well-known trope in Western anti-Semitism, which, however, I won't discuss here.
[41] However, Augustine, whose attitude toward Judaism was multifaceted (see, e.g., Fredriksen 2018), does not speak of Jews as envious of Jesus.

antidote to envy in recent psychological analyses.[42] Later in the history of philosophy we also find that Spinoza defines envy as a form of hatred, and so naturally considers love its opposite.

In the same sentence in which he opposes envy to love Augustine also claims that the mother of envy is pride ("Quia ergo caritati nihil adversius quam invidentia; mater autem invidentiae superbia est," *De Catechizandis Rudibus* 4, 8). This thought is left undeveloped by Augustine, but the relation between envy, pride, and what will soon be called capital vices are analyzed by his successors.

A.3.2   Seven Deadly Sins and Seven Heavenly Virtues: Gregory the Great, John Cassian, Giotto

Envy is notoriously one of the seven "deadly sins," a popular expression which is actually a misnomer derived from confusing mortal sins with capital or cardinal sins, the latter being the list to which envy belongs together with pride (*superbia*), greed (*avaritia*), lust (*luxuria*), gluttony (*gula*), wrath (*ira*), and sloth (*acedia*). These sins are called cardinal or capital because they are the origin ("caput" means "head" in Latin) of all the other sins. They can be mortal or venial (that is, forgivable) depending on the circumstances.

The capital sins designation originated in the Egyptian desert ascetic and monastic communities in the first centuries of the Christian era. Interestingly the first list, by Evagrius Ponticus (345–99 CE), contains eight sins, but does not include envy. John Cassian, a student of Evagrius who imported the classification to Europe, claimed that each cardinal sin generates the one that follows (gluttony > lust > avarice > sadness > anger > lethargy > vainglory > pride).[43]

In the sixth century Gregory the Great added envy to the list, merged sloth with sadness, and considered vainglory (that is, pride) to be the root of all sins. Envy was included on the grounds of being the source of many other sins, such as hate, whispering, slander, Schadenfreude, and

---

[42] See Exline and Zell 2008. For a contemporary defense of the virtue of charity as an antidote to the vice of envy, see Perrine and Timpe 2014. For my own views on love and envy see Chapter 4.

[43] Much has been written on the religious and philosophical aspects of this doctrine, and on its historical development. See Bloomfield 1967, May 1967, Fleming 1970, Fairlie 1988, Stafford 1994, Schwartz 1997, Schimmel 1997, Solomon 2000, Newhauser 2005, Taylor 2006, Kleinberg 2008, Tomlin 2008, Konyndyk DeYoung 2009. I owe this bibliography to Hud Hudson, whom I thank.

displeasure caused by another person's prosperity[44] (all of which Basil had talked about in his homily).[45]

In late antiquity a tradition of opposing the seven capital sins to seven heavenly virtues was started by Prudentius in his poem *Psychomachia*, which was very popular in the Middle Ages. The seven heavenly virtues are composed of four cardinal virtues of Platonic descent (prudence/wisdom, temperance, courage, and justice) and three theological virtues (faith, charity, and hope). However, what is perhaps the most famous iconographic representation of opposing virtues and vices in a Western Christian context, which can be found in the Scrovegni Chapel, is not about the seven deadly sins.

Italian painter Giotto di Bondone (1267–1337) paints seven pairs of vices and virtues in the lowest level of sidewall frescoes in the chapel (completed in 1308). They are: Prudence and Foolishness, Fortitude and Inconstancy, Temperance and Wrath, Justice and Injustice, Faith and Infidelity, Hope and Desperation, and finally Charity and Envy. According to Douglas Lackey, "Giotto's pairings of the virtues and vices provide an analysis of these virtues that is original with Giotto, psychologically interesting, and philosophically acute" (Lackey 2005, 556).

Envy is depicted allegorically as a horned, demonic woman with a snake coming out of her mouth only to blind her (to symbolize envy's "evil eye" and its malicious and self-defeating behaviors), a huge ear (for envious people are always alert and curious about other people's lot), and one hand protruding like a hook (motivated by the desire to deprive the envied of what one lacks) while the other is holding on to her own possessions. Charity instead seems indifferent to the bags of money lying at her feet, and looks up, offering her heart to God. As Lackey remarks, other visual representations of this kind, such as the ones in the Notre Dame and Amiens cathedrals, showcase Greed/Avarice, not Envy, in opposition to Charity (which was, incidentally, Prudentius' original opposition in *Psychomachia*). Lackey argues that the different attitude toward money (giving it to the poor vs. keeping it for oneself) is the salient difference

---

[44] Cf. *Moralia*, XXXI. 88.
[45] The evolution of the list reflects social changes. In ascetic and monastic environments, gluttony and lust are most threatening. In the ordered medieval society the social comparisons sins of envy and pride become much more salient. In the late Middle Ages increased opportunities of commerce and trade translated into an emphasis on greed, until a bourgeois mentality became more prevalent (see discussion of Giotto and Mandeville below).

between Giotto's allegory and more ancient ones.[46] Lackey attributes to Giotto a "proto-bourgeois" ideology due to his different choices, but he also acknowledges that, with regard to the virtues, Giotto is following Aquinas, to whom I now turn.

A.3.3   Thomas Aquinas

Aquinas' account of envy represents an interesting synthesis of the Aristotelian[47] and the Church Fathers' views, especially Gregory's. He discusses envy topically in the second part of the second part of *Summa Theologiae*, and also indirectly in many other parts of the same work. I do not discuss the remarks on envy in angels and demons, or other tangential references to envy, nor am I able to review the general structure of his complex moral psychology,[48] but, rather, I focus on the specific discussion in ST II-II Q. 36.[49]

Aquinas defines envy as "sorrow for another person's good," which is apprehended as one's own evil. ("Sorrow" is here a synonym for pain, or the opposite of pleasure.) In addition to envy there are other forms of sorrow that take as their object someone's good: fear,[50] zeal, and *nemesis*, all of which, unlike envy, are not necessarily wrong or sinful. Envy proper is characterized by being displeased by another person's fortune *insofar as it surpasses ours*, and thus decreases our reputation or excellence. Envy proper is a capital sin, albeit not necessarily a mortal one.

The differences between envy, on the one hand, and zeal and nemesis, on the other, are instructive regarding the way the Aristotelian approach is adapted to serve a Christian theory of value. Aquinas adopts the Aristotelian conception of zeal/*zēlos* according to which the agent is pained by the lack of the good, rather than by the other person's possession of the good. However, for Aquinas zeal is praiseworthy *only if* it is about virtuous,

---

[46] "The great poems of the 14th century, the *Divine Comedy, Piers Plowman,* the *Canterbury Tales,* all present personifications of Avarice, Lust, Gluttony, and Pride, as if these vices pose fundamental challenges in human life. In Giotto's chapel they play no role, and their place is taken up by a more strikingly modern repertoire of concerns: injustice, stupidity, idolatry, weakness of will. In Giotto's world, or at least in Scrovegni's world, it is no crime to make money, no sin to enjoy sex, food, and drink, and no vice to be proud" (Lackey 2005, 561).

[47] For the view that Aquinas's treatment of the passions in general owes to Aristotle's see Jordan 1986 and Green 2007, among others.

[48] A short and very clear review of some central concepts can be found in Green 2007, 405–12.

[49] I cite *Summa Theologiae* according to these abbreviations: ST, followed by Roman numbers for Part, Q. for Question, Art. for Article, s.c. for "sed contra" ("on the contrary"), co. for "corpus" or "respondeo" ("I respond that"), and ad. for replies to objections.

[50] Fear, in this context, is the very specific fear for an enemy's prosperity, which can be harmful to us.

spiritual, or eternal goods. If it is about what Aquinas terms in opposition "temporal goods," then zeal is either sinful or without sin (*"cum peccato, et sine peccato,"* ST II-II, Q. 36, Art. 2, co.), but not virtuous.

Relatedly, nemesis in Aristotle is deemed a virtuous passion, insofar as it is a sorrow for the good fortune of those who are unworthy of it. But Aquinas remarks that Aristotle is thinking here of temporal goods, which are accorded by God always justly "either for the correction of those men, or for their condemnation" (ST II-II, Q. 36, Art. 2, co.). Presumably man is not in a position to assess whether these material goods are assigned for the former or the latter reason. Furthermore, and more importantly, these temporal goods pale in comparison to the eternal goods, which always befall the virtuous man. Therefore, nemesis is not a virtuous passion either.

Envy is said to be contrary to pity and to charity – once again, an amalgamation of Aristotelian and Christian ideas. With regard to the relation to other passionate sins, he often appeals to the authority of Gregory's *Moralia* (e.g., ST II-II, Q. 36, Art. 4, s.c.). Envy is a capital sin because it gives rise to gossiping, slander, joy at another's misfortune, and hatred. (In turn, envy is begotten by another capital sin, vainglory or pride.)

Differently from Basil, Aquinas does not present envy as the most heinous sin. Contrary to popular perception, the doctrine of the capital sins does not imply that the capital sins are the most serious of all; on the contrary, their "daughters" may be more grave than the vices that beget them. Envy is most grievous – says Aquinas – when it is about spiritual goods (ST II-II, Q. 36, Art. 4, ad. 2). Envying another because of an increase in God's grace is a sin against the Holy Spirit.

Timothy Perrine (2011) has argued that Aquinas neglects the essentially comparative nature of envy, by which he means that envy necessarily entails a comparative notion of self-worth and a perception of inferiority toward the envied. Setting aside whether Perrine is right about envy, I think he is correct that Aquinas, like the Christian thinkers in general, does not analyze the psychological mechanisms at work in envy in detail, as modern philosophers will do. Christian thinkers mostly assume the Greeks' understanding of envy's psychology, and develop its normative implications according to a still-developing Christian theological doctrine.[51] As a consequence their judgment of envy is overall more

---

[51] Note also the difference between Plutarch (the Greeks more generally) and Aquinas on hatred. For the latter, hatred of persons is never justified nor morally permissible, because that kind of hatred is the antithesis of *charitas* (see Green 2007). For the Greeks, hatred for the enemy is perfectly justified and morally appropriate.

negative. Even zeal, arguably a form of benign envy, is not morally valuable unless its object is spiritual goodness. Envy proper is always sinful. However, there is one Christian philosopher who talks about envy in positive terms: Catherine of Siena.

A.3.4   Catherine of Siena

Catherine of Siena (1347–80) was a mystic and an influential figure in her time, the first woman (together with Teresa of Avila) to be declared a doctor of the Catholic church. In her main work, *The Dialogue of Divine Providence*, she talks about envy in several places, albeit never extensively.

First, she talks about envy as a product of *avaritia* (avarice/greed), which is often mingled with *superbia* (pride/greed). The three of them are said to be "miserable vices that destroy the heaven of the soul" (Catherine of Siena 1994, 43). In this discussion Catherine compares envy to an ever-gnawing worm (42), a novel variation of the familiar imagery of envy as a self-consuming vice, one that devours the agent from the inside.

Envy and self-love are said to hinder Jews' recognition of Jesus as God's son (43), an anti-Semitic accusation we already saw in Basil. A combination of envy, avarice, self-love, pride, and ignorance is presented as the cause for wickedness, more generally, with "inordinate self-love" (51), in particular, being identified as responsible for all evils. This is a theme that we have already seen in the first discussions of the capital sins, and which is developed by Rousseau.

The implicit opposition is between (an unhealthy form of) love for oneself and charity, love for God and one's fellow human beings, an opposition which is made explicit a bit later in the *Dialogue* where she discusses the "anointed ones" (104), that is, apostles and fathers of the Church such as Peter, Gregory, Augustine, and Thomas. Of them she speaks movingly thus:

> They wept with those who wept, and rejoiced with those who rejoiced; and thus sweetly they knew to give everyone his nourishment, preserving the good and rejoicing in their virtues, not being gnawed by envy, but expanded with the broadness of love for their neighbors, and those under them. They drew the imperfect ones out of imperfection, themselves becoming imperfect and infirm with them, as I told you, with true and holy compassion, and correcting them and giving them penance for the sins they committed – they through love endured their penance – together with them. (Catherine of Siena 1994, 104)

Once again, *charitas* and *invidia* are presented, and prescribed, as polar opposites. However, there is one place in the *Dialogue* where Catherine talks about envy in positive terms, which is worth citing in full:

> The obedient man wishes to be the first to enter choir and the last to leave it, and when he sees a brother more obedient than himself he regards him in his eagerness with a *holy envy*, stealing from him the virtue in which he excels, *not wishing, however, that his brother should have less thereof, for if he wished this he would be separated from brotherly love.* (Catherine of Siena 1994, 126–7, my emphases)

Catherine here departs from Aquinas in the letter, but follows him in the spirit. Aquinas had condemned envy for spiritual goods as the gravest form of envy, but he is thinking of someone who wishes, in Catherine's words, "that his brother should have less [virtue]." When she talks about "stealing" virtue Catherine is being sloppy, since what she means is instead that the holy envier acquires the same virtue that the envied has. That is, she is thinking of zeal (in Aquinas' terminology) with regard to virtue.

A.3.5 Envy in Medieval Islamic Philosophy: Al-Qushayrī and Al-Ghazálí

In this Appendix I focus on the Western tradition because it is the one I know best. But in this subsection I am going to briefly review two accounts of envy as they can be found in two medieval Islamic philosophers.

The first one is Al-Qushayrī (376–465 AH or 986/7–1072/3 CE), whose *Risala* (also known as *al-Risala al-Qushayriya* or *ar-Risala ila's Sufiya*, "The Epistle to the Sufis") contains many teachings of Sufism, or Islamic mysticism. One of the Risala's chapters is devoted to *ḥasad*. In Arabic there are actually two terms that can be translated as "envy" in English. *Ḥasad* (حسد) refers to the kind of malicious envy that I have been referring to when talking of *phthonos* or *invidia*. *ġabṭ* (غبط) refers to a more benign emotion, generally translated as "emulation."

In *Risala* we find many sayings that are congruent with the Christian doctrines we have already discussed. *Ḥasad* is one of the three sins that are "the root of all sins," together with greed and pride. Enviers are considered unbelievers insofar as they do not accept God's decree (presumably with regard to who deserves to be blessed). Among the signs of envy are said to be flattery (in presence of others), slander (in their absence), and joy at their misfortune (presumably the "others" in question are those whom the envier envies).

But we also find advice to shield oneself from the ill effects of envy, such as "If you wish to be safe from the envier, then conceal your affairs from him" (Al-Qushayrī 1990, 103). The belief in the *evil eye*,[52] the idea that a person can inadvertently cast a curse through their malevolent gaze, a widespread superstition in Mediterranean and Asian cultures, is surely at work here. Finally, we find a pragmatic take on the tension between personal love and envy, that is, the recommendation to not love the envier: "Beware lest you toil in loving one who envies you, for he will surely not accept your kindness" (ibid.).

We find similar teachings in the work of Al-Ghazálí (450–505 AH or 1058–1111 CE), one of the most prominent Islamic philosophers and theologians. Here I briefly review what he says about envy in two places: *The Beginning of Guidance* and *The Alchemy of Happiness*.

In *The Beginning of Guidance*, part III, Al-Ghazálí discusses the "sins of the heart," which are the vices that are "most prominent among the religious scholars of our times" (Al-Ghazálí 1994, 159). These are envy, hypocrisy, and pride. Similarly to the Christian philosophers of his time, he claims that these sins are not only "destructive in themselves [but also] [. . .] the roots of all other evil dispositions" (ibid.).

When discussing envy in particular, Al-Ghazálí defines it as a form of avarice, much like Catherine will claim a few centuries later. For both, envy stems from a begrudging and miserly attitude toward one's possessions. Al-Ghazálí, furthermore, specifies that the "leveling-down" motivation typical of *ḥasad* is so strong that the envier wants the envied to lose their advantage even if they themselves will gain nothing in return. Again, we find the theme of envy as a self-defeating vice, which brings about its own punishment, since there is always someone who is more fortunate than us, and thus the envier is constantly subject to torturous feelings. Al-Ghazálí also notes the tendency enviers have to slander the envied (Al-Ghazálí 1994, 164).

Purifying oneself from vice is a central tenet of Sufi mysticism, of which Al-Ghazálí was a fervid adherent, but Al-Ghazálí is particularly worried by the form these vices manifest among theologians and scholars. While Catherine's diagnosis will be that ignorance is one of envy's causes, Al-Ghazálí warns that "the greatest cause of these vices becoming established in the heart is the pursuit of knowledge in order to dispute with others and outshine them" (Al-Ghazálí 1994, 167). Knowledge, then, even knowledge of religious truths, is not sufficient to protect oneself from envy;

---

[52] Wikipedia provides a good overview: https://en.wikipedia.org/wiki/Evil_eye.

quite the contrary, it can exacerbate it. This is due to the fact that even scholars of religion can love this world too much, and "love of this world is the fount of all sins" (ibid.), according to Muhammad.

Al-Ghazálí is best known for his masterpiece, *The Revival of the Religious Sciences*. *The Alchemy of Happiness* is a Persian abridgment of the *Revival*, in which Al-Ghazálí talks about envy[53] and hatred as one arising from the other, a recurring idea in the history of philosophy. He reiterates that the first sins against God are pride, greed, and envy, and that the last of these caused the first murder in history (that of Abel). He shows the self-defeating effects of envy through a funny parable concerning someone who envied the king's advisor and plots against him, and ends up being decapitated as a result.

He also briefly talks of "emulation,"[54] in a passage worth quoting in full:

> if thou desirest that thou have something like that, but do not wish for its loss to another, and do not dislike (his having) it, then it is called emulation, and also called competition. In religious matters, this is praiseworthy and may be an obligation. God Most High says: For this, let (all) those strive who strive. (Q. 83:26) And He said: Race one with another for forgiveness from your Lord. (Q. 57:21) That is, put yourselves ahead of one another. (Al-Ghazálí 2007: 545)

On the surface this passage suggests a view similar to the one we saw in Aquinas concerning religious zeal. Al-Ghazálí's claim is even stronger, since it suggests that we ought to feel it – we ought to compare ourselves to others with regard to their religious blessedness and strive to be as blessed as they are.

Al-Ghazálí goes on to add that, even when we feel envy with regard to religious blessings, and thus we want the envied to lose their privileged status, if we do not actually act on our desire, and find it repugnant, then this is a natural feeling for which we cannot be held accountable. This idea is reiterated in several passages, and not only with regard to religious envy. He claims that nobody is immune to envy, and it is perhaps because of this belief that he indicates that envy that is not expressed or acted upon, and that is explicitly repudiated, is excusable.

Al-Ghazálí seems aware of the inescapability of envy more than the Christian thinkers:

> Thou art not required to change that nature, for it is not in thy power. However, thou art responsible for two things: one is that thou necessarily

---

[53] I do not know which Persian word is translated as "envy."
[54] Again, I do not know how the original Persian reads.

do not disclose this (feeling) by word or deed; and the other is that thou dislike this trait in thyself and reject it with thine intellect, and that thou be desirous of the elimination of that trait. When thou hast done this, thou hast escaped the sin of envy. (Al-Ghazálí 2007, 548)

While we cannot wholly change our human nature, we have power over some aspects of it; feeling envy is natural, but we can refuse to be dominated by it.

After all, the greatest punishment for the envier is internal: the envier is in constant pain, and "there is no sorrow greater than the sorrow of envy" (Al-Ghazálí 2007, 546). Al-Ghazálí, unlike other thinkers, does not seem to think that envy is dangerous to the envied, and he even says that "envy is injurious to oneself – in this world and the next, while it is beneficial to the envied person – in this world and the next" (ibid.), which is a somewhat odd claim in tension with the example of Cain's fratricide and the other biblical examples he cites.

It is worth noting that he often talks of "enviers" as opposed to envy, which seem to refer to people who are predisposed to feel envy, and this emphasis might justify his concern with the prudential costs of envy, as opposed to its harms to others. He also, like Basil, uses the simile of the stone thrown to strike the enemy but that returns to blind the striker. Again like the Christian thinkers, he talks of the vices that stem from envy: enmity, slander, lying, and repudiation of God, and lists among the causes of envy pride, vanity, hostility, and love of rank. In this respect, too, the Christian and Islamic tradition are congruent: authentic goodness lies in the world to come, and attributing excessive importance to temporal goods leads to sin.

These are the "roots [that] must be extirpated through earnest striving" (Al-Ghazálí 2007, 548): Al-Ghazálí devotes a section to the practical remedies of envy, and he advises to practice a sort of cognitive behavioral therapy, redirecting one's thoughts and habituating oneself to behave in opposite ways to the ones envy commands. Again, he talks of envy as a disease of the soul that ought to be extirpated for the sake of one's salvation, and the remedy to it is like a bitter medicine, hard to swallow but necessary.

A.4   Envy in the Modern Era

Passions and affects were an important area of philosophical study in the seventeenth and eighteenth century: philosophers were particularly interested in taxonomizing emotions correctly, and in the epistemological, metaphysical, and ethical implications of such taxonomies.[55] Whether or not they espoused a mechanistic explanation that focused on the physiological underpinnings of the emotions, they deepened the inquiry into the way the mind works, and in the way in which different emotions affect, or are part of, each other.

By the end of the Middle Ages the characteristics of envy, the conditions in which it arises, the kind of behaviors it motivates, the dispositions it is associated with, and its differences with cognate emotions like emulation, resentment, and Schadenfreude have all been discussed and identified. And yet the modern philosophers' reflections on envy are both rich and diverse, bringing to light novel concerns and perspectives.

As is the case for the authors analyzed above, the following review is unavoidably shallow and cannot delve into how accounts of envy are situated in the larger philosophical system of each author. Nevertheless, I hope this is a useful starting point for the reader interested in pursuing research on such connections.

A.4.1 Francis Bacon: A Modern Approach to Envy

Francis Bacon's 1625 essay *On Envy* is exemplary of the many topics that interest philosophers writing on envy in the seventeenth and eighteenth centuries. The essay begins with a startling juxtaposition: "There be none of the affections, which have been noted to fascinate or bewitch, but love and envy" (Bacon 1999: 18).[56] Both "have vehement wishes; they frame themselves readily into imaginations and suggestions; and they come easily into the eye" (ibid.). This connection between these two seemingly very different emotions is not, however, articulated further, and Bacon moves on to discuss envy only, and devotes a separate essay to love.

Bacon does not give a proper definition of envy. All we can derive from the initial remarks is that envy involves an intense conative state concerning an object. But we can infer more of his understanding of envy from the following passage:

> A man that hath no virtue in himself, ever envieth virtue in others. *For men's minds*, will either feed upon their own good, or upon others' evil; and who wanteth the one, will prey upon the other; and whoso is *out of hope*, to attain to another's virtue, will seek to come at even hand, by depressing another's fortune. (Bacon 1999, 18, my emphases)

---

[55] For a review, see Schmitter 2016. See also James 1997 for seventeenth century in particular.
[56] For a general overview of Bacon's moral philosophy, see Box 2006.

Bacon thus pays attention to the *mental mechanisms* that take place in the envious agent: a person can either focus on what they have or what they lack. When they lack virtues, they will note and resent others' virtues, and when they are *hopeless* with regard to improving their situation (by attaining the virtues they lack), they will attempt to "level down," to depress the other person's situation. We have seen that this notion was already present in Aristotle, and we shall see how it develops in later philosophical thought.

As a consequence, people who are disposed to envy and leveling down are those who tend to lack virtues and who are unlikely to improve their lot, such as "[d]eformed persons, and eunuchs, and old men, and bastards" (Bacon 1999, 19), and also those who are "busy, and inquisitive" (18). Those who are curious and don't mind their own businesses have more chances to compare their situation with that of others.

Another characteristic of enviers is fear of losing one's high status, as those of noble birth, who may envy the "the new men, when they rise. For the distance is altered, and it is like a deceit of the eye, that when others come on, they think themselves, go back" (19): once again, the importance of comparison is apparent, although he seems to suggest here that men should not base their self-assessment on such comparison, since it is deceiving. Worth should not be interpreted as relational but as absolute. We shall see that this point comes back in other authors, such as Kant. Also, Bacon's observation somewhat foreshadows Hume's claim (see Section A.4.2.1) that we can feel envy toward those who are socially inferior, when the distance between them and us is shortened.

He then highlights a feature that is characteristic of *all* enviers, and that is the similarity condition, which we have seen so often remarked upon. He connects it to the possibility of comparison: "where there is no comparison, no envy; and therefore kings are not envied, but by kings" (20). We shall see this point developed by Hume.

But who are the envied, instead? Those who are perceived as *undeserving* of their fortune are more envied than those who are perceived as deserving. This is why new men are more envied than nobles, since the latter are believed to have a right to their fortune, and why virtuous persons are less envied when successful, because they got what they deserved. However, in the long run the virtuous and the deserving are also envied because the memory of their work and toils pales. Those who are *most* envied are the arrogant and the insolent.

We shall see later that the relationship between envy and (perceived or actual) desert is a complicated one: Locke and Leibniz, for instance, diverge on this. For Bacon it is a matter of fact that we envy more those who are perceived as undeserving their fortune, because it is not their natural right, because they are not virtuous, or because they are conceited (although in this last case it is not clear to me if that makes them undeserving or just obnoxious). Whether envy necessarily involves a sense of subjective injustice, either at the descriptive or normative level, is still discussed in the contemporary literature (see Chapter 2 for details).

Bacon's overall assessment of envy is quite negative. He claims that it is the most painful of affections (possibly together with love) because it is continuous and never gives rest, and that it is the most depraved passion in that it is not only malicious but also subtle, secretive, and therefore devilish. (However, Bacon finds some goodness in public envy. See Section A.4.4.)

Bacon's essay contains three of *four interconnected threads* that can be tracked in a wealth of diverse approaches and definitions. First, the moderns dig deeper into the underlying *psychological mechanisms* of envy, and in particular they investigate the role played by comparison and imitation. Second, they think about *appropriateness conditions*, and in particular whether envy can ever be just or justified. Third, they *distinguish between the personal and the political sphere*, and realize that the individual and the collective domains are not isomorphic and that envy can be detrimental in one domain but beneficial in the other. Although it is sophisticated, Bacon's essay does not connect its qualified critique of envy *with a systematic view of human nature, human values, and moral education*, which is what we find in some other authors.

A.4.2 Psychological Mechanisms

A.4.2.1 Envy, Imitation, and Comparison in Spinoza, Mandeville, Smith, and Hume

Spinoza discusses envy and related emotions in several passages of the *Ethics* (1677). He defines it as "hatred, in so far as it induces a man to be pained by another's good fortune, and to rejoice in another's evil fortune" (III,d23), and goes on to explain that envy is generally opposed to *sympathy* (*misericordia*) which is a kind of love that "induces a man to feel pleasure at another's good fortune, and pain at another's evil fortune" (III,d24). Both emotions "arise from pleasure or pain accompanied by the idea of something external" (III,d24). He further stresses envy's hateful character in proposition 24, where he claims that envy "is nothing else but *hatred, in so far as it is regarded as disposing a man to rejoice in another's hurt, and to grieve at another's advantage*" (III,p24s, emphasis in the original). Thus, the traditional Christian opposition between *charitas* and *invidia* moves away from its theological characterization and assumes a psychological one, which is, however, still instrumental to ethical outcomes: being capable of empathetically engaging with another human being is key to morality – an idea that is still popular in contemporary discourse, and not just with regard to envy.

Bernard de Mandeville also investigates the role of social comparison in envy. He attributes our reluctance to admit envy to a deeply ingrained hypocrisy: we learn from an early age to "hide even from our selves the vast Extent of Self-Love, and all its different Branches."[57] Self-love is also responsible for our biased assessments: we tend to overestimate ourselves and underestimate others. It is a natural consequence, then, that seeing others in a position superior to our own upsets us, and that, to protect our sense of self-worth, our disappointment and hurt takes the form of perceived injustice and indignation. That is why envy is defined by Mandeville as a compound of anger and sadness. Mandeville's description of our reactions to upward social comparison, and our consequent post hoc rationalizations, is very close to what we find in contemporary social psychology.

Both Adam Smith and David Hume follow Spinoza and Mandeville in thinking of envy as an "odious and detestable passion" (*Theory of Moral Sentiments*, VI.III.16), and in investigating its connection with social comparison.

In the first part of the *Theory of Moral Sentiments* (1759), where he discusses the role of sympathy, Smith often mentions envy as the passion that hinders our natural sympathy toward others' joy (this idea is also reiterated later on, e.g., VI.II.24), how we struggle to rejoice with others. As a consequence he recommends that those who receive a great fortune behave modestly and smother their satisfaction so as to shield themselves from envy (I.II.5). Contemporary psychology has studied these behaviors and confirmed that boastful behaviors trigger much malicious envy (Silver and Sabini 1978). Anthropologists have also observed that many cultural norms of modesty or self-deprecation aim at preventing or shielding oneself from envy (Foster 1972).

Envy is further mentioned by Smith as one of the motivations, together with avarice and unjust resentment, to commit "inhuman murder" (III.I.95), and as one of the least honorable human passions (III.I.103).

---

[57] *Fable of the Bees*, Note N.

Originally it was not only attributed to the individual, but also to nations. Smith frequently discusses envy with regard to international relations (VI.II.27, 28, and 30), as responsible for enmity between countries.

However, we have to wait until VI.III.16 to find a proper definition: "Envy is that passion which views with malignant dislike the superiority of those who are *really entitled* to all the superiority they possess." This is interesting: in direct opposition to some of the previous definitions, Smith seems to think that envy cannot possibly be about *actual* unfairness ever. Envy is thus defined as necessarily malicious and also inherently inappropriate. This may be the reason why "we are *always* ashamed of our own envy" (I.III.4, my emphasis).

The idea that envy is shameful is not new (we have seen Plutarch's observation that we admit more readily to hate than envy), but it is modern philosophers who popularize this idea,[58] and surely many others.[59]

The connection between envy and the ways our sympathy works is investigated by Hume as well. Both thinkers reflect on how and why our feelings, actual or imagined, fail to fit with those of others. However, they differ in how they conceptualize the kind of comparison at stake: while Hume thinks about sympathy in cognitive terms, Smith characterizes it as affective in nature.

For Hume the passions of malice and envy derive from the principle according to which "objects appear greater or less by a comparison with others" (*A Treatise of Human Nature*, 2.2.7). This principle holds across very different domains, including measuring physical properties of objects, and derives from more general principles concerning the relations between ideas. When we compare a person's qualities to another's which are superior, we judge that person as defective, and similarly with regard to judgments about our own condition of fortune, happiness, wealth, power, or merit: rather than considering our lot in isolation we compare it to that of others.

"The misery of another gives us a more lively idea of our happiness, and his happiness of our misery. The former, therefore, produces delight; and

---

[58] In addition to Mandeville, as seen above, see De la Rochefoucauld ("We can often be vain of our passions, even the guiltiest ones; but envy is so sneaking and shameful that we never dare confess it" (*Maxims*, 27, de la Rochefoucauld 2008, 9)); Jeremy Taylor (1613–67) ("Many men profess to hate another, but no man owns envy, as being an enmity or displeasure for no cause but another's goodness or felicity"); John Wilmot ("Envy is a passion so full of cowardice and shame, that nobody ever had the confidence to own it").

[59] Jeremy Taylor and John Wilmot (1647–80) are quoted in several collections of quotes and aphorisms, but I could not retrieve the original sources.

the latter uneasiness" (*A Treatise of Human Nature*, 2.2.7). Interestingly, Hume thinks that we may experience something similar even with respect to our past selves, and even with respect to our present selves in some peculiar circumstances (as when we strongly empathize with a less fortunate friend, or when we feel remorse for a crime we committed, in both cases the effect being that, feeling uneasy about our present state of happiness, we inflict pain on ourselves).

Envy arises not only when we compare ourselves to someone who is superior to us (even though this is the most common case), but also when we compare ourselves to someone who is *inferior*. The reason is that "even in the case of an inferiority, we still desire a greater distance, in order to augment still more the idea of ourself. When this distance diminishes, the comparison is less to our advantage; and consequently gives us less pleasure, and is even disagreeable" (*A Treatise of Human Nature*, 2.2.7). As far as I know Hume is the only philosopher who discusses this issue. I do not know whether this phenomenon has been studied empirically. This is an important topic that bears on the discussion of political envy and racism in Chapter 5. Usually in the case of downward social comparison most people would expect to find only contempt and scorn, which are, in some, the opposite of envy. But the phenomenon observed by Hume helps explain how racists can smoothly move from feeling scorn to feeling envy.

As seen in Chapter 1, contemporary psychology has confirmed the Humean insight that our self-assessment is essentially tied to social comparison: it is only by comparing ourselves to others that we are able of assessing our standing, our social position, and our capabilities.

According to Gerald Postema, "[T]he key to unlocking the mystery of human passions, according to Hume, lay in the interaction between two fundamental psychological mechanisms or principles: sympathy and comparison. Both our sociality and our asociality find their psychic origins in the complex interaction between them" (Postema 2005, 251). But, as Amy Schmitter reminds us, "Hume's account does not achieve its originality *ex nihilo* but by adopting, adapting, reimagining, and reassembling previous views, by giving elements in them new prominence and new functions, and by crossbreeding them with seemingly alien positions" (Schmitter 2011, 256). Among Hume's predecessors and influences we arguably find Malebranche, Descartes, Hobbes, Spinoza, Mandeville, and Adam Smith,[60] *all of whom* analyze envy and other dark passions in a way that is, at least at first pass, both different from the moralistic approach of the

---

[60] For these relations, see Amy Schmitter (2011) and Susan James (1997).

Christian thinkers and disconnected from rhetorical and persuasive aims, as in Aristotle. Consequently, many of these thinkers see the bright side of these dark emotions. Unlike Aristotle, who can be seen as admitting a virtuous kind of envy, these authors think of vicious envy as having virtuous consequences.

Something similar can be said, albeit with important qualifications, of Immanuel Kant's view of envy. Envy is explicitly discussed in many places of the Kantian *opus*, so, once again, my review here cannot be but superficial. In this section, I focus on Kant's conception of envy as a vice, while in Section A.4.4 I discuss his approach to envy as a drive for civilization.

In *The Metaphysics of Morals*, in a section titled: *On the Vices of Hatred for Men, Directly Opposed to Love of Them*, Kant defines envy thus: "Envy (*livor*) is a propensity to view the well-being of others with distress, even though it does not detract from one's own; when it breaks forth into action (to diminish their well-being) it is called envy *proper*; otherwise it is merely *jealousy* (*invidentia*)" (4:458). So, it seems that Kant sees envy proper as an emotional disposition, not just an occurrent emotion, and a necessarily vicious one at that ("This vice is therefore contrary to a man's duty to himself as well as to others" (4:459)). He also argues that envy depends essentially on comparison and seeing a good as positional – often errone-ously, one presumes, given that earlier he said, "even though it does not detract from one's own."

Malice is a malevolent joy that is generated by others' haughtiness when their fortune is uninterrupted and by self-conceit in their good conduct, and is the direct opposite of sympathy. Malice proper (Schadenfreude) is active: it consists in bringing about evil or wickedness.[61]

In *Religion within the Boundaries of Mere Reason* (6:26, 27) Kant distinguishes between a "predisposition to animality" and a "predisposition to humanity." The predisposition to animality is a physical, mechanical, a-rational self-love, which aims at self-preservation, propagation of the species, and forming community with other human beings. When these three drives deviate the most from their natural ends they give rise to the *bestial* vices of *gluttony*, *lust*, and *wild lawlessness*.

The predisposition to humanity is a different kind of self-love: it involves comparison (so it requires reason) and it predisposes us to humanity. "Out of this self-love originates the inclination *to give worth in the opinion of others*" (6:27): initially we are just anxious to be of equal

---

[61] For a rich, but complex, commentary on these passages of the *Metaphysics*, see *Lectures of Ethics* (27:961–3).

worth and worried that others may do better than us, but gradually "an unnatural desire to acquire superiority for oneself over others" arises (6:27). It is from this predisposition that envy, ingratitude, and Schadenfreude arise, which Kant calls here *vices of culture,* an expression which recalls the artificiality of Rousseau's *amour propre* (on the relation between love and envy in Rousseau, see also Chapter 4). As in Rousseau, Kant recognizes the peculiarly human element of this form of self-love and its high potential for vice.

Later in the work Kant discusses the remedies to the vices engendered by the predisposition to animality and the predisposition to humanity. Every human being, even if morally well-disposed, is constantly exposed to evil. This is because of the arousal of passions, which "wreak such great devastation in his originally good predisposition" (6:93). The causes and circumstances of this vulnerability to sin do not come from his "raw nature" but *from the fact he stands in relation or association to other human beings.* Man considers himself poor only insofar as "he is anxious that other human beings will consider him poor and despise him for it. Envy, addiction to power, avarice, and the malignant inclinations associated with these, assail his nature, which on its own is undemanding, as soon as he is among human beings" (6:93–4).

The only hope for men is to unite forces and create an enduring society that aims to promote the moral good. Reason prescribes the human race to establish such a society, which is under the laws of virtue alone and is an ethical state, a kingdom of virtue. This community can completely overlap with a political community (in the sense that their members are the same), but they are different because they have distinct unifying principles, forms, and constitutions. We shall see, however, that even for Kant envy can have a positive role in the development of the human species.

A.4.2.2   *Envy and Emulation in Descartes, Hobbes, Butler, and Spinoza*

We have seen that modern authors go beyond Aristotle in investigating the cognitive underpinnings of envy. However, their approach to what Aristotle called *zēlos* and *phthonos* remains substantively the same, or is less sophisticated.

Descartes talks about envy and related emotions in several paragraphs of *The Passions of the Soul,* originally published in French in 1649.[62]

---

[62] For an overview of this work and a discussion of its philosophical significance, see Shapiro 2006. A naturalistic approach to passions can also be found in Malebranche, Hobbes, Spinoza, and Hume, among other modern thinkers (see Schmitter 2011).

The Passions of the Soul is one of the many treatises on the passions that flourished in the modern era, but the Cartesian perspective is characteristically naturalistic: passions are seen as psychophysical phenomena to be analyzed scientifically, thus inaugurating an approach that continues to this day.[63]

Envy (*envie*) and emulation (*émulation*) are presented as having opposite physiological natures: envy is cold while emulation is hot. Envy is "a kind of sadness mingled with hatred, which results from our seeing good coming to those we think unworthy of it" (II, Par. 182, Descartes 1985, 394). Cartesian *envie*, then, closely resembles Aristotelian *nemesis* (indignation), with the most notable difference being that Aristotle does not think of *nemesis* as mingled with hatred. (More on this aspect in Section A.4.3).

Paragraph 184 analyzes the physiological causes of envy, which, being a form of sadness mingled with hatred, is affected by the "movements of the blood" of both: hatred causes black and yellow bile to spread through the veins, and sadness slows down the blood's flow, and as a consequence enviers have a "leaden" complexion, that is, "pale, a mixture of yellow and black, like a livid bruise (hence the Latin word for envy is *livor*)" (Descartes 1985, 394). Envy is still popularly associated with "cold" hues and tones (light blue, bluish-yellow, green, grey), and Theodore Gericault's painting *La Folle Ou La Monomane de l'Envie* (1822) is a good representation of it.

In paragraph 172 Descartes discusses emulation, which is defined as "a heat which disposes the soul to undertake tasks in which it hopes to be able to succeed because it sees others succeed in them. Thus it is a species of courage of which the external cause is an example" (Descartes 1985, 391). Descartes' understanding of emulation as a species of courage and as a *heat* seems to put this emotion in stark contrast with the cold and implicitly craven envy, to which emulation is never compared as in other authors.

However, Descartes' account of emulation hints at an important element of positive emotional responses to upward social comparison: these responses cannot arise unless we see ourselves as in control of our position and capable of improving it. In his account, the target of emulation (the person who has succeeded) plays an evidential role: they are the proof that

---

[63] Lucrezia Marinella (1571–1653) argues in her *The Nobility and Excellence of Women and the Defects and Vices of Men* (1601) that the misogyny of philosophers such as Aristotle is rooted in envy. Marguerite Deslauriers (2017) argues that Marinella's work should be interpreted in the context of a general debate on men and women's physiological differences that began in antiquity and develops in the Renaissance. Thus, her analysis of envy can perhaps be taken to showcase a naturalistic approach to the emotions as well. I am grateful to Gary Ostertag for these references.

a certain objective is reachable. Of course, that by itself is poor evidence. There are many reasons why one succeeds where I cannot. In particular, Descartes does not mention the similarity condition, as Aristotle does when talking about *phthonos* and the fact that the success of similar others is a reproach to us. Social comparison is informative and diagnostic of one's own position only within a relevant comparison class (cf. Chapter 1). In the text, however, we find no indication that Descartes is aware of this.

It is striking that Descartes does not discuss emulation in conjunction with envy, especially since his contemporary, Thomas Hobbes, does so in chapter 6 of *Leviathan* (1651), work of which Descartes was aware: "Grief for the success of a competitor in wealth, honour, or other good, if it be joined with endeavour to enforce our own abilities to equal or exceed him, is called emulation: but joined with endeavour to supplant or hinder a competitor, envy" (Hobbes 2002, 47).

Pains are divided by Hobbes into two kinds: the ones coming from sensorial experience are called pains, while the ones related to "expectation of consequence" are called griefs. Dejection, shame, and pity are also griefs. Thus, envy and emulation are both mental pains caused by and concerned with the success of a competitor with regard to, it seems, any good on which one can compete. The only difference about the two rests on the behavior they motivate: if one is inclined to level up, then it's emulation; if one is inclined to level down, then it's envy. Thus, this definition is very similar to Aristotle's definition of *phthonos* and *zēlos* in the *Rhetoric*.[64]

Bishop Butler critiques Hobbes' definition a couple centuries later, since he explicitly rejects the notion that envy and emulation are griefs in themselves. Rather, he defines them as desires, from which grief can stem due to their intensity. Like Hobbes and Aristotle, however, he juxtaposes them and declares that the only difference between them resides in what I have called "leveling orientation": "Emulation is merely the desire and hope of equality with, or superiority over others, with whom we compare ourselves. [. . .] To desire the attainment of this equality or superiority by the *particular means* of others, being brought down to our own level, or below it, is, I think, the distinct notion of envy" (*Fifteen Sermons*, Sermon I, note 5, Butler 2017, 25, emphasis in the original). He also states that the different moral value of envy (its being "unlawful") resides exclusively in these different means to achieve the same end, namely "equality or superiority" (ibid.). Butler's account is also very similar to Aristotle. The

---

[64] For the complex relation between Aristotelianism and the seventeenth century philosophical approach to the passions, see James 1997.

only difference is that for Butler these emotions are essentially desires, whereas for Aristotle they are painful responses with a different focus of concern (the good or the envied), and the desire to level up or down is a consequence of that.

An intermediate position can be found in Spinoza, who does not define envy and emulation in conjunction with one another, but acknowledges that envy and emulation are "generally coupled," and refers us to the human tendency to *imitate* others – ingrained in us from a very early age – as the basis of envy, pity, and emulation. This imitational tendency is due to the fact that, "if we conceive that anyone takes delight in something, which only one person can possess, we shall endeavor to bring it about that the man in question shall not gain possession thereof" (*Ethics* III,p32,s). The idea seems to be that we perceive others' gains or losses in relation to ours. If it is a gain of something we want for ourselves and that cannot be shared, then we feel deprived by comparison, and feel pain, and develop hateful passions against that person. If it is a loss, and the person is sufficiently similar to us (a specification that is present in pity's definition but not in envy's), then we sympathize with them and feel pain. Pity and envy are incompatible because we cannot hate what we pity (III,p27,c2). Emulation is "the desire of something, engendered in us by our conception that others have the same desire" (def. 33). Imitation and emulation have the same cause, says Spinoza, although "it has become customary to speak of emulation only in him, who imitates that which we deem to be honourable, useful, or pleasant" (ibid.). So we do not talk of emulation when a person simply imitates someone's movements, for instance. Their common cause is explained in proposition 27: "By the very fact that we conceive a thing, which is like ourselves, and which we have not regarded with any emotion, to be affected with any emotion, we are ourselves affected with a like emotion (*affectus*)" (III,p27).[65]

A.4.3 *Appropriateness Conditions: Descartes, Locke, Leibniz*

Even though Descartes does not adopt the Aristotelian distinction between *zēlos* and *phthonos*, he still seems influenced by the Aristotelian approach to think of envy and pity as relating to the fortune of others. However, he

---

[65] According to Spinoza, since envy is a form of hatred it is extinguished by love, which is the most appropriate reaction to being envied. I argue against the idea that love is an antidote to envy in Chapter 4. Note that if it is true that envy is not extinguished by love and that hatred is, then we have reason to doubt that envy is a form of hatred.

Table A.2. *Summary of Descartes' views on responses to deserved and undeserved fortune*

Things that befall others	Deserved	Undeserved
Good	Joy	Sadness: envy
Evil	Joy plus laughter and derision	Sadness: pity

goes in quite a different direction with it unlike, for instance, Spinoza). In part II, paragraph 62 of the *Passions*, he presents a general distinction between passions that we feel when we think of the good or evil that happens to others. When we judge them worthy of their fate, whether it is a positive or negative one, then we feel joy. We feel joy, "in so far as we get some benefit from seeing things happen as they ought; and the joy aroused in the case of a good differs from that aroused in the case of an evil only in that the former is serious whereas the latter is accompanied by laughter and derision" (Descartes 1985, 351). Vice versa, when we deem the good or evil undeserved, we feel sadness. However, this sadness has two species: envy in the case of undeserved good and pity in the case of undeserved evil. Table A.2 summarizes these distinctions.

Envy is further discussed in paragraphs 182–4. Descartes is, to my knowledge, the first philosopher to state explicitly the difference between envy *as a vice* and envy *as an emotion*: "What we usually call 'envy' is a vice consisting in a natural perversity which causes certain people to be annoyed at the good they see coming to others. But I am using this word here to signify a passion which is not always vicious" (Descartes 1985, 394). Recall that envy is defined as a mixture of sadness and hatred, "which results from our seeing good coming to those we think unworthy of it" (par. 182, Descartes 1985, 394), which can be justified, presumably, when the judgment of undeservingness is correct.

However, Descartes is quick to acknowledge that that might not be the case, as with natural endowments, since "we received them from God before we were capable of doing any evil" (Descartes 1985, 394), and thus we are always worthy of them. Therefore, the passion of envy can be justified only with regard to goods of fortune.

The question of envy's appropriateness[66] is further discussed in paragraph 183, titled "How envy can be just or unjust." Here Descartes

---

[66] Descartes does not seem to distinguish between fittingness and the moral appropriateness or justification. Furthermore, he seems to use being excusable as a synonym for justifiable, as

reaffirms a connection between envy and "a zeal which may be excusable," especially if the envied's superior position can be used for evil purposes, as when one abuses the power of public office.

Descartes' use of "zeal" here does not seem to track the Scholastic notion of *zelus*, nor the Aristotelian one of *zēlos*, nor does he talk here of a notion equivalent to "emulation," which is discussed elsewhere, as we shall see promptly.

He does consider the case of an intense envy that stems from desiring a good for ourselves and being prevented from having it because it is possessed by someone who is less worthy of it. In this case the emotion is excusable if the envier is truly concerned with the unjust distribution and does not focus on the envied themselves. On the one hand, the focus on the good rather than the envied might make us think of *zēlos*. On the other hand, the emphasis on injustice points again in the direction of a moral emotion such as indignation, or, more precisely, *resentment*, which, like indignation, is a reaction to a perceived moral injury and which holds the perpetrator of the injury accountable, but from a first-personal perspective (Strawson 1962).

Thinking of envy as a moral emotion differentiates Descartes from many of the philosophers we have reviewed so far, and has not, overall, proved to be an influential or popular way of thinking of envy.[67] Both philosophers and psychologists adopt views according to which envy is a nonmoral emotion, which only masquerades as resentment or indignation. If envy was just the same as resentment then we would not be so ashamed to confess it. Also, as Leibniz observes later in response to Locke, we can experience being envious of someone while being well aware that the person is more deserving than us.

However, Descartes also admits that few people are so virtuous so as to not feel hatred toward the envied, and thus in practice envy is often unjust. Finally, he observes that glory is the most envied good. Glory is a positional good: in some sense we can all aspire to it, but the more one has glory the harder it is for others to acquire it. It is not really clear what the upshot of this observation is, but perhaps what Descartes intends is

opposed to the modern usage according to which a behavior being excusable means that we do not blame the agent even if the action or feeling is not justified.

[67] Among contemporary philosophers, only Marguerite La Caze (2001) takes an analogous position. Among contemporary psychologists. Richard Smith (1991) used to defend the view that envy contains a judgment of subjective injustice, although the introduction of the distinction between benign and malicious envy has complicated the issue (see, e.g., van de Ven et al. 2015). See chapter 2 for details.

that it is difficult to feel justified envy with regard to glory, because one is naturally predisposed to detest the envied.

John Locke also includes a judgment of undeservingness, albeit relative and not absolute, in his definition of envy in book II, chapter XX of *An Essay Concerning Human Understanding* (1690): "Envy is an uneasiness of mind, caused by the consideration of a good we desire, obtained by one, we think should not have had it before us."

Leibniz makes some very sensible objections to Locke in his book-length commentary on Lock's *Essay* (*New Essays on Human Understanding,* 1704). In book II, chapter XX, paragraph 13 Theophilius, Leibniz's alter ego, observes that Locke's notion implies that envy "would always be legitimate, at least in one's own opinion." However, Theophilius observes that we are often envious of people whose merits we acknowledge are deserved. A further proof of this – Theophilius adds – is that if the same envied qualities or goods were our own, we could not care to vilify them. What bothers us, *contra* Locke and Descartes, is not that the fortune is undeserved, but that someone else has it. Theophilius goes on to say that one may also envy "possession of a good which one would not care to possess for oneself: one would merely like to see them deprived of it, without thought of benefiting by their loss – and even with no possible hope of such benefit, for some goods are like paintings in fresco, which can be destroyed but cannot be removed." This makes a different criticism: Locke is wrong in saying that envy is caused by the consideration that someone else has something that one desires. We may be envious of things that we do not quite desire. He then draws the further conclusion that, when we envy a good that we don't actually want, the behavioral output is to want the envied deprived of their good. This further inference does not seem correct: there may be different reasons why one would want to level down. Leibniz is right, though, in pointing to gaps in Locke's simplistic definition. He also notices how leveling down may occur not only without the thought of benefiting from the envied's loss, but even without the hope of such benefit, such as in the case of goods that are non-transferrable or non-shareable.

A.4.4   *The Personal and The Political*

A central notion of Plato's *Republic* is that a healthy human soul and a well-functioning polity are isomorphic, that is, share the same structure. This is a version of a more general view that we could call the "collective harmony view," according to which the collective good and an individual's good coincide. Aristotle is critical of the Platonic ideal constitution, but does not challenge the larger picture of collective harmony.[68] Arguably, Augustine's metaphorical opposition between the "City of God" and the "City of Man" in *De Civitate Dei* implicitly relies on the same picture.[69] Even though there may have been dissenting voices,[70] most ancient philosophers seem to think along these lines. Modern philosophers not only see that there may be a gap between what is good for the individual and what is good for a community, but also realize the consequences that this has in the political sphere.[71]

One of the first authors in which we see how this different perspective affects the notion of envy is Bacon. While he condemns it harshly in the private domain, he remarks that "public envy" may do some good, because it keeps ambitious men under control: "For public envy, is as an ostracism, that eclipseth men, when they grow too great. And therefore it is a bridle also to great ones, to keep them within bounds" (Bacon 1999, 21).[72] The idea expressed here in passing is an innovative one: a vice, even a devilish vice such as envy, may have some positive features when we consider its effects on the public domain.[73]

Hobbes has a lot to say about the relation between individual and public morality, and his attention to the passions is connected to his larger

[68] *Politics* VII.9.1329a22–3.

[69] Thanks to Stephen Darwall for drawing my attention to the difference between the Platonic view and the more general picture.

[70] The Thrasymachean view may be one such case, although its interpretations vary widely and some doubt that at least the character of Thrasymachus as described by Plato in the *Republic* expresses a coherent position. Verity Harte (whom I thank) brought to my attention that one obvious case of conflict between the values of the *oikos* and the values of the *polis* is that of Antigone. Yet one could argue that the reason why Antigone's case counts as a tragic and genuine moral dilemma is precisely because it goes against the culturally entrenched idea that the rules of individual morality mirror and are harmonious with the rules of collective morality.

[71] Think for instance of the so-called *tragedy of the commons* (Hardin 1968), which Aristotle might have intuited, but which did not have a central role in his political thought ("what is common to the greatest number has the least care bestowed upon it. Everyone thinks chiefly of his own, hardly at all of the common interest" (*Politics*, XI. 3). Both Hobbes and Hume discuss versions of this problem. Frank 1999 shows how the tragedy of the commons can be caused by envy.

[72] The long-standing interpretation of the ancient Greek practice of ostracism as motivated by envy has been criticized recently by scholars. See Cairns 2003, 243–4.

[73] This partial rehabilitation of envy is paralleled in Bacon by the condemnation of erotic love in the context of the civic and political community: in both cases, a passion that appears to have a certain moral valence in a private domain has the opposite valence in the public domain. According to Box 2006, it is possible to find two conflicting perspectives in Bacon's moral philosophy. On the one hand, he gives priority to public morality and civic virtues over private morality and domestic virtues, and to action over contemplation. This is the perspective that underlies the analysis of passions in the *Essays*. On the other hand, he is driven by a traditional Christian conception of morality: he affirms that the highest good is Christian charity and defends the value of peace and domestic harmony in the *New Atlantis*. His analyses of love and envy reflect this tension.

political and philosophical projects. He discusses passions extensively in
several works, including the *Elements of Law, De Cive,* and *Leviathan.* His
conception is materialist: passions are internal motions of the body, by
which imagination drives us to act. All passions, in Hobbes' view, are
connected to the human *need for social recognition*: we can satisfy our
passions successfully only if we have power, where power is socially
constructed and stemming from others' recognition of it. The pursuit of
happiness coincides with the pursuit of power. In the state of nature we
strive to survive and satisfy our desires, but in the absence of a sovereign
authority and due to a combination of limited resources and roughly equal
abilities, the natural outcome is a strenuous competition.

In *Leviathan* Hobbes traces the origin of envy to the peculiarly human
tendency to compete for honor and dignity, which is absent in other social
non-human animals. As I show below, Hobbes argues that the highest joy
for humans is based on social esteem and is grounded in social comparison.
This competitive, honor-seeking, and envy-producing nature of man – says
Hobbes – is what produces a discrepancy between common and private
benefits: it is not true for human beings that attending to their private good
produces a common good.

He starts by noting that being rich exposes men to envy, and to
becoming their prey, when it is not shared with others, whereas shared
riches procure friends and servants, hence power (*Leviathan*, ch. 10, 4). In
chapter 17 he compares man to other social creatures such as bees and ants
in order to show that, while such simple creatures can live sociably with
one another even without speech and complex cognitive capacities, man
cannot. The first two differences between men and these creatures listed by
Hobbes are the following:

> First, that men are continually in competition for honour and dignity,
> which these creatures are not; and consequently amongst men there ariseth
> on that ground, envy, and hatred, and finally war; but amongst these not so.
> Secondly, that amongst these creatures the common good differeth not
> from the private; and being by nature inclined to their private, they procure
> thereby the common benefit. But man, whose joy consisteth in comparing
> himself with other men, can relish nothing but what is eminent.
> (Hobbes 2002, 127)

According to Hobbes, then, humans are by nature *competitive* with regard
to honor and dignity. Because of this feature, which is *continuously* at play,
envy and hatred, and consequently wars, arise. This competitive, honor-
seeking nature of man is what produces a discrepancy between *common*

and *private benefits*. Finally, man derives joy from comparison, and can *only* enjoy "what is eminent," that is, what makes him stand out from the crowd, what is comparatively excellent. We have seen how the psychological insights about comparison are developed by later philosophers. But here we also find the seeds for the that idea of "social asociality," which we find in Hume and Kant.

However, Hobbes' solution to this problem does not rely on a positive role for the antisocial passions, which is the theme, notoriously, of Mandeville's *Fable of the Bees*. In the parable told by Mandeville, individual vices are a source for public benefits. Even though "every Part was full of Vice," the sum of parts is virtuous: "the whole Mass a Paradise," at least in the sense that they make society prosper economically. Virtue derives from (or maybe is nothing but – depending on the interpretations) regimented and inhibited vice. Such cynicism about human nature also appears in his belief that envy is universal: "I don't believe there is a Human Creature in his Senses arriv'd to Maturity, that at one time or other has not been carried away by this Passion in good Earnest" (*Fable of the Bees*, Note N), thus agreeing with modern-day anthropologist George Foster that envy is a "pan-human phenomenon" (Foster 1972, 165). The modern-day advertising industry can be seen as providing supportive evidence for Mandeville's analysis, albeit with the important proviso that only certain kinds of envy spur consumers in the desired direction (Belk 2008).

A less psychologically subtle but perhaps more philosophically ambitious analysis of envy and its different roles at the individual and collective levels can be found in Kant. In *Idea for a Universal History with a Cosmopolitan Aim* he compares human beings who accept the hardship of a civic union to trees: "each needs the others, since each in seeking to take the air and sunlight from others must strive upward, and thereby each realizes a beautiful, straight stature, while those that live in isolated freedom put out branches at random and grow stunted, crooked, and twisted" (8:22). While a civic union is coercive to the individual, it is liberating for humanity: in limiting man's aggressive and antisocial tendencies it permits him to fully develop his potential: "All culture, art which adorns mankind, and the finest social order are fruits of unsociableness, which forces itself to discipline itself and so, by a contrived art, to develop the natural seeds to perfection" (8:22).

A natural interpretation of the passage read in isolation would be to think of envy in terms of *zēlos*, or anyway as an emotion that motivates to self-improvement. But that is actually far from what Kant means. Envy is among the antisocial passions that remain truly vicious at the individual level, but that are necessary for the species to develop its full potential. Without these antisocial passions human beings would live in an Arcadia of self-sufficiency and mutual love, but that would leave them in an animal state ("as good-natured as the sheep they tended"), with all their powers forever dormant. Social incompatibility, enviously competitive vanity, and insatiable desires for possession and power are fostered by nature to bring man to develop his excellent natural capacities.

Notice two differences between Kant's account and those of Bacon and Mandeville. First, Kant's perspective is diachronic, rather than synchronic. Second, and relatedly, the benefits brought about by envy are indirect. While in Bacon and Mandeville envy directly brings about some public and social benefits, in Kant it is indirectly responsible for progress: antisocial passions make necessary the institution of civil society, which in turn brings about progress.

A discordant note in this context is played by Adam Smith. As mentioned above, envy often recurs in the *Theory,* which is not surprising given that he, like Mandeville, is well aware of how tied the desire for wealth and material goods and the desire for social recognition are in the society of his time. As Thomas Horne nicely puts it:

> This desire for recognition sets off a competition that is intense, not moderate, because it is for goods that are very limited indeed. It is this competition that threatens individual morality and social harmony [...] . Envy destroys the ability to sympathize with others, and thus impedes the ability of the impartial spectator to mediate between the interests of the self and those of others. Smith understood this problem, preached against vanity, counselled moderation, but perhaps to no avail, for he also understood vanity to be the strongest motive to economic activity. (Horne 1981, 565)

As we have seen, his very definition of envy includes the idea that it is an inappropriate response against *deserved* good fortune. Envy is the wrong way to address an important social need, that of not letting undeserving people rise above oneself, either out of indolence, good nature, or "ill-judged magnanimity." This is a kind of weakness that "frequently gives place to a most malignant envy in the end, and to a hatred of that superiority, which those who have once attained it, may often become really entitled to, by the very circumstance of having attained it" (VI.III.16), Thus, envy arises out of a legitimate need "to defend our dignity and rank," but it then reveals itself to be the cure that is worse than the disease.

The reflection on envy's effects on the political sphere continues after the modern era, with Nietzsche and Freud finding in envy (and related emotions like *ressentiment*) the source (either historically or developmentally) of egalitarian ideals. The connection between envy and egalitarianism and the role of envy in a well-regulated society have been discussed by prominent political philosophers such as Rawls and Nozick, and are still relevant topics in the contemporary debate (see Chapter 5).

Finally, some of the modern philosophers' reflections on envy focus on a domain that is intermediate between the private and the public: the education of children and future citizens. Most of them see this role as a negative one.

Spinoza believes that education fosters the natural human tendency to feel hatred and envy, insofar as "parents are accustomed to incite their children to virtue solely by the spur of honour and envy" (*Ethics*, III,p15, note).

Both Kant and Rousseau join Spinoza in condemning the pedagogical use of envy. For Kant, children are rightly encouraged to look up to those who are roughly their equals. But since emulation and self-improvement are difficult, children end up being resentful and envious instead. Kant (2007b) therefore invites educators to develop in children the inclination to aspire to duty itself (*Lectures on Pedagogy* 9:491–2).

For Rousseau, children must be taught to free themselves from envy, pride, vanity, and all the other dangerous passions that arise from an inflamed *amour propre*. The right method to educate children to become virtuous men and citizens is to teach them to be self-reliant and confident in their own judgment. That way they will be capable of love, pity, and benevolence, and they will be genuinely happy and capable of rejoicing in others' happiness.

According to Neuhouser (2008), Rousseau's innovation consists in realizing that *amour propre* is a distinctive feature of human beings, which can be reformed and educated: it contains the seeds of both prosocial and antisocial emotions and attitudes. It is surprising, then, that Rousseau did not find a role for a morally positive counterpart to envy. Emulation is never mentioned in the *Discourse*. In *Emile* the term has either a negative connotation (when it refers to a passion associated with envy and rivalry) or a neutral one (when it refers not to a passion but to the tendency, shared with primates, to imitate someone else). This is interesting because it seems to indicate that Rousseau thought that social comparison cannot be used in favor of sociality. Once we are in the business of comparing our lot to that of others we are in the business of inflamed *amour propre* and injured self-esteem. This hypothesis, however, is in tension with Rousseau's approval of pity, which is also based on comparison (albeit downward comparison) and might therefore involve *amour propre.*

A dissonant voice in this choir of condemnations of envy in moral education is that of Mandeville's, who believes that further evidence for the ingrained place of envy in human nature is provided by the successful appeal to emulation in education. Mandeville warns us against thinking that such an appeal is efficacious because it arises from a virtuous disposition. Quite the contrary, "if we look narrowly into it, we shall find that this Sacrifice of Ease and Pleasure is only made to Envy, and the Love of Glory" (*Fable of the Bees,* Note N). A worry Mandeville has with this educational approach is that the children who are not "covetous, peevish, and quarrelsome" (ibid.) but "disinterested, good-humour'd, and peaceable" (ibid.) will become indolent and inactive. But, overall, he seems to think that, once again, the vice of envy brings about public benefits.

The topic of envy is not commonly discussed in modern pedagogy. Psychology can confirm that children do feel envy, and even often and with regard to more domains than adults, because their sense of identity and what matters to them is still underdeveloped (Bers and Rodin 1984). It is plausible that envy might be unavoidable among children, and therefore perhaps they should be educated to feel Aristotelian *zēlos.*[74]

A.5   Envy in John Rawls

Because of how influential John Rawls' approach to envy has been in political philosophy, and given his status as a classic, I devote the final section of this Appendix to a more detailed review of his treatment of envy. (Those who have read the shorter section in Chapter 5 will notice some overlapping.)

In *A Theory of Justice,* John Rawls stipulates that the highly rational individuals behind the veil of ignorance do not "suffer from envy" (Rawls 1999, 124). The choice of words is meaningful: envy as defined by Rawls is indeed something to *suffer* from – as opposed to simply feel – because it is not just unpleasant, but painful and vicious, a "form of rancor that harms both its object and its subject" (467). This definition has implications that I discuss momentarily.

Behind the veil of ignorance there is no envy in two senses: the parties in the original position not only do not *feel* envy, and thus are not motivated

---

[74] As proposed in Kristjánsson 2006.

by it in their deliberations, but also they do not *know* anything about envy and the role it plays in our social lives.

Rawls is aware that this assumption might be assessed as unrealistic, but he defends it on the grounds that his argument for the two principles of justice proceeds in two stages: he first ignores individual psychological propensities such as envy; then, after establishing the principles, he checks whether the resulting society is stable. It is at that point that he pauses to consider, in two very dense and still neglected sections (80 and 81), the "problem of envy" and its relation to inequality (464–80).

Rawls begins section 80 by reminding the reader that "the persons in the original position are not moved by certain psychological propensities" (464). Thus, Rawls justifies his exclusion of envy in two ways. First, because "accidental contingencies" (464) are best set aside to simplify the bargaining process. Among these accidental contingencies are psychological propensities of individuals, which include various emotions; Rawls mentions shame and humiliation alongside envy. He acknowledges that an adequate theory of justice will ultimately have to deal with these propensities. But why does Rawls discuss only envy and not also, for instance, shame and humiliation? I think the answer is that *only envy is believed to motivate egalitarianism.* A frequent accusation against egalitarians is that they are motivated by "class envy" and, since envy is deemed to be a vice, that is considered a strike against the view. Rawls faces this charge directly at the end of section 81. (Readers interested in what I call the Envious Egalitarianism argument are advised to take a look at the first part of Chapter 5.)

The second reason to reject envy that Rawls provides is that envy is a vice, and we do not want the parties to be motivated by any vice.[75] Thus, Rawls feels comfortable "for reasons both of simplicity and moral theory" (465) to eliminate envy in the first stage of his argument. However, once the principles of justice have been chosen, he admits that he has to reckon with it and ascertain whether "the well-ordered society corresponding to the conception adopted will actually generate feelings of envy and patterns of psychological attitudes that will undermine the arrangements it counts to be just" (465).

But it is not all kinds of envy that matter! Rawls distinguishes between several kinds of envy. His distinctions are both illuminating and confusing: he points out important differences, but he does not develop them

---

[75] In note 5, p. 466, he refers to both *Metaphysics of Morals* (II, 36) and *Nicomachean Ethics* (1107a11) as accounts of envy as a vice.

carefully (which is understandable given that his main preoccupation is dealing with the charge against egalitarians, rather than articulating a taxonomy of envy).

First, he distinguishes between *general* and *particular* envy. We feel general envy when we envy others for being better situated, for the kinds of goods they have. For instance, the upper classes are envied for their wealth. We feel particular envy when we envy others for some particular goods they have, for instance a specific job. According to Rawls this envy is unavoidable, since it has to do with personal rivalry and competition, and is not of concern for political theory. Thus, he sets particular envy aside.

Patrick Tomlin (2008) correctly points out that Rawls conflates two ways in which envy can be particular: with regard to the object and with regard to the target. Rawls talks about the former: envying others (presumably either individuals or groups) for general goods. But Tomlin uses the example of envying one's sibling, a particular individual, because of their superior position with regard to access to primary social goods, which is a general good. An implication of Tomlin's distinction is that envy can also be *general* in these two senses. Thus, we have four kinds of envy: envy that is general both with regard to target and object (e.g., poor people may envy rich people); envy that is general with regard to target but particular with regard to goods (e.g., women might envy men because they are advantaged in the run for president); envy that is particular with regard to target but general with regard to object (e.g., I may envy my brother because he has a job with better pension benefits); and finally envy that is particular both with regard to object and target (the many cases of envy we saw in the previous chapters, envying a particular person for a particular trait, position, or advantage they have).

Rawls' next distinction is orthogonal to general and particular. He distinguishes between *benign envy, emulative envy*, and *envy proper*. Benign envy consists in expressing the judgment that something is enviable in the sense of being valuable and/or desirable; this is only "envy" as a way of speaking. Emulative envy is an emotion that motivates us to achieve things similar to what others have in socially beneficial ways. Rawls does not say much more about this kind of envy. He refers to Bishop Butler's notion of emulation (see Section A.4.2.2), and implies that emulative envy requires feeling capable of overcoming one's disadvantage when he says that emulative envy may devolve into malicious envy "under certain conditions of defeat and sense of failure" (Rawls 1999, 467). Rawls' notion of emulative envy is thus compatible with mine, but he does not make any use of it since he never explicitly mentions it again. (Implicitly, he might be thinking of emulative envy when he discusses conditions that prevent envy proper from arising in section 81.)

Thereon, Rawls focuses exclusively on what he calls envy proper: "the propensity to view with hostility the greater good of others even though their being more fortunate than we are does not detract from our advantages" (466). This, you might recall, is Kant's definition of *livor* in the *Metaphysics of Morals* (4:458). Rawls says explicitly that he adopts Kant's definition. Thus, Rawls conceives of envy proper as a vice of mankind. But he goes beyond Kant's definition and thinks of envy proper as, we could say, "uberspiteful": "We envy persons whose situation is superior to ours ... and we are willing to deprive them of their greater benefits *even if it is necessary to give up something ourselves*" (Rawls 1999, 466, my emphasis). Not only are the envious willing to spoil the good, but even renounce some other good on top of that!

Harrison Frye (2016) has argued that Rawls defines envy so narrowly because of the assumption of close-knitness that is implied by the difference principle:

> The problem of envy pertains to the difference principle, which holds that social and economic inequalities are to be arranged so that they are to the greatest expected benefit of the least advantaged (TJ, 72). Included in Rawls's understanding of the difference principle is the assumption of close-knitness. When close-knitness holds, raising or lowering the economic expectation of any representative person will impact the economic expectations of other representative persons (TJ, 70).12 Consequently, Rawls is concerned with cases where regulation economically harms both the least advantaged and the more advantaged. (Frye 2016, 4)

What Frye has in mind here is, I think, a case such as the following: imagine that a new tax release is proposed, such that the richest 1 percent of a polity gets a more significant benefit than the other 99 percent of the population. The 99 percent's lot is still improved, but the inequality is massive[76] and it may be perceived, psychologically, as insulting and thus generate uberspiteful envy. This seems to be the kind of scenario that Rawls might be worried about: one in which the envier is willing to incur an additional cost for the sake of impeding the envied's advantage.

I find Frye's argument helpful in seeing an important difference between spiteful envy at the individual level and at the collective level.

---

[76] Of course, this massive inequality renders envy inappropriate. Resentment or indignation are the fitting responses here. Set that aside for the moment.

In an individual interaction spiteful envy is not self-defeating: even if the good is spoiled and the envier does not succeed in stealing it the envier is still comparatively better off. But at the collective level our assessment changes, especially if, like Rawls, we are evaluating the stability and flourishing of a society. If the parties are motivated by envy as defined – that is, uberspiteful envy – then they are willing to decrease the amount of primary goods available to another person, even if they themselves do not gain the goods or even lose something additionally. It is easy to see how socially disadvantageous such an approach would be, and how in tension with the difference principle ideal.

After having defined envy proper, Rawls goes on to perform his "stability test," that is, he checks whether a well-ordered society, regulated by his principles of justice, will be destabilized and undermined by excessive envy, particularly by "excusable general envy."

The difference between excusable and non-excusable envy is a further distinction in Rawls' pretty muddy taxonomy. It is worth citing in full the passage that introduces this notion:

> Thus vices are broadly based traits that are not wanted, spitefulness and envy being clear cases, since they are to everyone's detriment. The parties will surely prefer conceptions of justice the realization of which does not arouse these propensities. We are normally expected to forbear from the actions to which they prompt us and to take the steps necessary to rid ourselves of them. Yet sometimes the circumstances evoking envy are so compelling that given human beings as they are no one can reasonably be asked to overcome his rancorous feelings. A person's lesser position as measured by the index of objective primary goods may be so great as to wound his self-respect; and given his situation, we may sympathize with his sense of loss. Indeed, we can resent being made envious, for society may permit such large disparities in these goods that under existing social conditions these differences cannot help but cause a loss of self-esteem. For those suffering this hurt, envious feelings are not irrational; the satisfaction of their rancor would make them better off. When envy is a reaction to the loss of self-respect in circumstances where it would be unreasonable to expect someone feel differently, I shall say that it is excusable. (Rawls 1999, 468)

Even though Rawls does not mention him, this passage is resonant of Adam Smith's analysis of the relation between self-respect and possessing material goods like a clean shirt, as Harrison Frye also observes (Frye 2016, 6). Recent commentators have focused on the notion of excusable envy as a crucial tool to defend the rationality and even appropriateness of envy in the context of nonideal theory (see Chapter 5).

The mention of excusable envy allows Rawls to transition into section 81, where he explicitly tackles the accusation that egalitarians are motivated by envy, and the possibility that the well-ordered society might be destabilized by excessive envy. The implicit reasoning is that, insofar as this envy is excusable, *it is legitimate to be concerned with it*: we cannot dismiss it as conservatives would like us to do. If a society is such that it unavoidably brings many of its citizens to be prey of a terrible vice, thus harming them twice (in wounding their self-respect and in making them morally vicious), then something is wrong in this society and we have to change something.

Rawls believes that propensity to spiteful envy is caused by low self-esteem and a feeling of impotence. As a consequence, there are two social conditions that make this kind of envy worse: first, when the discrepancy between one's situation and others' is made visible and thus humiliating, one's self-esteem is lowered and one's (uberspiteful) envy is increased; second, when the least favored in society feel that they cannot improve their life prospects they are more prone to feeling envy. Even though Rawls does not provide any empirical reference to support his claims, we saw in Chapter 2 that his speculations are correct.

Rawls concludes that the well-ordered society will not risk generating excessive envy because its social institutions will mitigate the root psychological condition. A contractualist notion of justice reinforces citizens' self-respect and their sense of being treated as equal; Rawls expects citizens to be "bound by ties of civic friendship" (Rawls 1999, 470). People's claims to social resources are not adjudicated on the basis of excellence or virtue, therefore self-respect is not based on comparative elements. Rawls believes that the polity stemming from his principles of justice will make unavoidable disparities easier to tolerate. Furthermore, he expects the well-ordered society to be, in practice, less unequal than those that have existed: "the spread of income and wealth should not be excessive in practice, given the requisite background institutions" (470). It is worth noting that Rawls uses self-respect and self-esteem interchangeably in this context, something which has been amply critiqued in later discussion[77] and which will be relevant later.

As for the two social conditions that decrease self-esteem and increase sense of powerlessness, Rawls thinks that they are not likely to occur in the well-ordered society. Plurality of associations and the related possibility to

---

[77] The literature on self-respect and self-esteem in Rawls is vast. Some classic references are Shue 1975; Darwall 1977; Sachs 1981; Cohen 1989. More recent contributions include Moriarty 2009; Eyal 2005; Doppelt 2009; Laitinen 2012.

thrive in different ways should decrease the visibility and saliency of disparities, and he thinks that "a well-ordered society as much as any other offers constructive alternatives to hostile outbreaks of envy" (471). Rawls remains vague and noncommittal because he thinks the matter cannot be settled without "a more detailed knowledge of social norms available at the legislative stage" (471), a notion he reiterates when discussing self-respect and whether the distribution generated by the difference principle should be adjusted to avoid excusable envy (479).

Rawls' final verdict is thus that the well-ordered society is not likely to be destabilized by excessive envy. It is at this point that he finally tackles the charge against egalitarian conceptions of justice, under whose heading his two principles fall. Much like other egalitarians, he highlights how the problem is not inequality, but injustice, and that his focus is on improving the situation of the less advantaged. Furthermore, Rawls has a unique and original argument: the parties in the original position by hypothesis are not moved by envy. At most the parties might be moved by resentment, which is different from envy, *even more so* given the Rawlsian definition of envy as uberspiteful.

To sum up: Rawls' solution to *the* problem of envy is in fact a two-pronged solution, or rather two solutions to *two different* issues: one is to show that egalitarian ideals are not motivated by the vice of envy, the second is to show that the well-ordered society is not going to be plagued by excessive general envy. Rawls proposes the exclusion of envy from the original position to respond to the first problem, and believes that the difference principle together with other features will create a society that is moderately egalitarian and will not make its citizens feel too much destructive envy.

Even though he seems to initially intuit the complexity of envy, Rawls ends up shunning it completely, likely because he both inherits a very negative outlook (from the Aristotle of the *Ethics* and from Kant) and because of the pressure exerted by conservative political thinkers. As I show in Chapter 5, this move will have long-lasting and, in my view, detrimental consequences on the discussion of envy in the public sphere.

References

Al-Ghazálí. 1994. *The Faith and Practice of Al-Ghazali*, trans. W. Montgomery Watt. London: Oneworld.

2007. *Alchemy of Happiness*, Vol. 2, trans. Jay R. Crook. Chicago: Kazi Publications, Inc .

Al-Qushayrī, 1990. *Principles of Sufism*, trans. B. R. von Schlegell. South Jakarta: Mizan Press.

Anastasopoulos, Dimitris. 2007. "The narcissism of depression or the depression of narcissism and adolescence." *Journal of Child Psychotherapy* 33 (3): 345–62.

Appel, Helmut, Jan Crusius, and Alexander L. Gerlach. 2015. "Social comparison, envy, and depression on Facebook: A study looking at the effects of high comparison standards on depressed individuals." *Journal of Social and Clinical Psychology* 34 (4): 277–89.

Appel, Helmut, Alexander L. Gerlach, and Jan Crusius. 2016. "The interplay between Facebook use, social comparison, envy, and depression." *Current Opinion in Psychology* 9: 44–9.

Aquaro, George R. A. 2004. *Death by Envy: The Evil Eye and Envy in the Christian Tradition*. Lincoln, NB: Universe.

Archer, Alfred, and André Grahle, eds. 2019. *The Moral Psychology of Admiration*. London: Rowman & Littlefield International.

Aristotle. (*c.*340 BCE) 1920. *Ethica Nicomachea*, ed. I. Bywater. Oxford: Clarendon Press. .

(4th c. BCE) 1963. *Ars Rhetorica*, ed. W. D. Ross. Oxford: Clarendon Press.

(c.340 BCE) 1994. *Nicomachean Ethics*, trans. W. D. Ross, available online at http://classics.mit.edu/Aristotle/nicomachaen.html.

(4th c. BCE) 1998. *Politics*, trans. C. D. C. Reeves. Indianapolis: Hackett Publishing Co.

(4th c. BCE) 2004. *Rhetoric*, trans. W. Rhys Roberts. New York: Dover Thrift Editions.

Augustine of Hippo. (5th c. CE) 1952. *The City of God, Books VIII–XVI*, trans. Gerald G. Walsh, and Grace Monahan. Washington, DC: The Catholic University of America Press.

(c.400 CE) *De Catechizandis Rudibus* (in Latin), available online at www .thelatinlibrary.com/augustine/catechizandis.shtml.

(*c*.400 CE) *On the Catechising of the Uninstructed*, available online at www
.newadvent.org/fathers/1303.htm.

Austin, Emily A. 2012. "Fools and malicious pleasure in Plato's 'Philebus'."
History of Philosophy Quarterly 29 (2): 125–39.

Bacon, Francis. (1625) 1999. *The Essays, or Counsels Civil and Moral*, ed. Brian
Vickers. New York: Oxford University Press.

Bahns, Angela J., Kate M. Pickett, and Christian S. Crandall. 2012. "Social
ecology of similarity: Big schools, small schools and social relationships."
Group Processes and Intergroup Relations 15: 119–31.

Bankovsky, Miriam. 2018. "Excusing economic envy: On injustice and impotence." *Journal of Applied Philosophy* 35 (2): 257–79.

Barash, Susan S. 2006. *Tripping the Prom Queen: The Truth about Women and
Rivalry*. New York: St. Martin's Press.

Barnes, Elizabeth. 2016. *The Minority Body*. New York: Oxford University Press.

Barnidge, Matthew. 2018. "Social affect and political disagreement on social
media." *Social Media + Society* 4 (3). https://doi.org/10.1177/
2056305118797721.

Barrett, Lisa Feldman. 2006. "Are emotions natural kinds?" *Perspectives on
Psychological Science* 1 (1): 28–58.

2017. *How Emotions Are Made: The Secret Life of the Brain*. Boston: Houghton
Mifflin Harcourt.

Basil of Caesarea. (*c.* 364 CE) 1950. *Ascetical Works*, trans. Monica M. Wagner.
Washington, DC: The Catholic University of America Press, 463–74.

Belk, Russell W. 2008. "Marketing and envy." In *Envy: Theory and Research*,
edited by Richard H. Smith, 211–26. New York: Oxford University Press.

Bell, Macalester. 2005. "A woman's scorn: Toward a feminist defense of contempt
as a moral emotion." *Hypatia* 20 (4): 80–93.

Ben-Ze'ev, Aaron. 1990. "Envy and jealousy." *Canadian Journal of Philosophy* 20
(4): 487–516.

1992. "Envy and inequality." *The Journal of Philosophy* 89 (11): 551–81.

2000. *The Subtlety of Emotions*. Cambridge, MA: MIT Press.

2002. "Are envy, anger, and resentment moral emotions?" *Philosophical
Explorations* 5 (2): 148–54.

Berke, Joseph. 2012. *Why I Hate You and You Hate Me: The Interplay of
Envy, Greed, Jealousy and Narcissism in Everyday Life*. London: Karnac
Books.

Bers, Susan A., and Judith Rodin. 1984. "Social-comparison jealousy:
A developmental and motivational study." *Journal of Personality and Social
Psychology* 47 (4): 766–79.

Bloomfield, Morton. 1967. *The Seven Deadly Sins*. East Lansing: Michigan State
University Press.

Bloomfield, Paul. 2001. *Moral Reality*. New York: Oxford University Press.

Box, Ian. 2006. "Bacon's moral philosophy." In *The Cambridge Companion to
Bacon*, edited by Markku Peltonen, 260–82. New York: Cambridge
University Press.

Boyce, Christopher J., Gordon D. A. Brown, and Simon C. Moore. 2010. "Money and happiness: Rank of income, not income, affects life satisfaction." *Psychological Science* 21 (4): 471–5.

Bradley, Ben. 2005. "Virtue consequentialism." *Utilitas* 17 (3): 282–98.

Brighouse, Harry, and Adam Swift. 2006. "Equality, priority, and positional goods." *Ethics* 116 (3): 471–97.

Brisson, Luc. 2000. *Lectures de Platon*. Paris: Vrin.

Burgin, Victor. 1994. "Paranoiac space." In *Visualizing Theory: Selected Essays from V.A.R., 1990–1994*, edited by Lucien Castaing-Taylor, 230–51. London: Routledge.

Bushman, Briahna Bigelow, and Julianne Holt-Lunstad. 2009. "Understanding social relationship maintenance among friends: Why we don't end those frustrating friendships." *Journal of Social and Clinical Psychology* 28 (6): 749–78.

Butler, Joseph. (1729) 2017. *Fifteen Sermons Preached at the Rolls Chapel and Other Writings on Ethics*, ed. David McNaughton. Oxford: Oxford University Press.

Buunk, Abraham P., and Frederick X. Gibbons. 2006. "Social comparison orientation: A new perspective on those who do and those who don't compare with others." In *Social Comparison and Social Psychology: Understanding Cognition, Intergroup Relations, and Culture*, edited by Serge Guimond, 15–33. Cambridge: Cambridge University Press.

Cain, R. Bensen. 2017 "Malice and the ridiculous as self-ignorance: A dialectical argument in Philebus 47d–50e." *Southwest Philosophy Review* 33 (1): 83–94.

Cairns, D. L. 2003. "The politics of envy: Envy and equality in ancient Greece." In *Envy, Spite, and Jealousy: The Rivalrous Emotions in Ancient Greece*, edited by David Konstan and Keith N. Ruttner, 235–52. Edinburgh: Edinburgh University Press.

Carbado, Devon W., Kimberlé Williams Crenshaw, Vickie M. Mays, and Barbara Tomlinson. 2013. "INTERSECTIONALITY: Mapping the Movements of a Theory." *Du Bois Review* 10 (2): 303–12.

Catherine of Siena. 1994. *The Dialogue of Divine Providence*. www.catholicplanet.com/ebooks/Dialogue-of-St-Catherine.pdf.

Chan, Alan. 2012. "Laozi." *The Stanford Encyclopedia of Philosophy* (Fall 2012 Edition), edited by Edward N. Zalta. http://plato.stanford.edu/archives/fall2012/entries/laozi/.

Chaucer, Geoffrey. (1387–1400) 2011, *The Canterbury Tales*, trans. Cristopher Cannon and David Wright, ed. Cristopher Cannon. Oxford: Oxford University Press.

Cherry, Myisha. 2017. "The errors and limitations of our "anger-evaluating" ways." In *The Moral Psychology of Anger*, edited by Myisha Cherry and Owen Flanagan, 49–66. London: Rowman & Littlefield.

Cialdini, Robert B., Richard J. Borden, Avril Thorne, Marcus Randall Walker, Stephen Freeman, and Lloyd Reynolds Sloan. 1976. "Basking in reflected glory: Three (football) field studies." *Journal of Personality and Social Psychology* 34 (3): 366–75.

Cikara, Mina and Susan T. Fiske. 2012. "Stereotypes and Schadenfreude: Affective and physiological markers of pleasure at outgroup misfortunes." *Social Psychological and Personality Science* 3 (1): 63–71.

Clanton, Gordon. 2006. "Jealousy and envy." In *Handbook of the Sociology of Emotions*, edited by Jan Stets and Jonathan H. Turner, 410–42. Boston, MA: Springer.

Cohen, Betsy. 1986. *The Snow White Syndrome: All about Envy*. New York: Macmillan Publishing Company.

Cohen, Joshua. 1989. "Democratic equality." *Ethics* 99(4): 727–51.

Cohen-Charash, Yochi, and Elliott C. Larson. 2017. "An emotion divided: Studying envy is better than studying "benign" and "malicious" envy." *Current Directions in Psychological Science* 26 (2): 174–83.

Cooper, David E. 1982. "Equality and envy." *Journal of Philosophy of Education* 16 (1): 35–47.

Cooper, John. 1997. "Introduction." In *Plato: Complete Works*, edited by John Cooper and Douglas S. Hutchinson, vii–xxvi. Indianapolis: Hackett Publishing.

Corcoran, Katja, Jan Crusius, and Thomas Mussweiler. 2011. "Social comparison: Motives, standards, and mechanisms." In *Theories in Social Psychology*, edited by D. Chadee, 119–39. Oxford: Wiley-Blackwell.

Crenshaw, Kimberlé. 1989. "Demarginalizing the intersection of race and sex: A black feminist critique of antidiscrimination doctrine, feminist theory and antiracist politics." *University of Chicago Legal Forum*: Vol. 1989, Article 8. https://chicagounbound.uchicago.edu/uclf/vol1989/iss1/8.

Crusius, Jan, and Thomas Mussweiler. 2012. "When people want what others have: The impulsive side of envious desire." *Emotion* 12 (1): 142–53.

Crusius, Jan, and Jens Lange. 2014. "What catches the envious eye? Attentional biases within malicious and benign envy." *Journal of Experimental Social Psychology* 55: 1–11.

2017. "How do people respond to threatened social status? Moderators of benign versus malicious envy." In *Envy at Work and in Organizations*, edited by Richard H. Smith, Ugo Merlone, and Michelle K. Duffy, 85–110. New York: Oxford University Press.

MS. "Counterfactual thoughts distinguish benign and malicious envy." https://psyarxiv.com/kbqfv/.

Crusius, Jan, Manuel F. Gonzalez, Jens Lange, and Yochi Cohen-Charash. 2020 "Envy: An adversarial review and comparison of two competing views." *Emotion Review* 12 (1): 3–21.

Cuddy, Amy J., Susan T. Fiske, and Peter Glick, 2008. "Warmth and competence as universal dimensions of social perception: The stereotype content model and the BIAS map." *Advances in experimental social psychology* 40: 61–149.

D'Arms, Justin, and Daniel Jacobson. 2000. "The moralistic fallacy: On the "appropriateness" of emotions." *Philosophy and Phenomenological Research* 61 (1): 65–90.

2005. "Anthropocentric constraints on human value." *Oxford Studies in Methaethics* 1: 99–126.

D'Arms, Justin. 2009. "Envy." *The Stanford Encyclopedia of Philosophy*, archived version. https://plato.stanford.edu/archives/spr2009/entries/envy/.

2017. "Envy." *The Stanford Encyclopedia of Philosophy* (Spring 2017 Edition), edited by Edward N. Zalta. https://plato.stanford.edu/archives/spr2017/entries/envy/.

D'Arms, Justin and Alison Duncan Kerr. 2008. "Envy in the philosophical tradition." In *Envy: Theory and Research*, edited by Richard H. Smith, 39–59. New York: Oxford University Press.

Darwall, Stephen. 1977. "Two kinds of respect." *Ethics* 88 (1): 36–49.

2006. *The Second-Person Standpoint: Morality, Respect, Accountability*. Harvard, MA: Harvard University Press.

De la Rochefoucauld, François. (1665) 2008. *Collected Maxims and Other Reflections*. New York: Oxford University Press.

De Mandeville, Bernard. (1714) 1924. *The Fable of the Bees: Or, Private Vices, Publick Benefits*, ed. Frederick B. Kaye. Oxford: Clarendon Press.

De Pisan, Cristine. (1405) 1985. *The Book of the Three Virtues*, trans. Sarah Lawson. London: Penguin.

De Puixieux, Madeleine d'Arsant. 1750–1. *Les caractères*, available online (in French). https://archive.org/details/lescaractreso1madgoog.

Delcomminette, Sylvain. 2006. *Le Philèbe de Platon: Introduction à l'agathologie platonicienne*. Leiden: Brill.

Descartes, René. 1985. *The Philosophical Writings of Descartes*, Vol. 1, trans. John Cottingham, Robert Stoothoff, and Dugald Murdoch. New York: Cambridge University Press.

Deslauriers, Marguerite. 2017. "Marinella and her interlocutors: Hot blood, hot words, hot deeds." *Philosophical Studies* 174 (10): 2525–37.

Doosje, Bertjan E. J., Nyla R. Branscombe, Russell Spears, and Antony S. Manstead. 1998. "Guilty by association: When one's group has a negative history." *Journal of Personality and Social Psychology* 75: 872–86.

Doppelt, Gerald. 2009. "The place of self-respect in a theory of justice." *Inquiry* 52 (2): 127–54.

Driver, Julia. 2001. *Uneasy Virtue*. New York: Cambridge University Press.

Dryer, D. Cristopher, and Leonard M. Horowitz. 1997. "When do opposites attract? Interpersonal complementarity versus similarity." *Journal of Personality and Social Psychology* 72 (3): 592–603.

Dunn, Judy, and Carol Kendrick. 1982. *Siblings: Love, Envy and Understanding*. Cambridge, MA: Harvard University Press.

Ellman, Carolyn S. 2000. "The empty mother: Women's fear of their destructive envy." *Psychoanalytic Quarterly* 69: 633–57.

Elster, Jon. 1983. *Sour Grapes: Studies in the Subversion of Rationality*. Cambridge: Cambridge University Press.

Emerick, Barrett. 2017. "Forgiveness and reconciliation." In *The Moral Psychology of Forgiveness*, edited by Kathryn J. Norlock, 117–34. London: Rowman & Littlefield.

Exline, Julie E. and Anne L. Zell. 2008. "Antidotes to envy: A conceptual framework." In *Envy. Theory and Research*, edited by Richard H. Smith, 315–31. New York: Oxford University Press.

Eyal, Nir. 2005. "'Perhaps the most important primary good': Self-respect and Rawls's principles of justice." *Politics, Philosophy & Economics* 4 (2): 195–219.

Fairlie, Henry. 1988. *The Seven Deadly Sins Today*. Notre Dame, IN: University of Notre Dame Press.

Falcon, Rachael G. 2015. "Is envy categorical or dimensional? An empirical investigation using taxometric analysis." *Emotion* 15 (6): 694–8.

Farrell, Daniel M. 1980. "Jealousy." *The Philosophical Review* 89 (4): 527–59.

Farrell, Henry. 2012. "The consequences of the internet for politics." *Annual Review of Political Science* 15: 35–52.

Feather, Norman T. and Rebecca Sherman. 2002. "Envy, resentment, Schadenfreude, and sympathy: Reactions to deserved and undeserved achievement and subsequent failure." *Personality and Social Psychology Bulletin* 28 (7): 953–61.

Ferrante, Elena. 2012. *My Brilliant Friend*. London: Europa Editions UK.

2013. *Story of a New Name*. London: Europa Editions UK.

2014. *Those Who Leave and Those Who Stay*. New York: Europa Editions.

2015. *The Lost Daughter*. New York: Europa Editions.

Festinger, Leon. 1962. "Cognitive dissonance." *Scientific American* 207 (4): 93–106.

Fiske, Susan T. 2011. *Envy Up, Scorn Down: How Status Divides Us*. New York: Russell Sage Foundation.

Fiske, Susan T., Amy J. Cuddy, and Peter Glick. 2007. "Universal dimensions of social cognition: Warmth and competence." *Trends in Cognitive Sciences* 11 (2): 77–83.

Fleming, Ian, ed. 1970. *The Seven Deadly Sins*. Books for Library Press (online).

Foster, George M. 1972. "The anatomy of envy: A study in symbolic behavior." *Current Anthropology* 13: 165–202.

Frank, Robert H. 1999. *Luxury Fever: Why Money Fails to Satisfy in an Era of Excess*. New York: Free Press.

Frede, Dorothea. 1992. "Disintegration and restoration: Pleasure and pain in Plato's *Philebus*." In *The Cambridge Companion to Plato*, edited by R. Kraut, 425–63. Cambridge: Cambridge University Press.

1993. *Philebus*. Indianapolis: Hackett Publishing Company.

1996. "Mixed feelings in Aristotle's *Rhetoric*." In *Essays on Aristotle's Rhetoric*, edited by Amélie Oksenberg Rorty, 258–85. Berkeley: University of California Press.

Frey, Bruno S., and Alois Stutzer. 2002. *Happiness and Economics: How the Economy and Institutions Affect Human Well-Being*. Princeton: Princeton University Press.

Frye, Harrison P. 2016. "The relation of envy to distributive justice." *Social Theory and Practice* 42 (3): 501–24.

Frye, Marylin. 1983. "A note on anger." In *The Politics of Reality: Essays in Feminist Theory*, Marylin Frye, 84–94. New York: Crossing Press.

Fussi, Alessandra. 2017. "Schadenfreude, envy and jealousy in Plato's *Philebus* and Phaedrus." *Philosophical Inquiry* 5 (1): 73–90.

Galinsky, Adam D., Erika V. Hall, and Amy J. Cuddy. 2013. "Gendered races: Implications for interracial marriage, leadership selection, and athletic participation." *Psychological science* 24 (4): 498–506.

Gerhardt, Julie. 2009. "The roots of envy: The unaesthetic experience of the tantalized/dispossessed self." *Psychoanalytic Dialogues* 19: 267–93.

Gibbons, Frederick X. and Abraham P. Buunk, 1999. "Individual differences in social comparison: Development of a scale of social comparison orientation." *Journal of Personality and Social Psychology* 76 (1): 129–42.

Gill, Cristopher. 2003. "Is rivalry a virtue or a vice?" In *Envy, Spite, and Jealousy: The Rivalrous Emotions in Ancient Greece*, edited by David Konstan and Keith N. Ruttner, 29–51. Edinburgh: Edinburgh University Press.

Glick, Peter. 2002. "Sacrificial lambs dressed in wolves clothing: Envious prejudice, ideology, and the scapegoating of Jews." In *Understanding Genocide: The Social Psychology of the Holocaust*, edited by Leonard S. Newman, and Ralph Erber, 113–42. New York: Oxford University Press.

Green, Joshua E. 2013. "Rawls and the forgotten figure of the most advantaged: In defense of reasonable envy toward the superrich." *American Political Science Review* 107 (1):123–38.

Green, Keith. 2007. "Aquinas on attachment, envy, and hatred in the Summa Theologica." *Journal of Religious Ethics* 35 (3): 403–28.

Gregory the Great. (578–95 CE) 2012. *The Moralia in Job*, Vol. 3. Ex Fontibus Company, https://www.exfontibus.com/.

Guerrero, ed. 2020. *Do The Right Thing*. London: Bloomsbury.

Hackforth, Reginald. 1945. *Plato's Examination of Pleasure, A Translation of the Philebus, with Introduction and Commentary*. Cambridge: Cambridge University Press.

Halliwell, Stephen. 2008. *Greek Laughter: A Study of Cultural Psychology from Homer to Early Christianity*. Cambridge: Cambridge University Press.

Harcourt, Edward. 2013 "The place of psychoanalysis in the history of ethics." *Journal of Moral Philosophy*. https://doi.org/10.1163/17455243-4681030.

Hardin, Garrett. 1968. "The tragedy of the commons." *Science, New Series*, 162 (3859): 1243–8.

Harmon-Jones, Eddie, Tom F. Price, and Philip A. Gable. 2012. "The influence of affective states on cognitive broadening/narrowing: Considering the importance of motivational intensity." *Social and Personality Psychology Compass* 6: 314–27.

Harris, Adrienne. 2002. "Mothers, monsters, mentors." *Studies in Gender and Sexuality* 3 (3): 281–95.

Haslam, Nick, and Brian H. Bornstein. 1996. "Envy and Jealousy As Discrete Emotions: A Taxometric Analysis." *Motivation and Emotion* 20 (3): 255–72.

Hayek, Friedrich A. 1960. *The Constitution of Liberty, 2nd impression.* Chicago: University of Chicago Press.

Helm, Bennett. 2017. "Love." *The Stanford Encyclopedia of Philosophy* (Fall 2017 Edition), edited by Edward N. Zalta. https://plato.stanford.edu/archives/fall2017/entries/love/.

Henrich, Joseph, Steven J. Heine, and Ara Norenzayan. 2010. "The weirdest people in the world?" *Behavioral and Brain Sciences* 33 (2–3): 61–83.

Herrmann, F. G. 2003. "*Phthonos* in the World of Plato's *Timaeus.*" In *Envy, Spite, and Jealousy: The Rivalrous Emotions in Ancient Greece,* edited by David Konstan and Keith N. Ruttner, 53–83. Edinburgh: Edinburgh University Press.

Heyes, Cressida. 2020. "Identity politics." *The Stanford Encyclopedia of Philosophy* (Fall 2020 Edition), edited by Edward N. Zalta. https://plato.stanford.edu/archives/fall2020/entries/identity-politics/.

Hill, Sarah, and David Buss. 2008. "The evolutionary psychology of envy." In *Envy: Theory and Research,* edited by Richard H. Smith, 60–71. New York: Oxford University Press.

Hobbes, Thomas. (1651) 2002. *Leviathan,* ed. A. P. Martinich. Peterborough, ON: Broadview.

Horne, Thomas A. 1981. "Envy and commercial society: Mandeville and Smith on 'private vices, public benefits'". *Political Theory* 9(4): 551–69.

Hume, David. (1739–1740) 1978. *A Treatise of Human Nature.* Oxford: Oxford University Press.

Hursthouse, Rosalind. 1999. *On Virtue Ethics,* Oxford: Oxford University Press.

Hursthouse, Rosalind, and Pettigrove, Glen. 2018. "Virtue ethics." *The Stanford Encyclopedia of Philosophy* (Winter 2018 Edition), edited by Edward N. Zalta. https://plato.stanford.edu/archives/win2018/entries/ethics-virtue/.

Iyengar, Shanto, Gaurav Sood, and Yphtach Lelkes. 2012. "Affect, not ideology: A social identity perspective on polarization." *Public Opinion Quarterly* 76 (3): 405–31.

Jaggar, Alison M., 1989. "Love and knowledge: Emotion in feminist epistemology." *Inquiry* 32 (2): 151–76.

James, Susan. 1997. *Passion and Action: The Emotions in Seventeenth–Century Philosophy.* Oxford: Clarendon Press.

Johnson, Benjamin K., and Silvia Knobloch-Westerwick. 2014. "Glancing up or down: Mood management and selective social comparisons on social networking sites." *Computers in Human Behavior* 41: 33–9.

Jordan, Mark D. 1986. *Ordering Wisdom: The Hierarchy of Philosophical Discourses in Aquinas.* Notre Dame, IN: University of Notre Dame Press.

Kagan, Shelly. 1992. "The structure of normative ethics." *Philosophical Perspectives* 6: 223–42.

1998. *Normative Ethics.* New York: McGraw Hill.

Kant, Immanuel. (1797) 1996. *The Metaphysics of Morals*, trans. and ed. Mary J. Gregor. New York: Cambridge University Press.

(1793) 1998. *Religion within the Boundaries of Mere Reason*, trans. George Di Giovanni, ed. Allen W. Wood. New York: Cambridge University Press.

(1784) 2007a, *Idea for a Universal History with a Cosmopolitan Aim*, trans. Allen W. Wood, ed. G. Zöller and R. B. Louden. Cambridge: Cambridge University Press.

(1803) 2007b, *Lectures on Pedagogy*, trans. R. B. Louden, ed. G. Zöller and R. B. Louden. Cambridge: Cambridge University Press.

Kelly, Daniel, and Nicolae Morar. 2014. "Against the yuck factor: On the ideal role of disgust in society." *Utilitas* 26 (2): 153–77.

Kennedy, George A. 2007. *Aristotle, on Rhetoric: A Theory of Civic Discourse, Translated with Introduction, Notes and Appendices*. Oxford: Oxford University Press.

Khader, Serene J. 2011. *Adaptive Preferences and Women's Empowerment*. New York: Oxford University Press.

Kierkegaard, Søren. (1849) 1941. *The Sickness Unto Death: A Christian Psychological Exposition for Upbuilding and Awakening*. New York: Oxford University Press.

Kittay, Eva Feder. 2019. *Learning from My Daughter: The Value and Care of Disabled Minds*. New York: Oxford University Press.

Klein, Melanie. 1957. *Envy and Gratitude: A Study of Unconscious Forces*. New York: Basic Books.

Kleinberg, Aviad. 2008. *Seven Deadly Sins*. Cambridge, MA: Belknap Press.

Konstan, David. 2003. "Before jealousy." In *Envy, Spite, and Jealousy: The Rivalrous Emotions in Ancient Greece*, edited by David Konstan and Keith N. Ruttner, 7–27. Edinburgh: Edinburgh University Press.

2006. *The Emotions of the Ancient Greeks: Studies in Aristotle and Classical Literature*. Toronto: University of Toronto Press.

Konyndyk DeYoung, Rebecca. 2009. *Glittering Vices: A New Look at the Seven Deadly Sins and Their Remedies*. Grand Rapids: Brazos Press.

Krasnova, Hanna, Helena Wenninger, Thomas Widjaja, and Peter Buxmann. 2013. "Envy on Facebook: A hidden threat to users' life satisfaction?" In *Proceedings of the 11th International Conference on Wirtschaftsinformatik* (WI2013). Universität Leipzig, Germany.

Kristjánsson, Kristján. 2002. *Justifying Emotions: Pride and Jealousy*. New York: Routledge.

2006. "Emulation and the use of role models in moral education." *Journal of Moral Education* 35 (1): 37–49.

2018. *Virtuous Emotions*. Oxford: Oxford University Press.

Kumar, Victor. 2017. "Foul behavior." *Philosophers' Imprint* 17 (15): 1–17.

La Caze, Marguerite. 2001. "Envy and resentment." *Philosophical Explorations* 4 (1): 31–45.

Lacewing, Michael. 2013. "Could psychoanalysis be a science?" In *The Oxford Handbook of Philosophy and Psychiatry*, edited by Kenneth W. M. Fulford,

Martin Davies, Richard Gipps, George Graham, John Sadler, Giovanni Stanghellini, and Tim Thornton, 1103–27. Oxford: Oxford University Press.

Lackey, Douglas P. 2005. "Giotto in Padua: A new geography of the human soul." *The Journal of Ethics* 9: 551–72.

Laitinen, Arto. 2012. "Social bases of self–esteem: Rawls, Honneth and beyond." *Nordicum-Mediterraneum* 7 (2).

Lange, Jens, and Jan Crusius. 2015. "Dispositional envy revisited: Unraveling the motivational dynamics of benign and malicious envy." *Personality and Social Psychology Bulletin* 41 (2): 284–94.

Lange, Jens, Jan Crusius, and Birk Hagemeyer. 2016. "The evil queen's dilemma: Linking narcissistic admiration and rivalry to benign and malicious envy." *European Journal of Personality* 30 (2): 168–88.

Lange, Jens, Delroy L. Paulhus, and Jan Crusius. 2018. "Elucidating the dark side of envy: Distinctive links of benign and malicious envy with dark personalities." *Personality and Social Psychology Bulletin* 44 (4): 601–14.

Lange, Jens, Aaron C. Weidman, and Jan Crusius. 2018. "The painful duality of envy: Evidence for an integrative theory and a meta-analysis on the relation of envy and Schadenfreude." *Journal of Personality and Social Psychology* 114 (4): 572–98.

Lange, Jens, Lisa Blatz, and Jan Crusius. 2018. "Dispositional envy: A conceptual review." In *The SAGE Handbook of Personality and Individual Differences*, edited by Virgil Zeigler–Hill and Todd Shackelford, 424–40. Los Angeles: SAGE.

LaVerde-Rubio, Eduardo. 2004. "Envy: One or many?" *The International Journal of Psychoanalysis* 85 (2): 401–18.

Layard, Richard. 2005. *Happiness: Lessons From a New Science*. New York: Penguin Press.

Lazarus, Richard S. 1991. *Emotion and Adaptation*. New York: Oxford University Press.

Le Bon, Gustave. (1895) 1947. *The Crowd: A Study of the Popular Mind*. London: Ernest Benn. www.files.ethz.ch/isn/125518/1414_LeBon.pdf

Leach, Colin Wayne, Martijn van Zomeren, Sven Zebel, Michael L. W. Vliek, Sjoerd F. Pennekamp, Bertjan Doosje, Jaap W. Ouwerkerk, and Russell Spears. 2008 "Group-level self-definition and self-investment: A hierarchical (multicomponent) model of in-group identification." *Journal of Personality and Social Psychology* 95 (1): 144–65.

Leibniz, Gottfried. 1704. *New Essays on Human Understanding*.

Lewis, Michael. 2009. *Home Game: An Accidental Guide to Fatherhood*. New York: W. W. Norton & Company.

Liao, Matthew. 2015. *The Right to Be Loved*. New York: Oxford University Press.

Limberis, Vasiliki. 1991. "The eyes infected by evil: Basil of Caesarea's homily, on envy." *The Harvard Theological Review* 84 (2): 163–84.

Lin, Ruoyun, and Sonja Utz. 2015. "The emotional responses of browsing Facebook: Happiness, envy, and the role of tie strength." *Computers in Human Behavior* 52: 29–38.

Lindholm, Charles. 2008. "Culture and envy." In *Envy: Theory and Research*, edited by Richard H. Smith, 227–44. New York: Oxford University Press.

Livingstone Smith, David. 2011. *Less than Human: Why We Demean, Enslave and Exterminate Others*. New York: St. Martin's Press.

　2020. *On Inhumanity: Dehumanization and How to Resist It*. New York: Oxford University Press.

Locke, John. (1690) 1975. *The Clarendon Edition of the Works of John Locke: An Essay Concerning Human Understanding*, ed. Peter H. Nidditch. Oxford: Oxford University Press.

Lockwood, Penelope, and Ziva Kunda. 1997. "Superstars and me: Predicting the impact of role models on the self." *Journal of Personality and Social Psychology* 73 (1): 91–103.

Lorde, Audre. 1981. "The uses of anger: Women responding to racism." In *Sister Outsider: Essays and Speeches,* Audre Lorde (2012), 124–33. Freedom. CA: Crossing Press.

　1984. "Age, race, class and sex: Women redefining difference." In *Sister Outsider: Essays and Speeches,* Audre Lorde (2012), 114–23. Freedom, CA: Crossing Press.

Lutz, Catherine A. 1988. *Unnatural Emotions: Everyday Sentiments on a Micronesian Atoll and Their Challenge to Western Theory*. Chicago: University of Chicago Press.

McBride, Karyl. 2008. *Will I Ever Be Good Enough? Healing the Daughters of Narcissistic Mothers*. New York: Atria Books.

McDowell, John. 1979. "Virtue and reason." *The Monist* 62 (3): 331–50.

McIntyre, Alison. "Doctrine of double effect." *The Stanford Encyclopedia of Philosophy* (Spring 2019 Edition), edited by Edward N. Zalta. https://plato.stanford.edu/archives/spr2019/entries/double-effect/.

Mackie, Diane M., Eliot R. Smith, and Devin G. Ray. 2008. "Intergroup emotions and intergroup relations." *Social and Personality Psychology Compass* 2 (5): 1866–80.

Mackie, Diane M., 2010. "Unreasonable resentments." *Journal of Social Philosophy* 41 (4): 422–41.

MacLachlan, Alice. 2009. "Practicing imperfect forgiveness." In *Feminist Ethics and Social and Political Philosophy: Theorizing the Non-ideal*, edited by Lisa Tessman, 185–204. New York: Springer.

McRae, Emily. 2017. "Anger and the oppressed: Indo-Tibetan Buddhist perspectives." In *The Moral Psychology of Anger*, edited by Myisha Cherry and Owen Flanagan, 105–21. London: Rowman & Littlefield.

Mallon, Ron, and Stephen P. Stich. 2000. "The odd couple: The compatibility of social construction and evolutionary psychology." *Philosophy of Science* 67 (1): 133–54.

Masters, J.C. and L.J. Keil. 1987. "Generic comparison processes in human judgment and behavior." In *Social Comparison, Social Justice, and Relative Deprivation: Theoretical, Empirical, and Policy Perspectives*, edited by J. C. Masters and W. P. Smith, 11–54. Mahwah, NJ: Lawrence Erlbaum Associates, Inc.

May, Josh. 2014. "Does disgust influence moral judgment?" *Australasian Journal of Philosophy* 92 (1): 125–41.

May, William F. 1967. *A Catalogue of Sins*. New York: Holt, Rinehart, and Winston.

Miceli, Maria. 2012, *L'invidia. Anatomia di un'emozione inconfessabile*. Bologna: Il Mulino.

Miceli, Maria, and Cristiano Castelfranchi. 2007. "The envious mind." *Cognition and Emotion* 21 (3): 449–79.

Migliori, Maurizio. 1993. *L'uomo fra piacere, intelligenza e bene: commentario storico-filosofico al "Filebo" di Platone*. Milano: Vita e Pensiero.

Mills, Charles. 2005. "Ideal theory as ideology." *Hypatia* 20 (3): 165–84.

Morgan-Knapp, Cristopher. 2014. "Economic envy." *Journal of Applied Philosophy* 31 (2): 113–26.

Moriarty, Jeffrey. 2009. "Rawls, self–respect, and the opportunity for meaningful work." *Social Theory and Practice* 35 (3): 441–59.

Mussweiler, Thomas. 2003. "Comparison processes in social judgment: Mechanisms and consequences." *Psychological Review* 110 (3): 472.

Mussweiler, Thomas, Katja Rüter, and Kai Epstude. 2004. "The ups and downs of social comparison: Mechanisms of assimilation and contrast." *Journal of Personality and Social Psychology* 87 (6): 832.

Neaman, Judith S., and Carole G. Silver. 1995. *The Wordsworth Book of Euphemism*. Ware: Wordsworth.

Neill, M. A. F. 2006. *Othello, the Moor of Venice: The Oxford Shakespeare*. Oxford: Clarendon Press.

Neu, Jerome. 1980, "Jealous thoughts." In *Explaining Emotions*, edited by Amélie Oksenberg Rorty, 425–63. Oakland: University of California Press.

Neuhouser, Frederick. 2008. *Rousseau's Theodicy of Self-Love: Evil, Rationality, and the Drive for Recognition*. New York: Oxford University Press.

Newhauser, Richard G., ed. 2005. *In the Garden of Evil: The Vices and Culture in the Middle Ages*. Toronto: Pontifical Institute of Mediaeval Studies.

Nietzsche, Friedrich. (1887) 1994. *On the Genealogy of Morality*, trans. Carol Diethe, ed. Keith Ansell–Pearson. Cambridge: Cambridge University Press.

Nolen-Hoeksema, Susan, and Christopher G. Davis. 2002. "Positive responses to loss: Perceiving benefits and growth." In *Handbook of Positive Psychology*, edited by C. R. Snyder and Shane J. Lopez, 598–606. New York: Oxford University Press.

Norlock, Kathryn J., and Jean Rumsey. 2009. "The limits of forgiveness." *Hypatia* 24 (1): 100–22.

Norman, Richard. 2002. "Equality, envy, and the sense of injustice." *Journal of Applied Philosophy* 19 (1): 43–54.

Nozick, Robert. 1974. *Anarchy, State, and Utopia*. New York: Basic Books.

Nussbaum, Martha C. 1986. *The Fragility of Goodness: Luck and Ethics in Greek Tragedy and Philosophy*. New York: Cambridge University Press.

1990. *Love's Knowledge: Essays on Philosophy and Literature*. New York: Oxford University Press.

2001a. *Upheavals of Thought. The Intelligence of Emotions*. Cambridge: Cambridge University Press.

2001b. "Adaptive Preferences and Women's Options." *Economics and Philosophy* 17 (1): 67–88.

2013. *Political Emotions*. Harvard, MA: Harvard University Press.

2015. "Transitional anger." *Journal of the American Philosophical Association* 1 (1): 41–56.

2016. *Anger and Forgiveness: Resentment, Generosity, Justice*. New York: Oxford University Press.

2018. *The Monarchy of Fear: A Philosopher Looks at Our Political Crisis*. New York: Simon & Schuster.

Olesha, Yuri. 2012. *Envy*, trans. Marian Schwartz. New York: New York Review of Books.

Orbach, Susie, and Luise Eichenbaum. 1988, *Bittersweet: Facing Up to Feelings of Love, Envy and Competition in Women's Friendships*. London: Arrow Books.

Parfit, Derek. 2000. "Equality or priority?" In *The Ideal of Equality*, edited by Matthew Clayton and Andrew Williams. 81–125. Basingstoke and New York: Macmillan.

Parrott, W. Gerald. 1991. "The emotional experiences of envy and jealousy." In *The Psychology of Envy and Jealousy*, edited by Peter Salovey, 3–30. New York: Guilford Press.

Parrott, W. Gerald, and Richard H. Smith. 1993. "Distinguishing the experiences of envy and jealousy." *Journal of Personality and Social Psychology* 64: 906–20.

Parrott, W. Gerald, and Patricia Rodriguez Mosquera. 2008. "On the pleasures and displeasures of being envied." In *The Psychology of Envy and Jealousy*, edited by Peter Salovey, 117–32. New York: Guilford Press.

Perrine, T. 2011. "Envy and self-worth: Amending Aquinas's definition of envy." *American Catholic Philosophical Quarterly*, 85 (3): 433–46.

Perrine, T., and Kevin Timpe. 2014. "Envy and its discontents." In *Virtues and Their Vices*, edited by Kevin Timpe and Craig A. Boyd, 225–44. New York: Oxford University Press.

Pfaelzer, Jean. 2007. *Driven Out: The Forgotten War against Chinese Americans*. New York: Random House.

Platman, S. R., Robert Plutchik, and Bette Weinstein. 1971. "Psychiatric, physiological, behavioral and self-report measures in relation to a suicide attempt." *Journal of Psychiatric Research* 8 (2): 127–37.

Plato. 1997. *Plato: Complete Works*, ed. John M. Cooper. Indianapolis: Hackett Publishing Co.

Plutarch. (1st. c. CE) 1959. *De invidia et odio, Moralia*, Vol. 7. Loeb Classical Library. http://penelope.uchicago.edu/Thayer/E/Roman/Texts/Plutarch/Moralia/De_invidia_et_odio*.html.

(1st. c. CE) 2004. *De invidia et odio* (in Italian and Greek), trans. and ed. Silvia Lanzi. Napoli: M. D'Auria.

Plutchik, Robert. 2002. *Emotions and Life: Perspectives from Psychology, Biology, and Evolution*. Washington, DC: American Psychological Association.

Polledri, Patricia. 2003. "Envy revisited." *British Journal of Psychotherapy* 20 (2): 195–218.

Postema, Gerald J. 2005. "'Cemented with diseased qualities': sympathy and comparison in Hume's moral psychology." *Hume Studies* 31 (2): 249–98.

Prinz, Jesse. 2016. "Culture and cognitive science." *The Stanford Encyclopedia of Philosophy* (Fall 2016 Edition), edited by Edward N. Zalta. https://plato .stanford.edu/archives/fall2016/entries/culture–cogsci/.

Protasi, Sara 2014. "Loving people for who they are (even when they don't love you back.)" *European Journal of Philosophy* 24 (1): 214–34.

2016. "Varieties of envy." *Philosophical Psychology* 29 (4): 535–49.

2017a. "The perfect bikini body: Can we all really have it? Loving gaze as an antioppressive beauty idea." *Thought* 6 (2): 93–101.

2017b. "'I'm not envious, I'm just jealous!': On the difference between envy and jealousy." *Journal of the American Philosophical Association* 3 (3): 316–33.

2017c. "Invideo et amo: on envying the beloved." *Philosophia* 47: 1765–1784.

2019. "Happy self–surrender and unhappy self–assertion." In *The Moral Psychology of Admiration*, edited by Alfred Archer and André Grahle, 45–60. London: Rowman & Littlefield International.

Protevi, John. 2014. "Political emotion." In *Collective Emotions: Perspectives from Psychology, Philosophy, and Sociology*, edited by Christian von Scheve and Mikko Salmela, 326–40. Oxford: Oxford University Press.

Purshouse, Luke. 2004. "Jealousy in relation to envy." *Erkenntnis* 60 (2): 179–205.

Rangel, Marcos A. 2015. "Is parental love colorblind? Human capital accumulation within mixed families." *The Review of Black Political Economy* 42: 57–86.

Rawls, John. 1993. *Political Liberalism*. New York: Columbia University Press.

1999. *A Theory of Justice*, rev. ed. Cambridge, MA: Harvard University Press.

Roberts, Robert C. 2003. *Emotions: An Essay in Aid of Moral Psychology*. New York: Cambridge University Press.

Rousseau, Jean-Jacques. 1973. *The Social Contract and Discourses*, trans. G. D. H. Cole. London: Dent, and Everyman's library.

Ryff, Carol D. and Burton Singer. 2003. "Flourishing under fire: Resilience as a prototype of challenged thriving." In *Flourishing: Positive Psychology and the Life Well-lived*, edited by C. L. M. Keyes and J. Haidt, 15–36. Washington, DC: American Psychological Association.

Sachs, David. 1981. "How to distinguish self-respect from self-esteem." *Philosophy & Public Affairs* 10 (4): 346–60.

Salice, Alessandro, and Alba Montes Sánchez. 2019. "Envy and us." *European Journal of Philosophy* 27 (1): 227–42.

Salovey, Peter, and Judith Rodin. 1984. 'Some antecedents and consequences of social-comparison jealousy.' *Journal of Personality and Social Psychology* 47 (4): 780–92.

Salovey, Peter, and Alexander J. Rothman. 1991. "Envy and jealousy: Self and society." In *The Psychology of Envy and Jealousy*, edited by Peter Salovey, 271–86. New York: Guilford Press.

Sanders, Ed. 2014. *Envy and Jealousy in Classical Athens: A Socio-Psychological Approach.* New York: Oxford University Press.

Sayers, Dorothy. (1940) 1999. *Creed or Chaos? Why Christians Must Choose Either Dogma or Disaster (or, Why It Really Does Matter What You Believe).* Manchester, NH: Sophia Institute Press.

Schaubroeck, John and Simon S. K. Lam 2004. "Comparing lots before and after: Promotion rejectees' invidious reactions to promotees." *Organizational Behavior and Human Decision Processes* 94 (1): 33–47.

Scheman, Naomi. 1980. "Anger and the politics of naming." In *Women and Language in Literature and Society,* edited by Nelly Furman, Ruth Borker, and Sally McConnell-Ginet, 22–35. New York: Praeger.

Schimmel, Solomon. 1997. *The Seven Deadly Sins: Jewish, Christian, and Classical Reflections on Human Psychology.* New York: Oxford University Press.

    2008. "Envy in Jewish though and literature." In *Envy: Theory and Research,* edited by Richard H. Smith, 17–38. New York: Oxford University Press.

Schindler, Ines, Veronika Zink, Johannes Windrich, and Winfried Menninghaus. 2013. "Admiration and adoration: Their different ways of showing and shaping who we are." *Cognition & Emotion* 27 (1): 85–118.

Schindler, Ines, Juliane Paech, and Fabian Löwenbrück. 2015. "Linking admiration and adoration to self–expansion: Different ways to enhance one's potential." *Cognition and Emotion* 29 (2): 292–310.

Schmid, Hans Bernhard. 2014. "The feeling of being a group: Corporate emotions and collective consciousness." In *Collective Emotions: Perspectives from Psychology, Philosophy, and Sociology,* edited by Christian von Scheve and Mikko Salmela, 3–16. Oxford: Oxford University Press.

Schmitter, Amy M. 2011. "Family trees: Sympathy, comparison, and the proliferation of the passions in Hume and his predecessors." In *Emotion and Reason in Medieval and Early Modern Philosophy,* edited by Lisa Shapiro and Martin Pickavé, 255–78. Oxford: Oxford University Press.

    2016. "17th and 18th century theories of emotions." *The Stanford Encyclopedia of Philosophy* (Winter 2016 Edition), edited by Edward N. Zalta. https:// plato.stanford.edu/archives/win2016/entries/emotions-17th18th/.

Schoeck, Helmut. 1969. *Envy: A Theory of Social Behaviour.* San Diego: Harcourt, Brace & World.

Schwartz, Steven. 1997. *The Seven Deadly Sins.* Columbus, OH: Gramercy Books.

Senior, Jennifer. 2014. *All Joy and No Fun: The Paradox of Modern Parenthood.* New York: HarperCollins.

Shakespeare, William. (*c.*1603) 2006. *Othello,* ed. Michael Neill. Oxford: Oxford University Press.

Shapiro, Joseph P. 1993. *No Pity: People with Disabilities Forging a New Civil Rights Movement.* New York: Times books.

Shapiro, Lisa. 2006. "Descartes's passions of the soul." *Philosophy Compass* 1 (3): 268–78.

Shue, Henry. 1975. "Liberty and self-respect." *Ethics* 85 (3): 195–203.

Sidgwick, Henry. (1907) 1967. *The Methods of Ethics*, 7th ed. London: Macmillan.

Silver, Maury, and John Sabini. 1978. "The social construction of envy." *Journal for the Theory of Social Behaviour* 8: 313–32.

Singh, Jyotsna. 2003. "Post-colonial criticism." In *Shakespeare: An Oxford Guide*, ed. Stanley Wells and Lena Cowen Orlin, 492–507. Oxford: Oxford University Press.

Smith, Adam. (1759) 1976. *The Theory of Moral Sentiments*. Oxford: Clarendon Press.

Smith, Eliot R., Charles R. Seger, and Diane M. Mackie. 2008. "Can emotions be truly group level? Evidence regarding four conceptual criteria." *Journal of Personality and Social Psychology* 93 (3): 431–46.

Smith, Richard H. 1991. "Envy and the sense of injustice." In *The Psychology of Envy and Jealousy*, edited by Peter Salovey, 79–99. New York: Guilford Press.

———. 2000. "Assimilative and contrastive emotional reactions to upward and downward social comparisons." In *Handbook of Social Comparison: Theory and Research*, edited by Jerry Suls and Ladd Wheeler, 173–200. Berlin: Plenum.

Smith, Richard H., Sung Hee Kim, and Gerrod W. Parrott. 1988. "Envy and jealousy: Semantic problems and experiential distinctions." *Personality and Social Psychology Bulletin* 14: 401–9.

Smith, Richard H., Terence J. Turner, Ron Garonzik, Colin Wayne Leach, Vanessa Urch-Druskat, and Christine M. Weston. 1996. "Envy and Schadenfreude." *Personality and Social Psychology Bulletin* 22: 158–68.

Smith, Richard H., Gerrod W. Parrott, Edward F. Diener, R. H. Hoyle, and Sung Hee Kim. 1999. "Dispositional envy." *Personality and Social Psychology Bulletin* 25 (8): 1007–20.

Smith, Richard H., Caitlin A. J. Powell, David J. Y. Combs, and David Ryan Schurtz. 2009. "Exploring the when and why of Schadenfreude." *Social and Personality Psychology Compass* 3 (4): 530–46.

Solnick, Sara J. and David Hemenway, 1998. "Is more always better? A survey on positional concerns." *Journal of Economic Behavior & Organization* 37(3): 373–83.

———. 2005. "Are positional concerns stronger in some domains than in others?" *American Economic Review* 95 (2): 147–51.

Solomon, Robert C. 1976. *The Passions: The Myth and Nature of Human Emotion*. Garden City, NY: Doubleday.

———. 2000. *Wicked Pleasures*. London: Rowman & Littlefield.

Spinoza, Baruch. (1677) 1949. *Ethics*, ed. and trans. J. Gutmann. New York: Hafner Publishing Company.

Stafford, William S. 1994. *Disordered Loves: Healing the Seven Deadly Sins*. Cambridge, MA: Cowley.

Starmans, Christina, Mark Sheskin, and Paul Bloom. 2017. "Why people prefer unequal societies." *Nature Human Behaviour* 1 (0082): https://doi.org/10.1038/s41562-017-0082.

Staub, Ervin. 1989. *The Roots of Evil: The Origins of Genocide and Other Group Violence*. New York: Cambridge University Press.

Stein, Murray. 1990. "Sibling rivalry and the problem of envy." *Journal of Analytical Psychology* 35 (2): 161–74.

Stevens, Edward B. 1948. "Envy and pity in Greek philosophy." *The American Journal of Philology* 69 (2): 171–89.

Strawson, Peter F. 1962. "Freedom and resentment." *Proceedings of the British Academy* 48: 1–25.

Strohminger, Nina. 2014. "Disgust talked about." *Philosophy Compass* 9 (7): 478–93.

Tai, Kenneth, Jayanth Narayanan, and Daniel J. Mcallister. 2012. "Envy as pain: Rethinking the nature of envy and its implications for employees and organizations." *Academy of Management Review* 37 (1): 107–29.

Tandoc Jr., Edson C., Patrick Ferrucci, and Margaret Duffy. 2015. "Facebook use, envy, and depression among college students: Is facebooking depressing?" *Computers in Human Behavior* 43: 139–46.

Taylor, Gabriele E. 1988. "Envy and jealousy: Emotions and vices." *Midwest Studies in Philosophy* 13: 233–49.

2006. *Deadly Vices*. Oxford: Oxford University Press.

Terlazzo, Rosa. 2016. "Conceptualizing adaptive preferences respectfully: An indirectly substantive account." *The Journal of Political Philosophy* 24 (2): 206–26.

Tesser, Abraham, and James E. Collins. 1988. "Emotion in social reflection and comparison situations: Intuitive, systematic, and exploratory approaches." *Journal of Personality and Social Psychology* 55: 695–709.

Tesser, Abraham, Murray Millar, and Janet Moore. 1988. "Some affective consequences of social comparison and reflection processes: The pain and pleasure of being close." *Journal of Personality and Social Psychology* 54: 49–61.

Testa, Maria, and Brenda Major. 1990. "The impact of social comparison after failure: The moderating effects of perceived control." *Basic and Applied Social Psychology* 11: 205–18.

Thomas Aquinas. (1265–74) 1947–8. *Summa Theologica: Complete English Edition in Five Volumes*, trans. Fathers of the English Dominican Province. Notre Dame: Ave Maria Press.

Corpus Thomisticum: S. Thomae de Aquino Opera Omnia, available online. www.corpusthomisticum.org.

Thomason, Krista K. 2015. "The moral value of envy." *The Southern Journal of Philosophy* 53 (1): 36–53.

Tomlin, Patrick. 2008, "Envy, facts and justice: A critique of the treatment of envy in justice as fairness." *Res Publica* 14 (2): 101–16.

Tov-Ruach, Leila. 1980. "Jealousy, attention, and loss." In *Explaining Emotions*, edited by Amélie O. Rorty, 465–88. Oakland: University of California Press.

Tuske, Joerg. 2011. "The concept of emotion in classical Indian philosophy." *The Stanford Encyclopedia of Philosophy* (Spring 2011 Edition), edited by Edward

N. Zalta. http://plato.stanford.edu/archives/spr2011/entries/concept–emotion–india/.

Uchino, Bert N., Julianne Holt-Lunstad, Darcy Uno, and Jeffrey B. Flinders. 2001. "Heterogeneity in the social networks of young and older adults: Prediction of mental health and cardiovascular reactivity during acute stress." *Journal of Behavioral Medicine* 24: 261–382.

Van Kleef, Gerben A., and Agneta H. Fischer. 2015. "Emotional collectives: How groups shape emotions and emotions shape groups." *Cognition and Emotion* 30 (1): 3–19.

Van de Ven, Niels. 2016. "Envy and its consequences: Why it is useful to distinguish between benign and malicious envy." *Social and Personality Psychology Compass* 10 (6): 337–49.

2017. "Envy and admiration: Emotion and motivation following upward social comparison." *Cognition and Emotion* 31 (1): 193–200.

Van de Ven, Niels, Marcel Zeelenberg, and Rik Pieters. 2009. "Leveling up and down: The experiences of benign and malicious envy." *Emotion* 9 (3): 419–29.

2011. "Why envy outperforms admiration." *Personality and Social Psychology Bulletin* 37: 784–95.

2012. "Appraisal patterns of envy and related emotions." *Motivation and Emotion* 36: 195–204.

Van de Ven, Niels, Charles E. Hooglandb, Richard H. Smith, Wilco W. van Dijk, Seger M. Breugelmansad, and Marcel Zeelenberg. 2015. "When envy leads to Schadenfreude." *Cognition and Emotion* 29 (6): 1007–25.

Van de Ven, Niels, and Marcel Zeelenberg. 2015. "On the counterfactual nature of envy: 'It could have been me'." *Cognition and Emotion* 29(6): 954–71.

Van Dijk, Wilco W., Jaap W. Ouwerkerk, Sjoerd Goslinga, Myrke Nieweg, and Marcello Gallucci. 2006. "When people fall from grace: Reconsidering the role of envy in Schadenfreude." *Emotion* 6 (1): 156–60.

Van Kleef, Gerben A., and Agneta H. Fischer. 2016. "Emotional collectives: How groups shape emotions and emotions shape groups." *Cognition and Emotion* 30 (1): 3–19.

Van Zomeren, Martijn, Russell Spears, Agneta H. Fischer, and Colin Wayne Leach. 2004. "Put your money where your mouth is! Explaining collective action tendencies through group-based anger and group efficacy." *Journal of Personality and Social Psychology* 87: 649–64.

Verduyn, Philippe, David Seungjae Lee, Jiyoung Park, Holly Shablack, Ariana Orvell, Joseph Bayer, Oscar Ybarra, John Jonides, and Ethan Kross. 2015. "Passive Facebook usage undermines affective well-being: Experimental and longitudinal evidence." *Journal of Experimental Psychology: General* 144 (2): 480–8.

Vice, Samantha. 2017. "White pride." In *The Moral Psychology of Pride*, edited by J. Adam Carter and Emma C. Gordon, 191–210. London: Rowman & Littlefield.

Vigani, Denise. 2017. "Is patience a virtue?" *The Journal of Value Inquiry* 51 (2): 327–40.

Von Scheve, Christian, and Mikko Salmela. 2014. *Collective Emotions: Perspectives from Psychology, Philosophy, and Sociology.* Oxford: Oxford University Press.

Watson, David. 2000. *Mood and Temperament.* New York: Guilford.

Wert, Sarah R. and Peter Salovey. 2004. "A social comparison account of gossip." *Review of General Psychology* 8 (2): 122–37.

Wojcieszak, Magdalena E. and Diana C. Mutz. 2009. "Online groups and political discourse: Do online discussion spaces facilitate exposure to political disagreement?" *Journal of Communication* 59 (1): 40–56.

Wong, David. 2013. "Chinese ethics." *The Stanford Encyclopedia of Philosophy* (Spring 2013 Edition), edited by Edward N. Zalta. http://plato.stanford .edu/archives/spr2013/entries/ethics–chinese/.

Wreen, Michael J. 1989. "Jealousy." *Noûs* 23 (5): 635–52.

Wyatt, Jean. 1998. "I want to be you: Envy, the Lacanian double, and feminist community in Margaret Atwood's *The Robber Bride.*" *Tulsa Studies in Women's Literature* 17 (1): 37–64.

Young, Robert. 1987. "Egalitarianism and envy." *Philosophical Studies* 52 (2): 261–76.

Zeavin, Lynne. 2012. "The analyst's unconscious reactions to the baby in the consulting room." *Journal of the American Psychoanalytic Association* 60 (3): 517–25.

Zia, Helen. 2000. *Asian American Dreams: The Emergence of an American People.* New York: Farrar, Straus and Giroux.

Index

Page numbers followed by *f* indicate a figure on the corresponding page. Page numbers followed by *t* indicate a table on the corresponding page.

malice (cont.)
  defined, 195
  emulative envy as free from, 45
  envy and, 4, 193, 195
  envy free from, 28, 45, 56
  hatred and, 95
  Hume on, 193
  inert envy as free from, 56
  in malicious envy, 4, 167
  moral badness and, 69
  sympathy and, 195
  in women's friendships, 114
malicious envy
  aggressive envy and, 74–6
  Aristotle on, 32
  Ben-Ze'ev on, 32–3
  benign envy and, 53
  in Christianity, 168
  compliments and praise with, 58
  confessions of, 66
  deservingness and, 37
  desire in, 30
  emulative envy, 210
  fear and, 34, 58
  "It should have been me" scenario, 70–3
  leveling up/leveling down of envy, 32–4
  malice in, 4, 167
  between nations, 75
  perceived undeservingness correlation, 36–7
  Schadenfreude and, 77
  self-esteem and, 58
  shame and negative feelings with, 51
  sympathy and, 96
Mandeville, Bernard de, 192, 205–6, 208
Maxims (Rochefoucauld), 66
McDowell, John, 68
Menexenus (Plato), 165–6
mental health/state, 21, 54, 72, 80, 97, 155, 190, 198
metaphorical gaze of envy, 83
metaphysically vague transitional cases of jealousy, 19
Metaphysics of Morals (Kant), 123, 195–6, 211
misery, 3, 56, 193–4
misogyny as fear-envy, 130–1
"Mitfreude," defined, 4
modern era envy
  Bacon, Francis and, 189–91, 203, 206
  Descartes, René and, 50, 171, 196–202, 200t
  envy and emulation, 196–9
  Hobbes, Thomas, 21, 198, 203–5
  Hume, David and, 21–2, 193–5
  Kant, Immanuel and, 123, 195–6, 205–7, 211
  Leibniz, Gottfried Wilhelm, 202
  Locke, John, 21, 202

Mandeville, Bernard de and, 192, 205–6, 208
  overview of, 188–208
  Rousseau, Jean-Jacques, 104–5, 196, 207–8
  Smith, Adam and, 75, 142, 192–3, 206
  Spinoza, Baruch, 21, 191–2, 199, 207
moral badness
  aggressive envy and, 74–6
  aggressive envy as, 92–3
  inert envy and, 78–9
  malice and, 69
  political envy and, 119–20
  prudential badness *vs.*, 67–70
  spiteful envy and, 71
moral dimension of envy, 3–4, 32, 34–7, 90, 176
moral luck, 54, 60, 143
moral virtue, 69, 91, 159, 178
My Brilliant Friend (Ferrante), 113, 115–16
mythical norm, 135–6

nemesis, defined, 86, 169, 173–4, 182, 197
Neu, Jerome, 33
New Essays on Human Understanding (Leibniz), 202
Nicomachean Ethics (Aristotle), 102–3, 162–3, 173–4
Nietzsche, Friedrich, 207
noble love, 166–7
non-excusable general envy, 212
non-ideal theory perspective, 120–1, 124, 128–31
non-malicious envy, 32–3, 45, 52
nonprototypical jealousy, 10
normative dimension of envy, 35, 67, 83t, 83–5, 85t, 98–100, 108–9
Nozick, Robert, 126–8, 155–6, 207
Nussbaum, Martha, 69, 130–1, 158–9

object-envy, 35, 47
obsessive jealousy, 11, 13
obtainability of the good, 84–5
occurrent versions of Envious Egalitarianism, 122
The Office (TV show), 17–18
Old Testament jealousy, 13
On Envy (Bacon), 189–91
ontological dimension of envy, 67, 83t, 83–5, 85t
orgé, expression of, 164
Othello (Shakespeare), 11–12, 14, 136, 148–9
overlapping consensus notion, 140

painful nature of envy
  aggressive envy and, 62
  Aristotle on, 21
  emulative envy and, 51
  inert envy and, 55–7

White laborers, 144
White privilege, 144–5
White supremacists, 134, 136, 140, 145
wild lawlessness, 195
wise love, 100, 110–12
women suffrage movements, 144
wonder, 48. *see also* awe
wrath, 21, 68, 180–1

"Yellow Peril" movement, 134–9
Young, Robert, 127

Zell, Anne, 96
zēlos (emulation), 32–3, 83, 85–7, 162–3, 196, 199, 201, 208
zero-sum game, 10, 40, 58, 62, 89, 93, 111
Zia, Helen, 137

For EU product safety concerns, contact us at Calle de José Abascal, 56–1°, 28003 Madrid, Spain or eugpsr@cambridge.org.

www.ingramcontent.com/pod-product-compliance
Ingram Content Group UK Ltd.
Pitfield, Milton Keynes, MK11 3LW, UK
UKHW020354140625
459647UK00020B/2473